QUICK
ESCAPES®

Atlanta

27 WEEKEND GETAWAYS
FROM THE GATEWAY TO THE SOUTH

FOURTH EDITION

Carol and Dan Thalimer

The Globe Pequot Press

GUILFORD, CONNECTICUT

For Elaine, Debra, Cathy, and Matt,
for whom escape is no longer necessary

To buy books in quantity for corporate use
or incentives, call **(800) 962–0973, ext. 4551,**
or e-mail **premiums@GlobePequot.com.**

Text design by Nancy Freeborn
Maps by M. A. Dubé

ISSN 1552-7301
ISBN 0-7627-2516-8

Manufactured in the United States of America
Fourth Edition/First Printing

CONTENTS

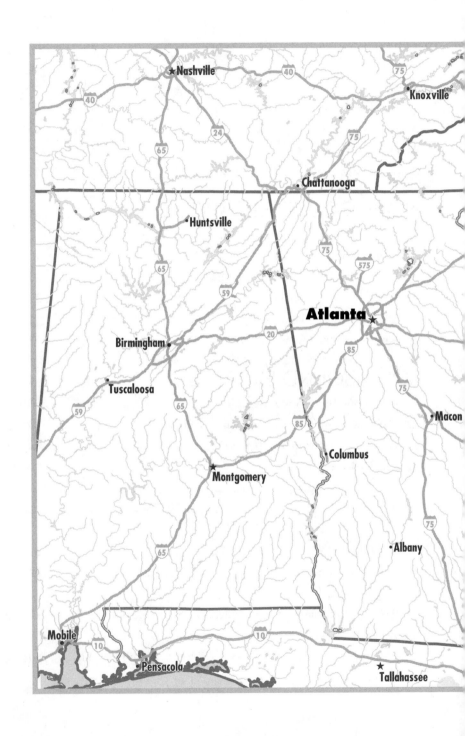

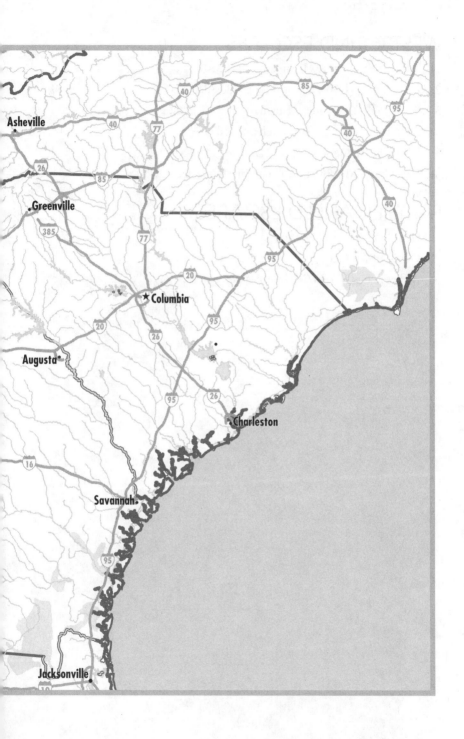

ACKNOWLEDGMENTS

This book wouldn't be possible without the help and forbearance of Paula Brisco, Justine Rathbun, Elizabeth Taylor, Laura Strom, and others at The Globe Pequot Press.

Among the many folks who helped us are: Heather Potts; Becky Bassett; Jeannie Buttrum; Mary Jo Dudley; Kitty Sikes; Britt Smith; Cheryl Smith, Dawn Townsend, and Fay Tripp with the Georgia Department of Industry, Trade, and Tourism; as well as June Murff, Greater Aiken Chamber of Commerce; Ami Simpson, Alabama Bureau of Tourism and Travel; Marla Tambellini, Asheville Convention and Visitors Bureau; Tim Brown, Athens Convention and Visitors Bureau; Mary Ashton Brown, Augusta Convention and Visitors Bureau; Vicki Ashford, Greater Birmingham Convention and Visitors Bureau; Kathy Vickers, Brunswick-Golden Isles Convention and Visitors Bureau; Rachel Crumbley, Callaway Gardens Resort; Amy Ballenger, Charleston Convention and Visitors Bureau; Amy Northern, Chattanooga Area Convention and Visitors Bureau; Kay Aogburn, Columbia Metropolitan Convention and Visitors Bureau; Shelby Guest, Columbus Convention and Visitors Bureau; Kate Brehe, Dahlonega-Lumpkin County Chamber of Commerce; Patty Tucker, DeKalb County Tourist Association; Karen Baker, Henderson County Travel and Tourism; Lee Sentell, Huntsville/Madison County Convention and Visitors Bureau; LaDonna Pettis, Knoxville Area Convention and Visitors Bureau; Ruth Sykes, Macon Convention and Visitors Bureau; Sandy Thomas, Montgomery Area Convention and Visitor Development; Amanda Fuller, Nashville Convention and Visitors Bureau; Jenny Stacy, Savannah Convention and Visitors Bureau; Barbara Parker, Tennessee Department of Tourist Development.

As always, we've had invaluable assistance from Geiger and Associates.

ABOUT THE AUTHORS

Carol and Dan Thalimer live near Atlanta and have been writing about travel since 1987. Their initial expertise on the subject came from the traveling they did during the seven years they owned several travel agencies. In addition to writing more than 500 articles for fifty magazines and newspapers such as *National Geographic Traveler, Ladies' Home Journal,* and the *New York Times,* they have written several other books *Georgia Outdoor Activity Guide, Georgia B&Bs, Country Roads of Alabama, Country Roads of South Carolina,* and *Country Roads of Georgia* (all from Country Roads Press); *Travel Smart Trip Planner: The Deep South* (Avalon Publishing); *Romantic Tennessee* (John F. Blair, Publisher); and *Romantic Days and Nights in Atlanta, Fun with the Family in Georgia, Recommended Country Inns: the South,* and *Recommended Bed and Breakfasts: the South* (all from The Globe Pequot Press).

INTRODUCTION

Although it has been said, with tongue in cheek, that "Atlanta is an island of sophistication in a sea of rednecks," in actuality the capital of the New South is conveniently located to explore a wide variety of classy destinations throughout the entire region. Accessible within one to five hours are gracious antebellum towns, the wilds of the Appalachian and Great Smoky Mountains, the ocean, and exciting cities such as Chattanooga, Nashville, Knoxville, Birmingham, Montgomery, and Huntsville.

Because Georgia is the largest state east of the Mississippi River and Atlanta is located in the northwest part of the state, some in-state areas are actually farther than cities and regions in neighboring states such as Alabama, Tennessee, and North and South Carolina.

You can get away every weekend all year long and still have plenty of places left to visit. The detailed itineraries in this book are driving tours complete with attractions, recreational activities, restaurants, lodgings, and some special shopping opportunities. For each getaway "Special Events" are listed, as are "Other Recommended Restaurants and Lodgings" in the area. "There's More" describes other attractions, activities, or events that will entice you to return. "For More Information" gives you contacts to help with planning your escape.

We've arranged almost all of these escapes so that you can avoid the heavy traffic of Friday night and Sunday evening. For most of these escapes, we recommend leaving on Friday morning or afternoon and returning on Sunday afternoon, although we have suggested a few Friday-to-Monday escapes. Another option is to leave on Saturday morning and return on Monday morning. The only problem with weekend escapes is that some museums and other attractions are closed on Sunday. Even those attractions that are open on Sunday generally aren't open until afternoon. All the Sunday activities we've suggested were open as of press time. Hours often change, however, so it's best to check ahead. If you can make a trip during the week, all the better. You can avoid crowds and take advantage of discounts.

Most of the lodgings and restaurants are moderately priced. If some are more expensive, we've indicated that. Because they're so changeable, we don't include prices or hours of operation for any of the places we describe.

Several of the escapes we've created are in the same general area or have one city or town in common and could be combined if you have an extra day, so we suggest reading all the escapes in a region before planning your trip.

Although traveling without a specific itinerary or reservations can be fun, we recommend that you make advance reservations anyway. You can always cancel them. In particular, you shouldn't just show up at a quaint bed-and-breakfast and expect to get a room.

We travel so much that we keep an overnight bag packed with some essentials: toiletries, jackets, ponchos, umbrellas, bathing suits, sunscreen. Some other items you might want to pack include binoculars, a camera, long pants and walking shoes, a corkscrew, and picnic gear. Don't forget a detailed map. The directions and maps we've provided are for general information. You should still get the latest map available for an area.

Look into a Georgia ParkPass. In addition to getting free entry into the state parks by purchasing the $25 annual pass, you help provide the extra funds necessary to repair and maintain cottages, campsites, nature trails, picnic shelters, historic sites, and all the other amenities that make state parks so special. The pass can be purchased at a state park or historic site. For more information or a free color brochure, call (404) 656–3530 in metro Atlanta or out of state or (800) 3GA–PARK in the rest of Georgia.

ALABAMA
Alabama Bureau of Tourism and
  Travel
401 Adams Avenue
Montgomery, AL 36103-4309
(334) 242–4169

FLORIDA
Visit Florida
P.O. Box 1100, Tallahassee, FL 32302
(888) 7FLAUSA

GEORGIA
Georgia Department of Industry,
  Trade, and Tourism
P.O. Box 1776, Atlanta, GA 30301
(404) 656–3590

NORTH CAROLINA
North Carolina Department of
  Commerce, Travel and Tourism
  Division
430 North Salisbury Street
Raleigh, NC 27611
(919) 733–4151

SOUTH CAROLINA
South Carolina Division of Tourism
P.O. Box 71, Columbia, SC 29202
(803) 734–1700

TENNESSEE
Department of Tourist Development
State of Tennessee
320 Sixth Avenue North
Nashville, TN 37202
(615) 741–2159

NORTHBOUND
ESCAPES

NORTHBOUND ESCAPE ONE

Asheville, North Carolina

Biltmore and Much More / 2 Nights

Those who haven't visited Asheville owe it to themselves to spend a day at the Biltmore Estate—that luxurious monument to unparalleled turn-of-the-twentieth-century opulence. The largest private home in America, it was built as a summer home for the George Vanderbilts.

- ☐ Art deco downtown
- ☐ Museums
- ☐ Biltmore House
- ☐ Winery

But don't stop there. Asheville also offers stunning mountain scenery, clear skies, comfortable temperatures, and friendly citizens, as well as a variety of attractions to lure the naturalist, the sports enthusiast, the arts-and-crafts aficionado, the literary buff, the architectural historian, the theater lover, and the gastronome. Concentrate on one area or sample from all of them. Several years ago the city's convention and visitor bureau inaugurated an ambitious TV ad campaign with the slogan "Asheville—It will lift your spirit." Obviously, thousands have agreed. Rand McNally's *Places Rated Almanac* consistently ranks Asheville as one of the best places to live in the United States among small metropolitan areas. *Vacations* magazine has named the city one of its "10 Best" weekend getaway destinations. In the Asheville area visitors can enjoy unspoiled countryside and yet have access to elegant lodgings and delectable meals.

Day 1 / Afternoon

Leave Atlanta via I–85 and go northeast across the Georgia/South Carolina line. Take the first exit in South Carolina onto SC 11—the **Cherokee Foothills Scenic Highway,** on which you will continue to US 25N. Take it to I–26 and go north to Asheville. You could stop on the way in Clemson, Pendleton, or Seneca. The attractions in those towns are described in the "Follow the Tiger Paws" escape, page 142.

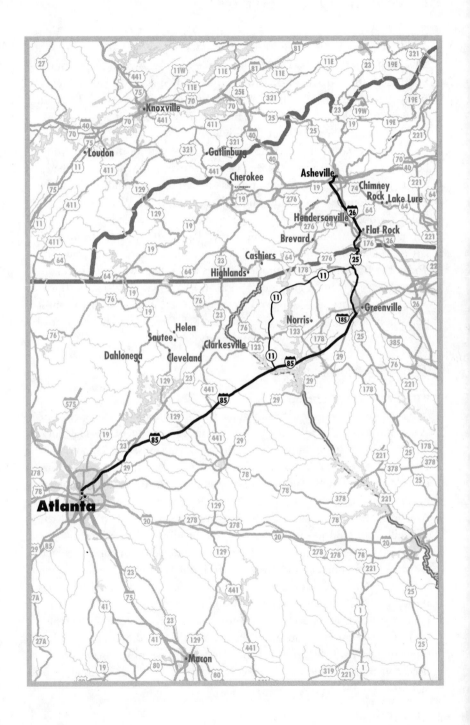

Evening

DINNER AND LODGING: One of the most renowned resorts in the Southeast is the **Grove Park Inn Resort and Spa,** 290 Macon Avenue (828–252–2711 or 800–438–5800; www.groveparkinn.com). Built in 1913 from boulders hewn from the mountain on which it sits, it was the brainchild of medicine vendor Dr. Edwin W. Grove. This inn is considered a remarkable feat of engineering no matter how you look at it, but you'll be even more amazed to learn that Grove's son-in-law, who was in charge of the construction, had no training as an architect or builder. The lobby is 120 feet long, 80 feet wide, and 24 feet high; the cavernous fireplaces hold 12-foot logs; and the elevator is cleverly concealed in the rocks behind one of the chimneys. The Grove Park Inn contains the nation's largest collection of mission oak furniture from the Arts and Crafts era. Today the hotel sports two modern wings and offers two museums, golf, tennis, fitness facilities, an indoor pool, an award-winning spa, as well as several restaurants and lounges. During warm weather one of the most popular places to eat is Chops at the Sunset Terrace on the enormous veranda, with its sweeping vistas of the city.

Day 2 / Morning

BREAKFAST: At the hotel.

Pick up a brochure for a self-guided 1.7-mile walking tour called the **Asheville Urban Trail** from Asheville City Development, 29 Haywood Street (828–232–4500), or from the Asheville Visitors Center, 151 Haywood Street (828–258–6100 or 888–667–3000). Guided walking tours leave from Pack Place on Saturday at 3:00 P.M. Allow two-and-a-half hours for the tour. March through December, seventy-five-minute Asheville Historic Trolley Tours leave from the visitor center. Call the Asheville Arts Council at (828) 258–0710 for more information.

Poverty helped preserve Asheville's extensive historic district. Covering several blocks and boasting 170 buildings, the whole downtown is on the National Register of Historic Places. From the late 1800s through 1929, Asheville boomed as a summer resort and center for thera-peutic health treatments. Artisans who were brought in for the construc-tion of the Biltmore Estate, the Biltmore Village, and the Grove Park Inn often remained in the area, creating a treasure trove of Victorian and art deco construction. The stock market crash, however, brought prosperity to an end.

At the onset of the Great Depression, Asheville was the hardest-hit city in the nation. Although other cities defaulted on depression debts, Asheville's city fathers vowed to repay every penny—a promise that took more than forty years to accomplish. The debt burden turned out to be a blessing in disguise, however; because no money was available for what would have been considered urban renewal—in reality the destruction of historic buildings for parking lots and modern monstrosities—Asheville's historic buildings remain. Now that money is available, the structures are being restored rather than removed. Surprisingly, Asheville contains more art deco architecture than any other Southeastern city except Miami Beach. For example, **City Hall,** 70 Court Plaza (828–259–5600), is an extravagant structure topped with a pink-and-green-tiled octagonal roof that resembles a rhododendron bud. The art deco dome of the **First Baptist Church** of Asheville, I–240 and Charlotte Street (828–252–4781), designed by Douglas Ellington, is created of colored tiles graduating from green to red and features other art deco detailing.

Another architectural gem is the **Basilica of St. Lawrence,** 97 Haywood Street (828–252–6042), an Italian renaissance Catholic church built by Rafael Guastavino, who worked on the Biltmore House. The basilica boasts two Spanish Baroque towers and a huge unsupported tile dome—the largest in the country.

One of the country's first enclosed malls, the Neo–Tudor Gothic **Grove Arcade,** Public Market, 1 Page Avenue (828–252–7799), which takes up a square block bounded by Page, O. Henry, Battery Park, and Battle Square, has spiral staircases inside and is adorned on the outside with glazed terra-cotta as well as griffins that guard the roof's parapets. The Arcade is filled with shops and restaurants.

LUNCH: Cafe on the Square, 1 Biltmore Avenue (828–251–5565), is located in a transformed drugstore that overlooks historic Pack Square. The menu at the chic eatery is varied and imaginative; portions are generous.

Afternoon

Asheville has a proud literary heritage. Thomas Wolfe grew up here in his mother's boardinghouse, called the Old Kentucky Home. Later he used that house, its lodgers, the city, and many of its citizenry for his semiautobiographical novel *Look Homeward, Angel.* The boardinghouse, now the **Thomas Wolfe Memorial,** 52 North Market Street (828–253–8304), has been fully restored after an arson fire several years ago, and it's once again open for tours daily except Monday and major holidays. Start at the visitor center, where you can watch an informative video and see exhibits about Wolfe. After touring the house, stroll through the heirloom gardens. A three-day festival in October includes lectures, walking tours, and special performances. In early December, Christmas at My Old Kentucky Home offers an evening tour.

Asheville is well known for its concentration of artisans. The nation's preeminent organization that represents the southern Appalachians craft culture is the Southern Highland Craft Guild (828–298–7928), founded in 1930. Since 1980 it has been located in the **Folk Art Center** at milepost 382 on the Blue Ridge Parkway. At the center, you'll find artisans demonstrating their crafts on a rotating basis. For example, you might see demonstrations of leather working, basketry, and the creation of miniatures. A large gift shop sells the wares of more than 200 local artists. Upstairs in the exhibition hall, you'll find displays of traveling shows or local work.

Asheville's museums include the Antique Car Museum and North Carolina Homespun Museums at the Grove Park Inn. The Pack Place cultural center downtown, 2 South Pack Square, houses the Asheville Art Museum (828–253–3227), the Colburn Mineral Museum (828–254–7162), the Health Adventure (828–254–6373), the Diana Wortham Theatre (828–257–4530), and the YMI Cultural Center (828–252–4614).

Evening

DINNER: Savor a leisurely evening meal at one of the many restaurants at the Grove Park Inn or a delightful repast at **Gabrielle's** at the Richmond Hill Inn, 87 Richmond Hill Drive (828–252–7313 or 800–545–9238; www.richmondhillinn.com). Specializing in continental cuisine, the restaurant features menu items that can be ordered a la carte, or you can choose the five-course fixed price Grand Menu with or without wine. Reservations are required, as is a coat for gentlemen. Closed Tuesday.

LODGING: The Grove Park Inn.

Day 3 / Morning

BREAKFAST: At the inn.

The **Biltmore Estate** off Biltmore Avenue/US 25 (828–225–1333 or 800–624–1575; www.biltmore.com), established as a country home for G. W. Vanderbilt at the turn of the twentieth century, is the largest private residence (255 rooms) in the country. The French château–like mansion, designed by Beaux Arts interpreter Richard Morris Hunt, contains priceless family antiques and works of art as well as sixteenth-century Flemish tapestries and Meissen porcelains. Upstairs/downstairs tours include the elegant family quarters, as well as the below-stairs working heart of the manor. Begin with the exquisite Winter Garden, a glass-domed, conservatory-like room. The Billiard Room, Smoking Room, and Gun Room make up a suite of rooms created for men's entertainment. The most stunning room in the mansion is easily the Banquet Hall. Seventy-two feet long and 42 feet wide, the medieval baronial hall is crowned by an arched ceiling 70 feet high. The 90-foot-long Gallery features three magnificent tapestries. The Library holds more than 10,000 volumes.

The basement contains family playrooms such as the Halloween Room, left decorated as it was for a long-ago party; an indoor pool with seventeen dressing rooms; a gymnasium; and a bowling alley. The working part of the basement includes three kitchens—one just for preparing pastries—as well as laundry rooms, storage rooms, pantries, and other working rooms. A "Behind the Scenes" tour focuses on restoration-in-progress in rooms previously closed to the public. Don't miss the Carriage House with its harness, saddle, blanket, and tack rooms or the "Rooftop Tour" to see the gargoyles and stunning views.

The 250 acres immediately surrounding the château still reflect the vision of its creator, Frederick Law Olmstead—designer of Central Park in New York and Piedmont Park in Atlanta—in his last, largest, and most loved project. A 3-mile approach road keeps the visitor in suspense until the Esplanade is reached. The formal Library Terrace and Italian Gardens hug the mansion. A Shrub Garden or Ramble guides you by transition to the formal Walled Garden, which contains the large Rose Garden and Victorian Conservatory, which boasts exotic tropical plants similar to those grown during George Vanderbilt's time. The natural Azalea Glen contains one of the largest collections of native azaleas in America—rivaling that of Callaway Gardens in Pine Mountain, Georgia. The entire estate is surrounded by dense forests.

There's always something new at the Biltmore Estate. The **Historic Horse Barns** have been newly converted into display space for interpretive exhibits and antique equipment. Farmyard animals wander freely, and space has been set aside for the type of kitchen garden the estate would have had in the Vanderbilts' time.

You can now stay at Biltmore (too bad, not in the mansion) in the palatial new **Inn on Biltmore Estate** (828–225–1600). With four acres

Conservatory at the Biltmore Estate, Asheville

of space under roof and 250 rooms, the inn is decorated in the style of English and French manor houses. Several restaurants, a pool, and a fitness center mean you would never have to leave the estate. Packages include tickets to the estate and/or tickets to special events.

LUNCH: The **Stable Cafe,** in the estate's Carriage House, where horse stalls have been converted to booths; the **Deerpark Restaurant,** located in a converted calving barn; or the **Bistro,** located at the winery.

Afternoon

Biltmore Winery is the most visited in the United States, as well as one of the fastest-growing producers. Vanderbilt conceived, from the very beginning, a working estate. A dairy and vegetable gardens were early additions. In keeping with that dream, present owner William A. V. Cecil, Vanderbilt's grandson, created the winery during the 1970s. Not just any wines would do for his pet project—they had to reflect the tradition of elegance and appreciation of fine wines established during the Vanderbilt era. To this end, Cecil began planting vines in the early 1970s. By the end of the decade, he had located a French wine master. The first wines were produced in 1978, but the winery didn't go into full production in the converted dairy until 1984. From more than one hundred acres of grapes, the winery produces premium European-style red and white wines and *méthode champenoise* wines.

The tour begins in an impressive foyer that contains stained-glass windows from a former New York Vanderbilt home, as well as artifacts that depict the history of wine, such as an Egyptian wine cup from 1400 B.C. and a Grecian *kylix* (a shallow, two-handled drinking cup) from the fifth century B.C. You'll see a short film about the vineyards and winery. The production rooms are lined with sleek stainless-steel tanks. State-of-the-art chemical and biological laboratories monitor every step of the winemaking process. The only resemblance to medieval winemaking is the cavelike tunnels where sparkling wines are stored during their two-year fermentation. In Burgundy, conditions are known to be ideal when a certain mold grows on the walls. California winemakers tried unsuccessfully to import it, but at Biltmore the mold grows naturally. You'll complete the tour in the tasting room/shop.

As you leave the estate, you will come out of the massive gate into **Biltmore Village,** which was created by Vanderbilt as a place for the workmen and artisans who built the mansion to live and shop. Today the English Tudor buildings house cafes and craft, jewelry, and clothing shops.

Return to Atlanta via I–26 south to US 25, I–185 west, and I–85 to Atlanta.

There's More

Outdoor activities. Within a 60-mile radius of Asheville, you can find fifteen golf courses, seventy-five hiking trails, three rivers for white-water rafting, tennis courts, two ski resorts, rockhounding and rock climbing, and fishing, as well as ten campgrounds. Nine of North Carolina's eleven major waterfalls are located nearby. The Pisgah National Forest covers 497,000 acres.

Special Events

April–May. Festival of Flowers, Biltmore Estate. A profusion of flowers inside the Biltmore House and in the gardens accompanies a schedule of special activities that celebrate spring. (828) 225–1600 or (800) 624–1575.

Summer. During summer weekends, "Biltmore Estate Evenings" (888–543–2961) are especially popular. Big-name concerts are held on the lawn after the Biltmore House closes.

August. Held annually since 1928, Asheville's Mountain Dance and Folk Festival is the oldest festival of its kind in America. The festival celebrates mountain music and other distinctive aspects of Appalachian Mountain life and lore with hundreds of musicians, a dozen clogging teams, bluegrass and string bands, storytellers, balladeers, and an annual quilt competition. The three-day festival is held at the Diana Wortham Theatre, 2 South Pack Square (828–258–6101, ext. 789).

November–December. Candlelight Christmas at Biltmore, Biltmore Estate. The estate re-creates an elaborate Victorian Christmas like the one celebrated when the home was completed on Christmas Eve 1895. Daily and candlelight tours. Reservations are required for candlelight tours. (828) 225–1600 or (800) 624–1575.

Other Recommended Restaurants and Lodgings

Asheville has one of the largest concentrations of bed-and-breakfasts we've seen outside Charleston and Savannah. Most lodgings take full advantage of the setting, with either a view of the mountains from below or a panorama of the city from above. Contact the Chamber of Commerce for a complete listing of lodgings (828–258–6101).

Among the outstanding B&Bs are the Albemarle Inn, 86 Edgemont Road (828–255–0027 or 800–621–7435); the Black Walnut Bed and Breakfast Inn and Carriage House, 288 Montford Avenue (828–254–3878 or 800–381–3878); the Cedar Crest Victorian, 674 Biltmore Avenue (704–252–1389 or 800–252–0310); the Colby House, 230 Pearson Drive (828–253–5644 or 800–982–2118); Inn on Montford, 296 Montford Avenue (828–254–9569 or 800–254–9569); the Lion & the Rose, 276 Montford Avenue (828–255–ROSE or 800–546–6988); and the Wright Inn and Carriage House, 235 Pearson Drive (828–251–0789 or 800–552–5724).

The Richmond Hill Inn, 87 Richmond Hill Drive (704–252–7313 or 888–742–4554; www.richmondhillinn.com), a rambling Victorian, was named one of Uncle Ben's Top Ten Inns in the United States. The inn is recognized nationwide for its superior service. Many guest rooms have fireplaces. AAA Four Diamond restaurant.

If you like room to spread out and want to be in the center of town, the historic but completely renovated Haywood Park Hotel, 1 Battery Park Avenue (828–252–2522 or 800–228–2522; www.haywoodpark.com), consists of thirty-three suites, a restaurant, and shops.

For an intimate dinner try the Flying Frog Cafe and Wine Bar, a restaurant at the Haywood Park Hotel, 1 Battery Park Avenue (828–254–9411; www.flyingfrogcafe.com). The extensive menu at this cozy restaurant announces elegant meals served in generous portions.

The Market Place Restaurant, 20 Wall Street (828–252–4162), has been noted since 1979 for its award-winning cuisine and a wine list that features more than 150 wines from around the world.

For More Information

Asheville Convention and Visitors Bureau, 151 Haywood Street, Asheville, NC 28802-1010. (828) 258–6102 or (888) 247–9811; www.explore asheville.com.

Blue Ridge Parkway Headquarters, 200 BB&T Building, One Pack Square, Asheville, NC 28801. (704) 259–0701.

Blue Ridge Parkway Information Line. (704) 271–4779.

Chattanooga, Tennessee

Crossroads Then and Now / 2 Nights

In a region today characterized by waterfalls and white-water rivers, green-clad mountains, steep-sided gorges, cool limestone caves, broad-shouldered plateaus, and verdant farming valleys, geologists say that marine organisms in the limestone formations indicate the area once had a climate similar to that of the Bahamas. More than 300 species of trees and 900 varieties of wildflowers grow in this section of eastern Tennessee, more than anywhere else on Earth except central China.

- ☐ Aquarium
- ☐ Chattanooga Choo Choo
- ☐ Rock gardens
- ☐ Underground waterfall

Native Americans lived here for thousands of years before Hernando de Soto, the first white man, passed through in 1540. By that time the "Great Indian Warpath," a trail that once stretched from Alabama to New York, and another Native American track that ran from Manchester, Tennessee, to St. Augustine, Florida, were worn 3 feet deep by moccasin traffic. The region was the last capital of the Cherokee Nation. Located between the Appalachian and Cumberland Mountains, the city was established in 1816 as a trading post called Ross's Landing by Cherokee chief John Ross. Ironically, the city later served as an incarceration area for the Cherokee before they were expelled to Oklahoma via the infamous Trail of Tears.

A new name was chosen for the city in 1838. The word *Chattanooga* is believed to have been a Native American expression that means a "rock that comes to a point," referring to Lookout Mountain. By the 1860s Chattanooga's position as a major rail center ultimately led to its pivotal role during the Civil War. After the war, the city continued to have important rail facilities and became one of the few southern cities to build a center for heavy industry. Chattanooga is the geographic center of the

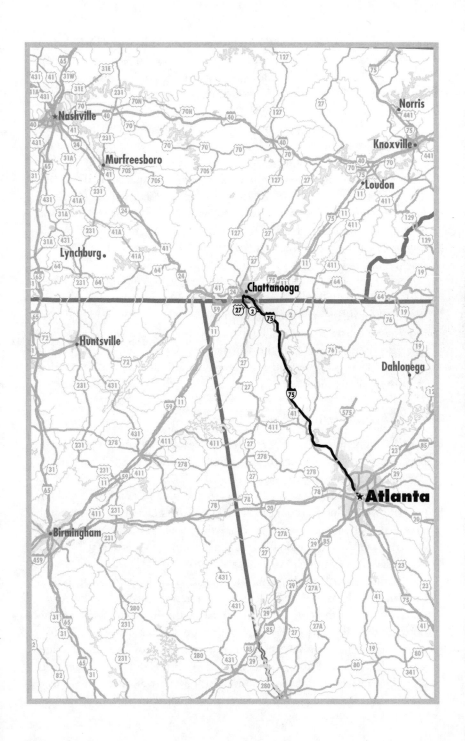

seven-state region served by the Tennessee Valley Authority (TVA), which was created in the 1930s. Glenn Miller's 1941 recording of "Chattanooga Choo Choo," the record industry's first gold record, brought the city national recognition. Today the community abounds with varied attractions and sporting opportunities.

One of the many pleasures of this small city is that so many of its delightful attractions are located compactly downtown within easy walking distance of one another: Ross's Landing Park and Plaza, Chattanooga Visitors Center, Tennessee Aquarium, Tennessee Aquarium 3D IMAX Theater, Walnut Street Bridge, *Southern Belle,* Chattanooga Regional History Museum, Creative Discovery Museum, and the International Towing and Recovery Hall of Fame and Museum. The Bluff View Arts District, with its galleries, restaurants, and bed-and-breakfasts, can be reached on foot from Ross's Landing as well.

Several bus services that run between major attractions and connect with each other will make any visit to Chattanooga easier and more pleasant for the tourist—allowing you to park your car in one spot and leave the driving to someone else. The free Downtown Shuttle transfers passengers from the aquarium to the Chattanooga Choo Choo, with stops at every block in between, and runs every five minutes. Get a shuttle map from the visitor center.

Day 1 / Afternoon

Take I–75 north from Atlanta to Chattanooga. Before you get to the state line, exit at GA 2 and proceed west to US 27, where you will turn north. Located near Rossville, Georgia, is the **John Ross House,** on McFarland Avenue (706–375–7702), a memorial to the great Cherokee chief. The two-story log house was built in 1797 by John McDonald, Ross's Scottish maternal grandfather, using plank flooring, rock chimneys, and pegged construction. It is the oldest remaining structure in northwest Georgia. Open daily June through September 1:00 to 5:00 P.M.

Continue on US 27 into Chattanooga. Make your first stop **Ross's Landing Park and Plaza,** along the Tennessee River. Considered the "front porch" of the city, the four-acre park, just one section of an ambitious 22-mile Riverpark master plan, presents Chattanooga's history, natural beauty, and cultural significance through innovative architecture, native plantings, and historical icons. A series of grassed, paved, or waterscaped bands depicts various periods of history; a stream course represents the river; artworks and artifacts portray the geology and people of the region. Significant historical periods, events, or people commemorated here include the earliest recorded human settlements on Moccasin Bend, Chattanooga's railroad heritage, the world's first Coca-Cola bottling operation, legendary blues singer Bessie Smith, and the civil rights movement. Distinctive architectural features include raised planted arches, representing the mountains, from which you can see panoramas of the river; an entry fountain; fabricated bluffs; and a waterfall. Ross's Landing is the home of the Chattanooga Visitors Center and the Tennessee Aquarium.

At the **Visitors Center,** 2 Broad Street (423–756–8687), ask the friendly staff for information and suggestions about seeing Chattanooga, including several historical and architectural walking tours. You can buy attraction tickets and souvenirs as well as pick up a Chattanooga Value Book full of discount coupons.

Go next door to the spectacular **Tennessee Aquarium,** 1 Broad Street (423–265–0695 or 800–262–0695; www.tnaqua.org), the world's largest exhibit of freshwater life. Tennessee is an appropriate choice for the first major freshwater life center in the world because it has more species of freshwater fish than any other state in the nation and is the home of more varieties of plants and animals than any comparable inland, temperate zone in the world. Thousands of plants, fish, birds, and other animals, representing more than 350 different species, reside in some forty realistic exhibits.

The stunning building features a 70-foot-high, pyramid-shaped glass roof. Inside, seven major freshwater tanks and two terrestrial environments are arranged in five main galleries. Your tour through the aquarium traces a drop of water from the Tennessee River's source in the high mountain forest of the Smoky Mountains through the reservoir system created by the TVA and finally to the Gulf of Mexico. In addition, the aquarium has displays of six of the world's great river systems in Africa, North and South America, Asia, and Siberia. The aquarium's only saltwater tank is an exhibit about the Gulf of Mexico.

Adjacent to the aquarium is the **IMAX 3D Theater,** 201 Chestnut Street (423–266–4629 or 800–262–0695), where films are shown continuously from 11:00 A.M. to 6:00 P.M., with extended summer hours. Combo tickets are available for the aquarium and theater.

Also from Ross's Landing, you can get a different view of the Tennessee River by walking across the **Walnut Street Bridge,** 1 River Street (423–757–5152). At 2,370 feet it is the longest pedestrian bridge in the world. Originally opened in 1891, the old truss bridge was the first multiuse structure across the Tennessee. Fully restored, it is now stronger than the original. The bridge is an ideal spot from which to gaze into the swirling depths of the river, watch the wildlife on Maclellan Island—an Audubon Society sanctuary (423–892–1499)—ogle the Fourth of July fireworks, or relish the Christmas boat parade. A section of one of the stone piers is set up for wall-climbing enthusiasts. **Coolidge Park** awaits you at the end of the bridge with a restored, antique, hand-carved carousel and a delightful interactive play fountain.

You can't go to Chattanooga without visiting the legendary **Chattanooga Choo Choo,** 1400 Market Street (423–266–5000 or 800–TRACK29 [872–2529]; www.choochoo.com). The glamorous Beaux Arts–style Terminal Station, opened in 1909, is now the gateway to numerous attractions at the complex. In its heyday the bustling station had fourteen tracks, with sixty-eight trains arriving and departing each day. The last train left Chattanooga in 1970, but the glorious station is preserved. An 85-foot dome, the highest freestanding vault in the world, soars over the Grand Lobby, once the main waiting room. The dome is supported by four arches embellished with intricate plaster-of-paris filigrees. The marble floor, ticket window, and station sheds where railroad cars are anchored are all original.

Visitors can ride a trolley, enjoy an impressive model train display, prowl through numerous shops, stroll through the formal gardens, or enjoy a meal at one of several eating establishments that range from snack stands to formal dining.

DINNER: Delightful choices at the Chattanooga Choo Choo are **Dinner on the Diner,** an elegant gourmet meal aboard an authentic railroad dining car; southern-style specialties in the **Gardens Restaurant;** a meal in the **Station House** served by a singing wait staff; **Cafe Espresso,** a dessert and sandwich shop; and the **Silver Diner** for pizza.

Evening

On Friday nights, the **Mountain Opry,** held in the Walden Ridge Civic Center, Fairmount Road atop Signal Mountain in Walden, Tennessee (contact Ray P. Fox, 423–886–5897), features spontaneous, informal mountain and bluegrass music from some of the best talents in southeastern Tennessee, northern Georgia, northern Alabama, and the world. Players have ranged from ages seven to 101 and have come from as far away as Norway and Japan.

LODGING: All the grandeur and exceptional service of an intimate European hotel are found at the **Mayor's Mansion Inn Bed and Breakfast,** 801 Vine Street (423–265–5000 or 888–446–6569; www .mayorsmansioninn.com). The majestic historic Victorian Romanesque home in the Fort Historic District was originally built in 1889 for the mayor of the city. Sixteen-foot coffered ceilings, magnificent moldings, and original hardware set an elegant backdrop for the exquisite furnishings and floor, window, and wall coverings of the public spaces and fifteen spacious guest rooms, which also feature all the modern conveniences. Full breakfast is included, and the inn also features a gourmet restaurant open to the public for dinner Friday and Saturday by reservation.

Day 2 / Morning

BREAKFAST: At the bed-and-breakfast.

Up to fifteen years ago, you could hardly drive anywhere in the South without seeing the red and black birdhouses or barns that said SEE ROCK CITY. Although not many of those landmarks are left, you'll still see a few reminders here and there. **Rock City Gardens,** 1400 Patten Road, Lookout Mountain, Georgia (706–820–2531; www.seerockcity.com), is one of this country's most unusual geologic formations. Millions of years ago an ocean receded and exposed the land to erosion. Ice and earthquakes caused the hard sandstone cap to crack. Wind, rain, and ice have continued to carve the rock into huge, bizarre formations.

Enchanted Rock City, as it exists today, began in the 1920s as the private rock garden of Garnet and Frieda Carter. Eventually they opened it to the public, and additions such as the Fairyland Caverns and Mother Goose Village were made. Enjoy the unique rock formations, lush gardens with more than 400 species of wildflowers, waterfall, overlooks, swinging bridge, and spectacular view, not only of Chattanooga but also of seven states—if the weather is perfect and there is no haze. The Seven States Flag Court salutes Tennessee, Georgia, Alabama, Kentucky, Virginia, and North and South Carolina. During the summer cuddly, life-size fairy-tale characters wander around, to the delight of children. A herd of unusual white fallow deer lives in Rock City's Deer Park.

LUNCH: Enjoy the sweeping vistas while having lunch at **Cliff Terrace Restaurant** at Rock City, or eat at the Big Rock Cafe.

Afternoon

Nearby is **Ruby Falls,** 1720 South Scenic Highway (423–821–2544; www.rubyfalls.com), a 145-foot underground waterfall. The attraction is not only the falls but the gigantic cavern. You're transported 1,120 feet underground by elevator, then begin a fascinating tour through the caverns sculpted with white onyx stalactites, stalagmites, and intriguing rock formations that resemble steak and potatoes, an angel's wing, an elephant's foot, and more, until you finally emerge at the base of the falls, bathed in multicolored but mostly ruby light. More than 300 gallons of water plunge ferociously into a small pool every minute before exiting the cave. Parts of the cave were used for centuries as hideouts by Native Americans, outlaws, and both Confederate and Union Civil War soldiers, but it wasn't until 1928 that the falls were discovered.

When you return to the surface, climb the castlelike observation tower for a stunning view of Chattanooga.

DINNER: The **Loft,** 328 Cherokee Boulevard (423–266–3601), voted "Chattanooga's First Choice in Dining" twenty years in a row, serves a fine selection of beef, chicken, and seafood in a casual atmosphere.

Evening

Check before you leave home, when you get to the Chattanooga Visitors Center, or directly with the **Tivoli Theater,** 709 Broad Street (423–757–5050), to see if there are any performances at the magnificently restored, 1920s Baroque theater, often called the Jewel Box of the South. The theater hosts concerts, dance, opera, and traveling Broadway shows. Admire the regal splendor of the theater's high, domed ceiling; grand lobby; crystal chandeliers; and elegant foyer. Traveling concerts and Broadway shows sometimes use the **Soldiers and Sailors Memorial Auditorium,** 399 McCallie Avenue (423–757–5042), so check with the auditorium or your concierge.

LODGING: Mayor's Mansion Inn.

Day 3 / Morning

BREAKFAST: At the bed-and-breakfast.

Railroad buffs will enjoy the **Tennessee Valley Railroad,** 4119 Cromwell Road and 2202 North Chamberlain Avenue (423–894–8028; www.tvrail.com)—the largest operating historic railroad in the South.

Steam trains provide a 6.5-mile round-trip hourly, including a trip through a pre–Civil War tunnel under Missionary Ridge. At either end of the line you can explore exhibits, watch the steam engine being turned around at the roundhouse, see engines and cars being restored, and tour historic railcars of all types, including a 1917 office car with three bedrooms and four bathrooms, a 1926 dining car, a 1929 caboose, and a Pullman sleeping car. The stations offer light meals and gift shops. Between Memorial Day and Labor Day, the *Downtown Arrow* provides passenger service between the Chattanooga Choo Choo Hotel downtown and the Grand Junction complex. The railroad sponsors special annual excursions such as those to see fall foliage.

LUNCH: Between April and October you can experience another mode of transportation while you enjoy lunch and a sightseeing cruise along the Tennessee River aboard the **Southern Belle,** Chattanooga Riverboat Company, Ross's Landing, Riverfront Parkway (423–266–4488 or 800–766–2784). The luncheon cruise features the "Build-Your-Own-Sandwich" buffet with an assortment of meats, cheeses, breads, and condiments. Depending on the time of year and day of the week, the company also offers breakfast sightseeing cruises; dinner cruises with such themes as Dixieland music, gospel music, or Nashville Nite BBQ; and moonlight cruises.

Afternoon

Spend the afternoon visiting Chattanooga's startlingly different museums. One of the finest permanent collections of eighteenth-, nineteenth-, and twentieth-century American art in the Southeast is displayed at the **Hunter Museum of American Art,** 10 Bluff View (423–267–0968; www.huntermuseum.org). Situated on a limestone bluff looming 90 feet over the Tennessee River and downtown, the museum occupies several disparate buildings renovated with a bold look that unifies the 1904 Classical Revival mansion, a contemporary structure, and a new West Addition. Fronting the museum is a striking outdoor sculpture garden. Pieces in the 1,500-piece collection represent art ranging from 1790 to the present and are rotated, so visitors can make numerous visits and see different artwork. Closed Monday.

Antiques, glass, china, furniture, and other fascinating items from the eighteenth and nineteenth centuries are displayed at the **Houston Museum of Decorative Arts,** 201 High Street (423–267–7176). Housed in an 1880s mansion across the street from the Hunter Museum of American Art, in addition to antique art glass and early American pressed glass, the museum's collection of lusterware is one of the largest and finest in the world. Beyond the scope and magnitude of the collection is the amazing fact that it was amassed by one woman, Anna Safley Houston. Even more astounding, she was of modest means, and until her death hardly anyone had ever seen any of the items. Houston—nicknamed "Antique Annie" and reputed to have married nine times—lived in virtual poverty in a rustic, barnlike structure she built with her own hands. It was packed to the rafters with treasures she collected (and refused to part with) over the years, including her 15,000 pitchers. Houston willed the entire collection to the city of Chattanooga. The collection is so large that only a fraction of it can be displayed. In addition to the art glass, the museum displays numerous important pieces of antique furniture. Changes in the items exhibited are made periodically, so repeat visitors will most likely see things they haven't seen before.

Return to Atlanta via I–75.

There's More

Black heritage. The Chattanooga African-American Museum and Research Center, 200 East Martin Luther King Boulevard (423–266–8658; www.caamhistory.com), exhibits African and African-American artifacts, historical documents, and photos. One room of the museum is devoted to one of Chattanooga's most illustrious citizens—the "Empress of the Blues," Bessie Smith. Interactive displays allow you to hear some of her old recordings, and jazz, blues, and gospel performances are given periodically. Closed Sunday.

Civil War sites. Chattanooga has a significant number of Civil War sites. Ride the Lookout Mountain Incline Railway, 827 East Brow Road or 3917 St. Elmo Avenue (423–821–4224), to the top of the mountain to explore some of the Civil War sites or simply to enjoy the ride and the spectacular views from the summit. Known as America's Most Amazing Mile because of its incredible 72.7 percent grade, the railroad has provided fast, inexpensive transportation and entertainment to residents and visitors for more than one hundred years.

Outdoor activities. Raccoon Mountain Caverns and Campground, 319 West Hills Drive (423–821–2283 or 800–823–2267; www.raccoon

mountain.com), boasts a concentrated collection of rock formations. The Lake Winnepesaukah Amusement Park, 1115 Lakeview Drive, Rossville, Georgia (706–866–5681; www.lakewinnie.com), has thirty rides, miniature golf, and Sunday entertainment by famous country and oldies crooners. Open April through September.

Shopping. The city draws thousands of Atlanta shoppers to its Prime Outlets at Warehouse Row, 1110 Market Street (423–267–1111), a complex of thirty elegant, upscale outlets offering designer fashions and other items in beautifully renovated, turn-of-the-twentieth-century railroad warehouses. Food court.

Special Events

June. The three-day Chattanooga Traditional Jazz Festival presents various bands playing New Orleans Dixieland jazz. (423) 266–0944.

Riverbend Festival, Chattanooga's biggest outdoor event, is a nine-day festival at Ross's Landing with world-class entertainment, sporting events, street performers, children's activities, fine-art exhibits, and fireworks. (423) 756–2211; www.riverbendfestival.com.

Other Recommended Restaurants and Lodgings

212 Market Restaurant, 212 Market Street (423–265–1212; www.212 market.com), provides upscale dining in elegant, comfortable surroundings. In addition to an excellent selection of wines, the restaurant serves divine desserts and offers monthly wine dinners.

Bluff View Inn, 412 East Second Street (423–265–5033 or 800–725–8338; www.bluffviewinn.com), offers restaurants and bed-and-breakfast accommodations in several historic mansions overlooking downtown and the river. Within walking distance of River Gallery, Sculpture Garden, Hunter Museum of Art, Tennessee Aquarium, and more. Four restaurants serve lunch, dinner, and Sunday brunch. Evening and brunch reservations requested.

Holiday Inn, at the Chattanooga Choo Choo, 1400 Market Street (423–266–5000 or 866–608–9330). Although the hotel contains three modern buildings, you can choose to stay in a historic railcar. No, you won't be sleeping in bunk beds in a tiny compartment. Each passenger car has been gutted and divided into two luxurious bedrooms decorated in opulent Victorian style, each with private bath. Other hotel amenities include tennis courts, an indoor pool, and an outdoor pool with water slide.

The Read House Hotel and Suites, 827 Broad Street (423–266–4121 or 800–691–1255; www.readhousehotel.com), is a beautifully restored historic building downtown. Green Room Restaurant for elegant dinner and Sunday brunch. Madelyne's Tavern for light fare three meals daily and entertainment.

For More Information

Chattanooga Area Convention and Visitors Bureau, 2 Broad Street, Chattanooga, TN 37401. (423) 756–8687 or (800) 322–3344; www .chattanoogafun.com.

Clarkesville/Helen/Sautee, Georgia

Georgia's Little Germany / 2 Nights

About twenty-five years ago, Helen was barely a blip on the landscape—a small, dying logging town in northeast Georgia. As residents cast far and wide for ideas to save their tiny town, they came up with a unique concept: to re-create Helen as a tourist attraction—a replica of a German, Swiss, or Austrian alpine village, complete with Bavarian facades on the buildings and narrow cobblestone alleys to explore. Shops would feature European items, and restaurants would highlight European cuisine.

- ☐ Alpine village
- ☐ Antiques and crafts shopping
- ☐ Waterfalls
- ☐ International restaurants
- ☐ Indian mound
- ☐ Old general store
- ☐ Covered bridge

The idea caught on and was immensely successful—perhaps too successful. Helen continues to grow unchecked. Dozens of motels, outlet malls, and tasting rooms from several of Georgia's wineries have mushroomed on the outskirts of town. Some kind of festival is being celebrated practically all the time. Traffic and parking can be problems.

Day 1 / Morning

Head north from Atlanta on I–85 and turn onto I–985, which ends at US 23. Follow the signs east to **Cornelia,** home of two unusual attractions. In the center of town is the **Big Red Apple Monument,** at 102 Grant Place. Said to be the world's largest apple monument, it is dedicated to the apple growers of north Georgia.

Elvis fans can peruse memorabilia to their hearts' content at the **Loudermilk Boarding House Museum,** 271 Foreacre Street (706–778–2001). Among the 30,000 treasures in owner Joni Mabe's

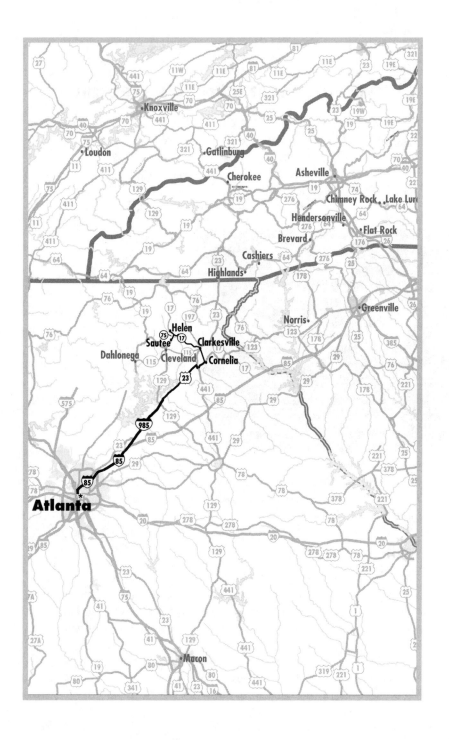

Panoramic Encyclopedia of Everything Elvis is a wart removed from the singer's right wrist in 1958 and a toenail that is believed to be his. Open Friday and Saturday 10:00 A.M. to 5:00 P.M. from April to November or by appointment.

Retrace US 23 to **Clarkesville**—renowned for its mountain crafts and antiques stores. "Goin' up to Clarkesville" has been a pastime of Georgians since the 1830s, when travelers made what was then an arduous journey to the mountains for the cool temperatures. For more information, check www.clarkesville.org, which will give you a driving tour past historic homes, churches, and cemeteries.

Stop at the **Habersham County Chamber of Commerce Historic Welcome Center,** 458 Jefferson Street (706–754–2296), located in the Mauldin House. The large nineteenth-century Victorian cottage with an adjacent millinery shop was first occupied by A. M. Mauldin and his wife, who was a hat maker. Today the house and shop contain exhibits about the mountain heritage of the area.

Many one-of-a-kind treasures can be found at the **World of Dreams Museum,** 4000 State 17 (706–754–0174). You'll see everything from gold discovered aboard the *Attocha* when it was raised by Mel Fisher to a car once owned by George Jones to Olympic memorabilia.

Spend the rest of the morning exploring Clarkesville's shops, galleries, and restaurants.

LUNCH: Located just off the square in a 1907 drugstore and soda fountain, **Stephen's,** 1460 Washington Street (706–839–1077), serves contemporary California cuisine.

Afternoon

Several options await. You could go west out of town on State 115 to see **Big Holly Cabin,** a primitive log house built in the early nineteenth century. Or take State 197 about 10 miles north of Clarkesville to the **Mark of the Potter** (706–947–3440), situated by a waterfall on the Soque River. The rustic, sixty-plus-year-old Grandpa Watts's Mill houses the potter's studio and a gift shop selling quality crafts from forty local artists.

Return to town and take State 17 west to **Helen.** Although most visitors go to Helen to buy Bavarian goods, others enjoy simply window-shopping and people-watching. Sitting at an open-air restaurant along a gurgling stream while sipping a German beer or wine and savoring a German dish is remarkably soothing. Pick up some information on what

The alpine town of Helen

to see and do at the **Helen Welcome Center** in the City Hall building at 726 Brucken Street (706–878–2181; www.helenga.org).

Hearkening back to the days even before Helen was a bustling logging town, the **Alpine Antique Auto and Buggy Museum,** 115 Escowee Drive (706–878–0072), displays more than one hundred horse-drawn buggies and wagons, including an 1840 hearse and a Civil War ambulance. In addition you can feast your eyes on antique cars from the early 1900s through the late 1970s.

See the Old World in a new way at **Charlemagne's Kingdom,** 8808 North Main Street (706–878–2200). A favorite for all ages, the fascinating exhibit provides an educational and unique trip through a miniature Germany. Stretching from the North Sea to the Alps, the realistic display re-creates that nation with an accurate topological landscape, bridges, autobahns, towns, villages, lakes, and rivers. This isn't just any tabletop display, mind you—it includes mountains 22 feet tall and two levels of viewing so you can actually walk through the country amid 300 buildings, more than 400 feet of HO-scale railroad track, a model railroad with computerized trains, and 800 painted figures. You'll also marvel at six 4-foot-tall carved German Glockenspiel figures in colorful traditional dress dancing to German music three times daily in the Gingerbread House.

DINNER: **Hofbrauhaus Inn International,** 1 Main Street (706–878–2248), overlooks the river near the tiny town square and offers international cuisine with, naturally, emphasis on German dishes.

LODGING: **Georgia Mountain Madness Adult Resort Cabins,** 190 Mountain Madness Drive (706–878–2851 or 888–534–6452; www.gamountainmadness.com), located in secluded woods 4 miles from Helen on GA 356, offers one- and two-bedroom cabins, some with private hot tubs and fireplaces. Adults only.

Day 2 / Morning

BREAKFAST: Sample the hearty breakfast buffet at the **Lodge at Unicoi State Park,** State 356 (706–878–2201).

Anna Ruby Falls, off State 356 near Unicoi State Park, is actually a double falls created by the junction of Curtis and York Creeks, both of which rise from underground springs on Tray Mountain. Curtis Falls is a 150-foot drop; York Falls only about 50 feet. A short paved trail from the visitor center leads to the falls. There are rest stops and descriptive signs along the way. In the late spring you can see rare red ferns. The Lion's Eye Nature Trail offers activities for the visually impaired along the way.

See rescued native Georgia black bears as well as grizzlies, Himalayans, Syrian browns, and other bears at the **Black Forest Bear Park and Reptile Exhibit,** 8160 South Main Street (706–878–7043), where you can learn more about each species and its habitats. The reptile exhibit has numerous large snakes, including representatives of all the poisonous snakes found in North America.

Return to town and continue your explorations and shopping in Helen.

LUNCH: **International Cafe,** State 75 (706–878–3102), a casual eatery alongside a shaded stream, serves a variety of dishes from several countries.

Afternoon

Leave Helen by traveling south on State 75, where you will find the **Nora Mill Granary,** 7101 South Main Street (706–878–2375 or 800–927–2375; www.noramill.com), a working gristmill built in 1876 on the banks of the Chattahoochee River. You can watch the miller operate the water-powered grinding stones and produce many wholesome stone-ground grain mixes as well as grits and cornmeal, all of which you can purchase. The mill also sells jams and Grandma's home-baked pies.

Continue south on State 75 and step into another world—one of natural beauty and pioneer heritage. At the intersection of State 17 and State 75 is the **Sautee-Nacoochee Indian Mound,** built by ancient Native Americans thousands of years ago and much later reputed to be the resting place of tragic young lovers from warring Cherokee and Chickasaw tribes.

Turn east on State 17 and travel to **Sautee.** At the intersection of State 17 and State 255 is the **Old Sautee General Store** (706–878–2281 or 888–463–9853; www.sauteestore.com). The legendary emporium has stood at the junction of the Nacoochee and Sautee Valleys, in the center of what was once the Cherokee Nation, for more than one hundred years. Just as when it served the needs of pioneers, the store museum today displays unusual old-time merchandise, old store fixtures, posters, and other memorabilia. None of the items are for sale; they are just to enjoy. Adjacent to the old store are shops selling fine Scandinavian imports and Christmas merchandise.

Turn north on State 255 to the **Sautee-Nacoochee Community Center,** 283 State 255 (706–878–3300), which operates as a history museum featuring memorabilia from the two valleys, as well as an art gallery, a performing arts hall, and the home of the annual Echota Performing Arts Festival each July and August.

Farther along State 255 is the **Stovall Covered Bridge.** Built in 1895, it is the smallest covered bridge in Georgia. The highway has been rerouted around the bridge, but you can park, admire the Kingpost design, and take pictures.

DINNER AND LODGING: The **Stovall House Country Inn and Restaurant,** 1526 State 255 North (706–878–3355; www.stovallhouse .com), offers five guest rooms in a restored 1837 house. Its restaurant serves gourmet cuisine, and *Georgia Trend* magazine named the restaurant as one of its "Best 50 in the State." From rockers on the ample porches, guests can enjoy the 360-degree view of the valley backed by mountains. Dinner is served Thursday through Saturday and brunch is served on Sunday.

Day 3 / Morning

BREAKFAST: Enjoy a hearty continental-plus breakfast at the inn.

Take State 17 through Clarkesville and get back on I–985 to return to Atlanta.

There's More

Helen

Canoeing and rafting. Flea Market Tubing, Alpine Valley Complex Flea Market (706–878–1082), offers free shuttles and changing rooms with its Chattahoochee River float trips. Cool River Tubing, Edelweiss Street (706–878–COOL; www.coolrivertubing.com), is also a good choice.

Theater. On Saturday throughout the year, visitors to Helen's Remember When Theatre, 115 Escowee Street (706–878–SHOW; www.remember whentheatre.com), can take a stroll down memory lane with such shows as *Mark Pitt's Tribute to Elvis*, *Richard Sammon's Legends of Rock, Rhythm, and Blues*, and other acts.

Winery. Habersham Winery, 7025 South Main Street (706–878–9463; www.habershamwinery.com), one of Georgia's oldest wineries, operates a satellite outlet where you can sample wines while you view the tank room, oak barrel room, and bottling line.

Fred's Famous Peanuts, 17 Clayton Road (706–878–3124), purveys boiled, roasted, and Fred's Famous Fried Peanuts as well as peanut brittle, apples, cider, pumpkins, and mountain craft products. You'll know the place by the life-size soft-sculpture old couple resting a spell on a bench out front.

Sautee

Shopping. The Gourd Place, 2319 Duncan Bridge Road (706–865–4048; www.gourdplace.com), offers interesting items made from gourds as well as a gourd museum and a nature trail around the lake. Closed January through March.

Scarlett's Secret, 1902 State 17 (706–878–1028; www.scarlettsecret.com), located in a plantation-style house, is furnished in the period of *Gone with the Wind* and contains memorabilia related to the movie and the Civil War. They sell vintage and new *Gone with the Wind* memorabilia.

Special Events

Clarkesville

May. Mountain Laurel Festival, held downtown on Washington Street, features arts and crafts, food, and a juried art show of artists from the area and all over the Southeast. (706) 754–4216.

Helen

September–November. Helen's famous Oktoberfest (which really lasts two months) features live Bavarian music, German food and beverages, and dancing. The area is one of the most popular in the state during fall foliage season at the end of October and the beginning of November. (706) 878–2181.

Other Recommended Restaurants and Lodgings

Clarkesville

The Burns-Sutton House, 85 Washington Street (706–754–5565), located in a 1901 asymmetrical Queen Anne Victorian mansion, operates as a bed-and-breakfast.

Glen-Ella Springs Inn, 1789 Bear Gap Road (706–754–7295 or 877–456–7527; www.glenella.com), is a historic country inn on seventeen acres. It offers a gourmet restaurant, pool, gardens, and theme weekends. Glen-Ella's restaurant serves breakfast and lunch to guests only. It is open to the public for dinner.

Helen

Bavarian Brook Lodge and Rentals, 359 Edelweiss Drive (706–878–2840 or 800–422–6355; www.bavarianbrookrentals.com), on the riverfront within walking distance of attractions, offers motel rooms as well as condos with fireplaces, kitchens, and Jacuzzis.

Innsbruck Resort and Golf Club, 2400 State 75 (706–878–2100; www.innsbruckresort.com), is a premier family resort with three-bedroom villas. Golf, tennis, swimming, hiking trails.

The Troll Tavern, Main Street (706–878–3117), specializes in prime rib and seafood and presents weekend music and a comedy show.

Unicoi State Park Lodge, State 356 (706–878–2201 or 800–573–9659), is a modern lodge with one hundred rooms, a restaurant, and a craft shop. The park also has thirty cottages as well as campsites.

Sautee

Edleweiss German Country Inn, 747 Duncan Bridge Road (706–865–7371; www.edelweissgermaninn.com), offers bed-and-breakfast accommodations, cabins, and a restaurant.

Nacoochee Valley Guest House and Restaurant, 2220 State 17 (706–878–3830; www.letsgotobernies.com), is a bed-and-breakfast, restaurant, bakery, and gift shop, all housed in a 1920s home.

For More Information

Alpine Helen Convention and Visitors Bureau, Chattahoochee Street, Helen, GA 30545. (706) 878–2181 or (800) 858–8027; www.helenga.org.

Habersham County Chamber of Commerce, 668 Clarkesville Highway, Cornelia, GA 30531. (706) 778–4654 or (800) 835–2559.

Great Smoky Mountains National Park Area

Land of the Blue Mist / 2 Nights

Awaken in a quaint bed-and-breakfast enveloped in a Smoky Mountain mist clinging to the hills and hollows. When the vapor burns off, the sun reveals natural wonders such as miles of rushing trout streams and deep virgin forests. Your activities for the day might include points of scenic and historic interest, rest and relaxation, or physical activity.

☐ Rugged mountains

☐ Spectacular views

☐ Outdoor dramas

☐ Native American heritage

☐ Arts and crafts

The spirits of the Cherokee, who called the mountains the "Great Blue Hills of God," "Land of the Blue Mist," or "Place of Blue Smoke," and of the early settlers, who translated the name to "Smoky Mountains," linger in the hills and valleys. Cherokee legend says the pinnacles were created by a Great Buzzard that, when the earth was soft and still forming, flew too close to the surface. As its wing tips pushed the ground down, the mountains popped up. Geologists have defined the Appalachians, of which the Smokies are a part, as the oldest mountains in the world.

The Cherokee have occupied this land for more than 10,000 years. The lands once claimed by the Cherokee encompassed parts of what are now eight states: Kentucky, Tennessee, Alabama, Georgia, Virginia, West Virginia, and North and South Carolina—a total of 135,000 square miles. Unfortunately, caucasians decided they wanted the lands. In the 1830s the Cherokee were rounded up and expelled. Their tragic journey to reservations in Oklahoma is remembered as the Trail of Tears. The descendants of those displaced Cherokee are called the Western Band of Cherokee. About a thousand Cherokee were able to evade capture, however, by hiding in the Smoky Mountain forests and little-known caves. Their 10,000 descendants are known as the Eastern Band of Cherokee, and their history and culture

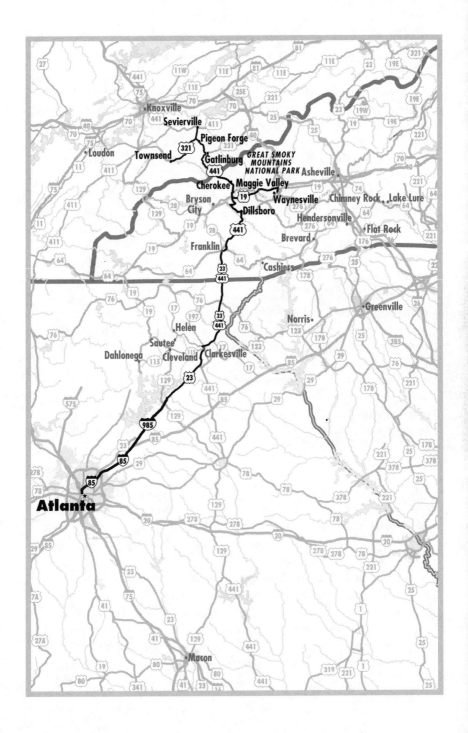

are kept alive in the 56,572-acre Cherokee Indian reservation known as the Qualla Boundary, a sovereign land held in trust specifically for the tribe by the U.S. government.

Great Smoky Mountains National Park, which straddles the Tennessee/North Carolina border for 60 miles, is America's most popular national park, visited by eight million people annually. Within its 520,000 acres are more species of trees and plants than on the whole of the European continent. Nine hundred miles of hiking and horseback riding trails have been developed within the park. The elevation varies from 840 feet at the mouth of Abrams Creek to 6,643 feet at the summit of Clingman's Dome—the highest mountain in the park, the second highest in the East, and the highest point on the Appalachian Trail. Popular landmarks include Mount LeConte, Chimney Tops, Ramsay Cascades—a 100-foot waterfall—and scenic and historic sites at Cataloochee Valley, Cades Cove, and Oconaluftee.

Several small cities and towns around the park offer mountain crafts, museums, country and bluegrass music, and outdoor activities: Maggie Valley, Waynesville, and Bryson City on the North Carolina side of the park and Gatlinburg, Pigeon Forge, Sevierville, Townsend, and Walland on the Tennessee side.

You can visit the Smokies any time of year, but because of the severe winters that make skiing possible, many attractions, lodgings, and restaurants are closed for several months. Accordingly, check ahead so you won't be disappointed.

Day 1 / Afternoon

Leave Atlanta and take I–85 to I–985, which becomes US 23/441. Before you get to Franklin, North Carolina, stop at the **Smoky Mountain Host of North Carolina,** 4437 Georgia Highway (800–432–HOST), for regional information and interpretive exhibits. Sometimes the center holds mountain craft demonstrations.

Next you'll come to **Dillsboro,** from which you can introduce yourself to the mountains aboard the **Great Smoky Mountains Railway,** 119 Front Street (828–586–8811 or 800–872–4681; www.gsmr.com). Open-air cars allow you to be at one with nature—the wind tousling your hair, the mists caressing your cheeks—as the train roars or crawls through narrow passages, over craggy mountains, and alongside surging rivers. For the more fainthearted, closed cars are available, too. The railroad offers four half-day excursions from different stations in the Smokies. On the Tuskasegee River Excursion from Dillsboro, the highlight is passing the spectacular train-wreck site from the movie *The Fugitive*. Although the climactic crash took two months to set up, it took only sixty seconds to film. Round-trip prices are based on distance traveled, type of seating you choose, and whether the train is pulled by a steam or a diesel locomotive. During December, when the Santa Express makes round-trips between Dillsboro and Whittier, festive onboard activities end with a visit from Santa. The Easter Bunny hops aboard in the spring. New activities include a dinner train excursion, a murder-mystery dinner train excursion, and an overnight excursion with accommodations at the Tuttle House Bed and Breakfast.

While you're in Dillsboro, visit the **Floyd McEachern Historic Railway Museum** (866–914–5200) at the depot from which the train departs. Then browse through Dillsboro's maze of forty gift and arts-and-crafts shops.

Continue north on US 441 to **Cherokee,** arriving in time for dinner.

DINNER: **Harrah's Casino,** US 19N/US 441 Business (828–497–7777; www.harrahs.com/our_casinos/che), offers three restaurant options: Seven Sisters, Fresh Market Square Buffet, and Selu Garden Cafe.

Evening

If you are in Cherokee between mid-June and the end of August, attend a performance of **Unto These Hills,** a tragic but triumphant drama that relives Cherokee history from 1540, when Spanish explorer Hernando de Soto was the first white man to encounter the Cherokee, through the Trail of Tears in the 1830s. One hundred actors and actresses, battle sounds, and music re-create the story at Mountainside Theater, Drama Road (828–497–2111; www.untothesehills.com). In the forty-plus years the production has been running, more than five million people have attended.

LODGING: **Holiday Inn–Cherokee,** US 19 (828–497–9181 or 800–HOLIDAY), features beautiful rooms and gardens. Indoor and outdoor pools. Chestnut Tree Restaurant.

Day 2 / Morning

BREAKFAST: **Hungry Bear Restaurant,** US 441 (828–497–2073), specializes in Carolina country ham. Beautiful mountain view with outdoor seating. Open daily for breakfast; lunch and dinner on Saturday and Sunday.

The Cherokee, who called themselves the "Principal People," were not nomadic; they farmed and lived in log cabins. Several attractions on the reservation provide an overview of Cherokee history and culture.

Visit the **Museum of the Cherokee Indian,** US 441 North at Drama Road (828–497–3481; www.cherokeemuseum.org). You'll be greeted outside by a 20-foot hand-carved statue of Sequoyah, inventor of the Cherokee alphabet, hewn from California redwood. Because of his efforts, the Cherokee were the first Native Americans to have a written language. Throughout the spacious facility are outstanding examples of ancient craftsmanship, some as old as 10,000 years: weapons, household items, farming utensils, and art forms such as pottery and baskets—not only of the Cherokee but from other Native American tribes around the country as well. Various audiovisual presentations walk you from prehistoric times to the present. Special "hearphones" allow you to hear the Cherokee language spoken. Ancient legends about creation, fire, and life are passed on through the Myth Keepers display. Books, crafts, artwork, and other Native American items are for sale in the gift shop.

Located in a natural wooded setting, the **Oconaluftee Indian Village,** US 441 on the reservation (828–497–2111; www.untothese hills.com), re-creates a Cherokee village from circa 1750. The two-hour tour includes lectures and demonstrations by various Cherokee craftspeople. You'll see basket weaving, carving, pottery making, mask making, and hewing of dugout canoes. At the ceremonial grounds, in addition to learning the purpose of the grounds, you'll hear explanations about dances and the use of masks, rattles, and feathers. In the seven-sided council house, you'll hear about treaties, territories, language, and other nonceremonial topics. The village also contains a sweat lodge and typical eighteenth-century homes. Adjacent to the village is a mile-long nature trail with a variety of trees, plants, and flowers indigenous to western North Carolina. Open May through October.

Although there are a lot of tacky, trashy souvenir shops in and around Cherokee, take the time to browse around in the stores, ferreting out the quality arts-and-crafts items. The largest retailer of authentic Native American goods is **Qualla Arts and Crafts Mutual, Inc.,** US 441 North at Drama Road (828–497–3103). Formed as a cooperative in the 1940s, the outlet represents 300 Cherokee artisans. Fifteen other stores on the reservation specialize in or exclusively offer crafts, clothing, paintings, or jewelry made by local craftspeople or other Native Americans.

Traditional to the town of Cherokee are the costumed chiefs who station themselves at strategic spots to be photographed with visitors. If you've already toured the Oconaluftee Village or some of the museums, you'll realize that these aren't really chiefs and their costumes are not representative of the Cherokee—it's just showbiz. The chiefs usually charge a small fee or ask for a tip when photographs are taken.

LUNCH: Jernigan's Country Restaurant, US 411 South (828–497–2307), serves great sandwiches, blue plate specials, and fish.

Afternoon

Take US 19 east to **Maggie Valley,** just off the Blue Ridge Parkway near the east entrance to the park. The name of the town was chosen by the postmaster general in 1909 to honor one of his daughters. A year-round resort, the town bills itself as the Clogging Capital of the World. This spirited mountain dance evolved from old Scottish and Irish reels and jigs brought to the area by early pioneers. Watch or join in at the **Stompin' Ground Dance Hall,** 3116 Soco Road (828–926–1288; www.stomping groundpresents.com).

Continue east on US 19 until you come to US 23, then turn south to **Waynesville,** home of the outstanding North Carolina International Folk Festival—Folkmoot USA and the oldest ramp-eating festival in the country. (Ramps are related to onions, leeks, and garlic.) Shelton House is the home of the **Museum of North Carolina's Handicrafts,** 49 Shelton (828–452–1551). Waynesville, named for Revolutionary War hero Gen. "Mad" Anthony Wayne, offers many spectacular views, such as those at Soco Gap and Mile High Heintooga Overlook on a spur of the Blue Ridge Parkway. A beautiful spring drive is Pigeon Loop through Pigeon Gap and past the blooms of numerous orchards. The loop follows US 276, NC 100, and US 19.

DINNER AND LODGING: The **Swag Country Inn,** Hemphill Road (828–926–0430, 828–926–3119, or 800–789–7672; www.the swag.com). "God lives here," says a guest as he surveys the 50-mile panorama from atop the 5,000-foot private mountain at this rustic inn. The main lodge—constructed from several old buildings collected by the owners—and two other cabins are exquisitely furnished in mountain primitive and feature steam showers or whirlpool baths. Meals included.

View from the Swag Country Inn, Maggie Valley

Restaurant open to nonguests. Situated on 250 acres, the property shares a 1-mile boundary with the national park. Gift shop, sauna, racquetball court, lawn games, library. Open from the end of May through November.

Day 3 / Morning

BREAKFAST: At the Swag Country Inn.

Return to Cherokee and take US 441, which is Newfound Gap Road, across the North Carolina line to Gatlinburg/Pigeon Forge/Sevierville, Tennessee. This side of the park is much more developed (in our opinion, overdeveloped). Here's where you'll find miles of wall-to-wall souvenir shops, wax museums, haunted houses, miniature golf courses, theme parks, water parks, and, of course, Dollywood. We'll leave their descriptions to other folks and concentrate on the less commercial sights.

Begin at the **Gatlinburg Welcome Center,** Foothills Parkway–Gatlinburg Spur (800–822–1998; www.gatlinburg.com), for information relating to the park. Then visit the **Great Smoky Arts and Crafts**

Community, US 321 (865–436–3301), an 8-mile loop of the shops, studios, and galleries of eighty artists and craftspeople. You can drive or take the Arts and Crafts Trolley.

The **Old Mill,** 160 Old Mill Avenue, Pigeon Forge (865–453–4628), built in 1830 and in operation ever since, is a water-powered mill that still grinds corn, wheat, rye, and buckwheat into twenty-eight kinds of meal, flour, grits, and pancake mixes.

LUNCH: Enjoy a hearty lunch at the **Applewood Farmhouse Restaurant,** at the Apple Barn and Cider Mill, 230 Apple Valley Road, Sevierville (865–428–1222), then stock up on fresh apples, fried apple pies, and apple cider. Sample the wines being produced by Applewood's winery.

Afternoon

Take US 441 back to Pigeon Forge, then go west on US 321 to **Townsend,** an old railroad and lumber company town. **Little River Railroad and Lumber Company Museum,** US 321, East Lamar Parkway (865–448–2211; www.littleriverrailroad.org), presents mementos of the railroad and lumber operations from early settlements to the present.

Retrace your route on US 321 until you reach US 23/441 at Pigeon Forge, which will take you south back to Atlanta.

There's More

Fishing. There are 30 miles of trout streams on the reservation. The Cherokee trout season is from the end of March though the end of the following February. A tribal fishing permit is required, but not a state fishing license. Call Cherokee Fish and Game Management at (828) 497–5201.

Gambling. Harrah's Casino, US 19N/US 441 Business (828–497–7777), offers various electronic wagering games. Tribal Bingo, US 19N, Cherokee (828–497–4320), holds games nightly except Sunday.

Horseback riding. Walden's Creek Horse Back Riding, 2709 Walden's Creek Road, Sevierville, Tennessee (865–429–0411); Cades Cove Stables, 4035 East Lamar Alexander Parkway, Walland, Tennessee (865–448–6286); and Davy Crockett Riding Stables, 505 Old Cades Cove Road, Townsend, Tennessee (865–448–6411).

Skiing. Cataloochee Ski Area at Maggie Valley, North Carolina (800–768–0285), has a vertical drop of 740 feet.

White-water rafting/canoeing/tubing. Cherokee River Trips schedules outings between June 1 and Labor Day. Call the visitor center at (828) 497–9195.

Special Events

Cherokee, North Carolina

Special events take place throughout the year but, with the exception of Christmas, are concentrated from April to October. Powwows and most of the other special events are held at the Ceremonial Grounds. For more information call (828) 497–9195 or (800) 438–1601.

Other Recommended Restaurants and Lodgings

North Carolina Side of the Park

Bryson City

Fryemont Inn, Fryemont Road (828–488–2159 or 800–845–4879), is a rustic inn built in 1923. Dining room, specializing in trout, operates from the end of April through October and weekends in November.

Cherokee

There are forty-three lodgings on the reservation. Among the better known are Best Western Smoky Mountain Inn, US 441 at Acquoni Road (828–497–2020); Hampton Inn, US 19S (800–HAMPTON); Holiday Inn–Cherokee, US 19S (800–HOLIDAY); and Pioneer Cottages and Motel, US 19S (828–497–2435). There are numerous other motels, cabins, and campgrounds in the immediate vicinity.

Dillsboro

One of the friendliest places to stay at the gateway to the Smokies is the Squire Watkins Inn, 657 Haywood Road (828–586–5244 or 800–586–2429). Located in a Queen Anne Victorian house on three landscaped acres, the inn is within walking distance of shops and studios and the Great Smoky Mountains Railway depot.

Maggie Valley

At the Cataloochee Ranch (a resort), 119 Ranch Road (828–926–1401 or 800–868–1401), you can explore valleys and mountains on horseback. Accommodations are in the Ranch House—a converted barn, seven cabins, and two suites. Restaurant open to nonguests by reservation. Wagon rides, overnight trail rides, tennis, fishing, hot tub, skiing, gift shop.

Waynesville

Old Stone Inn, 900 Dolan Road (828–456–3333 or 800–432–8499), a simply furnished 1940s inn, is nestled on six shady acres. Accommodations are in the main lodge and several cottages. Restaurant open to nonguests by reservation. Hillside hot tub.

Tennessee Side of the Park

All major hotel chains are represented in Gatlinburg, Pigeon Forge, and Sevierville and are scattered elsewhere. Best Western has the best variety. On the budget side there's a heavy presence of Family Inns and Hampton Inns. Campgrounds, cabin and condo rentals, and resorts abound.

Cosby

The Front Porch, US 321 (865–487–2875), the world's only Mexican-bluegrass restaurant, has been voted eastern Tennessee's "Best Mexican Restaurant" by the *Knoxville Journal*. Self-described as Mountain-Mex, the made-from-scratch cuisine is that of central Mexico. On Friday, Saturday, and Sunday local fiddlers, banjo players, guitar and mandolin strummers, and country singers dispense authentic bluegrass music. Slapped-together decor includes paper flowers, puppets, and miniature chili lights.

Gatlinburg

Buckhorn Inn (a B&B), 2140 Tudor Mountain Road (865–436–4668; www.buckhorninn.com), captures the feel of early, unspoiled Gatlinburg. Near the celebrated Smoky Mountains Crafts Community. Built in the 1930s, it is located on thirty wooded acres and has its own self-guided nature walk. Six rooms, four cottages, two guest houses. Full breakfast included. Six-course gourmet dinner (additional cost) available to nonguests by reservation.

Sevierville

Blue Mountain Mist Country Inn (a B&B), 1811 Pullen Road
(865–428–2335; www.bluemountainmist.com), is a graceful, antiques-
filled Queen Anne Victorian farmhouse furnished in country charm.
Eleven rooms, one suite, five rustic cabins, and a full country breakfast.
Some Jacuzzis, private porches.

Townsend

Richmont Inn, 220 Winterberry Lane (865–448–6751; www.richmont
inn.com), a romantic, ten-room and two-suite B&B built in the style of
the famous Appalachian Cantilever Barn, is on eleven secluded acres
within the sanctuary of the Laurel Valley resort. Full breakfast and late-
evening candlelight dessert. Exquisitely furnished. Some Jacuzzis, fireplaces, and private porches. Golf and dining privileges at Laurel Valley
Country Club.

Walland

Blackberry Farm, 1471 West Millers Cove (423–984–8166), is a sprawling
stone-and-frame country manor house with a matching guest house and
several cottages. The forty-four-room retreat—on a 1,100-acre estate—
specializes in luxury and pampering: exquisite art and antiques, feather
beds, down comforters, three gourmet meals a day, and impeccable service.
Formal but not stuffy; guests do dress for dinner. Pool, tennis, putting
green, fishing—almost everything is included. Spa services are extra.

For More Information

Cherokee Visitors Center, Main Street, Cherokee, NC 28719. (828)
497–9195 or (800) 438–1601.

Great Smoky Mountains National Park, 107 Park Headquarters Road,
Gatlinburg, TN 37738. (865) 436–1200; www.nps.gov/grsm/.

Dahlonega/Cleveland, Georgia

Thar's Gold in Them Thar Hills / *2 Nights*

In 1828, long before the cry of "gold in them thar hills" enticed prospectors to California, America's first major gold rush struck the northeast Georgia mountains. Treasure hunters, seduced by the anticipation of swift and easy wealth, arrived in droves. The inundation of dreamers and schemers catapulted the region into a booming prospecting and mining mecca. Almost overnight, two towns—Dahlonega and Auraria—developed. Dahlonega takes its name from the Cherokee word *talonaga,* which means "precious metal." Cherokees were the inhabitants of northeast Georgia long before the discovery of gold. Plans were already under way to remove them, but the gold rush hastened their relocation to Oklahoma and Arkansas—beginning the infamous Trail of Tears.

- ☐ Dahlonega
- ☐ Panning for gold
- ☐ Home-style Southern cooking
- ☐ Antiques and crafts shopping
- ☐ Mountains
- ☐ Waterfalls
- ☐ Highest point in Georgia
- ☐ Birthplace of Cabbage Patch Kids

A U.S. mint was built west of town in 1837, making Dahlonega one of only seven official mints in the country. Although the residents of Lumpkin County opposed southern sentiment in 1861 by voting against secession from the Union, the area was compelled to follow the rest of the state into the Confederacy. The federal government therefore closed the Dahlonega mint. Although it operated as a Confederate assay office during the Civil War, it was captured by the Union in 1865 and eventually burned. However, portions of the old mint can be seen today in the lower

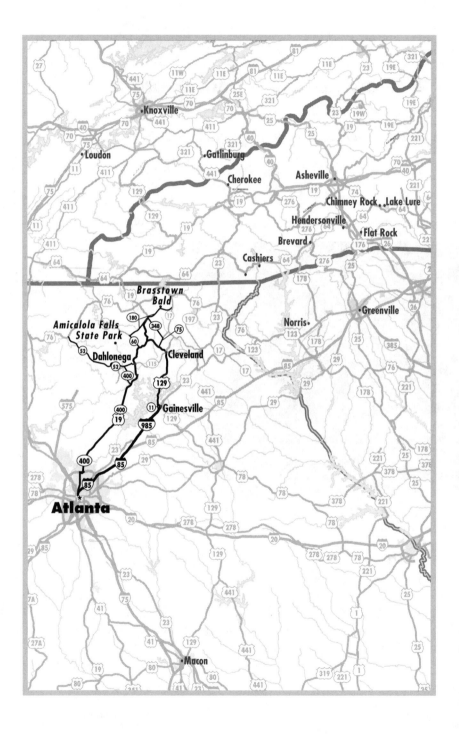

level of Price Memorial Hall, which was built on the foundation in 1878 at North Georgia College and State University.

The dome of Georgia's capitol in Atlanta is embellished with gold leaf from Dahlonega. During the dome's restoration several years ago, the gold was carted to Atlanta by wagon train, just as it had been when the dome was first gilded. Although the major seams of gold have long been depleted, enough traces are left to provide entertainment and excitement for visitors. It is said that there's still enough gold in the hills around Dahlonega to pave the town square around the courthouse with gold 1 foot deep.

Today a new breed of prospector—the tourist—is discovering Dahlonega. Although it's a small town of about 5,000, it's not a sleepy little village. Between its own attractions and its location as one of the gateways into the mountains, the home of North Georgia College and State University is always bustling with tourists drawn by the aura of gold. In fact, no matter when you visit, you're sure to find golden moments in Dahlonega.

Day 1 / Afternoon

Head north from Atlanta to **Dahlonega** on State 400. When the divided highway ends, turn left onto State 60 North, which will take you right to Dahlonega's quaint town square and historic district, which is listed on the National Register of Historic Places. The centerpiece of the district is the **Dahlonega Courthouse Gold Museum** (706–864–2257; www .dahlonega.org), one of the most visited historic sites in the state. Built in 1836 on the site of an original log cabin, it is the oldest public building in north Georgia. The traditionally styled brick and white-columned building began life as the county courthouse.

Tourists will get gold fever while examining exhibits that trace the history of the county, gold mining techniques, ore processing, and lifestyles of early residents. Of course, all the exhibits are well protected by display cases and alarm systems, but the sight of gigantic blocks of shiny ore and piles of coins are awe inspiring. An immense old safe from that era shows how gold was protected before modern technology. Enlargements of historic photos line the walls, as do miners' implements.

Several locations around town offer visitors the opportunity to pan for gold: the **Smith House Inn,** 84 South Chestatee (706–867–7000 or 800–852–9577; www.smithhouse.com); **Crisson Gold Mine,** 2736

Morrison Moore Parkway (706–864–6363), a strip-mine site with the only working stamp mill in Georgia; and **Consolidated Gold Mine Tours,** 185 Consolidated Gold Mine Road (706–864–8473; www.consolidated goldmine.com), where you can experience what gold mining was like. Although the mine, which began operation in 1847, closed in the 1930s, it was the largest mining operation east of the Mississippi and is still owned by the fourth generation of a gold-mining family. Their gift shop sells gold nuggets and handmade gold jewelry. Whether you pan for it or buy it, lucky vacationers can walk away with the precious ore.

DINNER: The **Smith House Inn,** 84 South Chestatee Street (706–867–7000 or 800–852–9577; www.smithhouse.com), is famous for its home-style southern cooking served family-style. The house, which was built as a family home in 1899, has served as an inn and restaurant since the 1920s. If you're lucky, you won't have to wait in line, but folks are more than willing to endure long delays to indulge in the profusion and variety of food. Play it safe and make reservations. Once in the dining room, diners are seated together at large tables, thus giving you the opportunity to get to know others. You may be surprised to learn that some of your tablemates are from other states and even other countries, so widespread is the fame of the Smith House.

LODGING: The atmosphere at the **Worley Homestead Inn,** 168 Main Street West (706–864–7002), located within walking distance of the historic district, is that of a very upscale stagecoach stop. Built in 1845, the home in which the bed-and-breakfast is located is in mint condition and is furnished with exquisite antiques.

Day 2 / Morning

BREAKFAST: You'll enjoy a hearty full breakfast at the Worley Homestead Inn.

Surrounding Dahlonega's square on all four sides are historic buildings. Although not from the gold rush era, most of these structures were erected before the turn of the twentieth century. Today they house nostalgic shops and quaint restaurants catering to tourists. These shops overflow with Appalachian folk arts and other items that exemplify and preserve the region's mountain heritage. Pick up the brochure *Once Around the Square* from the Welcome Center to learn the history of these venerable buildings and the lively stories connected with them. A second walking tour brochure you can get from the Welcome Center describes the Hawkins Street National Historic District.

Price Memorial Hall at North Georgia College and State University, West Main Street (706–864–1400; www.ngcsu.edu), was built on the foundation of the old mint. Its gold-covered steeple not only rises above the building that serves as the college's administrative offices but is a major landmark in Dahlonega and the surrounding countryside. The lower level includes the ramp where the carts dumped gold into the basement of the old mint, original pillars, and walls from 1833.

LUNCH: Wylie's Restaurant, 19 North Chestatee Street (706–867–6334), is located in a historic building on the square and serves delicious soups, salads, and sandwiches as well as steaks and seafood in an upscale atmosphere.

Afternoon

Stop by the Welcome Center on the square to get ideas about other things to do in the Dahlonega area. The Chamber of Commerce (www.dahlonega.org) has created **Dahlonega's Mountain Magic Self-Guided Auto Tour,** which takes you through the Chattahoochee National Forest for glimpses of picturesque lakes, secluded valleys, bubbling streams, and spectacular waterfalls.

West of town on State 52 is **Amicalola Falls State Park** (706–265–4703, park; 706–265–8888, lodge; www.gastateparks.org/info/amicalola/). At 729 feet, Amicalola Falls, named for the Cherokee word that means "tumbling waters," is the highest waterfall not only in Georgia but east of the Mississippi. You can drive to vantage points where you can get a close-up view of the falls from the bottom or the top. Trails lead partway up or down, but they don't meet, so you can't hike the entire expanse. Be forewarned that the trail is quite steep; however, there are handrails and resting places—some with benches. The valley faces south, so if you want to take pictures, don't wait until too late in the afternoon or the falls will be in shadow.

Return to Dahlonega and head north out of town on US 19/129. This area is covered with thick forests, numerous state parks, and myriad waterfalls. At the intersection of US 19 and State 60 is **Princess Trahlyta's Grave,** a pile of stones that marks the resting place of a Native American princess. Legend, which was probably started by caucasians who wanted to publicize nearby Porter Springs, says that her tribe, living on

Cedar Mountain, got eternal youth from the magic springs of a witch. Trahlyta was kidnapped by a rejected suitor and taken far away, where she lost her youth and beauty. When she was dying, the warrior Wahsega promised to bury her near her home and the magic springs—a promise he kept. It is customary to drop a stone on her grave to bring good fortune. **DeSoto Falls Scenic Area,** US 129, has three waterfalls. One is reached by an easy walk, one by a moderate hike, and the third is recommended only for experienced hikers.

Not far from Dahlonega, the Appalachian Trail rises out of the Chattahoochee National Forest at Springer Mountain and crosses the highway several times. Native Americans called this area the "Land of the Dancing Rabbits." It was also a territory of moonshine stills, pioneer cabins, and logging camps. A recommended stop is the **Neel's Gap Lookout Point and Mountain Crossings** at **Walasi-Yi Information Center,** US 19 (706–745–6095). At the rustic center, built in 1937, you can buy handmade crafts, hiking gear, maps, guidebooks, and picnic supplies. The overlook offers a stunning view.

Helton Creek Falls, off US 19/129, one of our favorites, also has three falls, but all are from the same stream, so you can easily hike to all of them.

Vogel State Park, US 19/129 (706–745–2628; www.gastate parks.org/info/vogel/), one of Georgia's first state parks, features camping sites, cottages, fishing, swimming, hiking, pedal boats, and miniature golf.

Take State 180 east, then the State 180 Spur to **Brasstown Bald** (706–896–2555 or 706–896–2556), Georgia's highest mountain. The summit rises 4,784 feet above sea level. From the peak you can see a 360-degree panorama of four states, tour the museum in the visitor center, and watch an audiovisual presentation. There are four hiking trails here, ranging from 0.5 to 6 miles.

Go west on State 180 and turn south on State 348 to State 75, where you will go south to US 129. Turn east to **Cleveland**—home of BabyLand General Hospital, which you'll visit tomorrow.

Get information about the area from the **White County Welcome Center,** located in a 1901 former jail building at 122 North Main Street (706–865–5356). The **Old White County Courthouse** on the square (706–865–3225) was built between 1857 and 1859 and houses the county historical society. The museum is open Thursday through Saturday from 10:00 A.M. to 3:00 P.M. Downtown, **Merchants Square** brims with crafts, novelties, and restaurants.

DINNER: **Ma Gooch's,** 318 North Main (706–865–2023), serves the well-known cook's country cuisine.

LODGING: Return to the Worley Homestead to spend the night.

Day 3 / Morning

BREAKFAST: At the inn.

Mine for gold and gems at **Gold 'n Gem Grubbin,** Town Creek Road off State 115 (706–865–5454), a historic operating gold mine. The log cabin Gem Shack features gift items, custom gem cutting, and gold jewelry. Miniature golf is a new addition.

LUNCH: The **Creekside Deli,** US 129 (706–865–3666), serves sandwiches.

Afternoon

BabyLand General Hospital, 19 Underwood Street (706–865–2171; www.cabbagepatchkids.com), is a fanciful world of make-believe where you can witness a "birth" and then adopt one of Xavier Roberts's original, soft-sculptured Cabbage Patch Kids. "Doctors and nurses" assist in the births and adoptions at the turn-of-the-twentieth-century medical clinic. Each Cabbage Patch Kid is different and has a name. When you take the Oath of Adoption, you "promise with all your heart to be the best parent in the world." The gift shop has everything an adoptive parent will need to care for a new addition. The general store also carries unusual items that reflect the folklore of the mountain surroundings.

Take US 129 south to State 11 and continue south to **Gainesville.** From there you can take I–985 to I–85 and back to Atlanta or take State 53 west across Lake Lanier to US 19/State 400, which you will take south to Atlanta.

There's More

Canoeing and rafting. Appalachian Outfitters (706–864–7117), whose canoe outpost is on State 60.

Fishing. Waters Creek Trophy Trout Stream, on Forest Service Road 34 off US 19 (706–535–5498), is managed only in trout season for rainbow, brown, and brook trout. Smith Gall Woods on Duke's Creek (706–864–6173) is also popular with serious fishers.

Hayrides. Burt's Farm, State 52, Dawsonville (706–265–3701), offers a 2-mile hayride past pumpkin fields and over a covered bridge, September through Thanksgiving. The farm also sells pumpkins, gourds, squash, Indian corn, boiled peanuts, and fall decorations.

Hiking. Yonah Mountain—named for the bear-killer Chief Gadalulu—is, at 3,156 feet of elevation, the highest point in White County.

Special Events

Cleveland

March or April. Easter Eggstravaganza, held Friday and Saturday of Easter weekend, downtown (706–865–5356), features a parade, 30,000-plus egg hunt for children, treasure hunt for adults, 5K run and 2K walk, and an arts-and-crafts fair.

December. Activities for an Appalachian Christmas at BabyLand General Hospital (706–865–2171) begin with a Christmas tree lighting and caroling the weekend after Thanksgiving.

Dahlonega

The region surrounding Dahlonega is beautiful during any season, from the pastel flowers that paint the hillsides during spring to the brilliant colors splashing the mountains in fall. Sometimes you'll even see snow. Fairs and festivals occur constantly. Each focuses on some exciting feature or historical event that celebrates the county. For information on all the festivals, contact the Dahlonega–Lumpkin County Chamber of Commerce, 13 South Park Street; (706) 864–3711.

October. The 1828 Gold Rush is re-created with buck dancing, greased-pig chasing, a beard-growing contest, a pioneer parade, and 300 arts and crafts exhibitors.

December. During the first weekend in December, Dahlonega's square is filled with the aromas of mountain pine, hot spiced punch, and Christmas baked goodies. The air is filled with a symphony of carolers, bands, and choruses. In addition to the twinkling lights of the gigantic Christmas tree, thousands of other tiny lights flicker from store- and housefront decorations, as well as nearly every tree and bush in the center of town. If you haven't finished your Christmas shopping by then, it's a great opportunity to do so. If you have, just enjoy the Christmas cheer.

Other Recommended Restaurants and Lodgings

Dahlonega

These bed-and-breakfasts and restaurants are within walking distance of the historic district:

Caruso's, on the square (706–864–4664), features Italian food and a casual setting.

Jack's Cafe, 44 Public Square (706–864–9169), serves sandwiches, burgers, soups, and salads.

Park Place, South Park on the square (706–864–9678), serves casual home-style meals.

The Smith House Inn (see *Dinner,* Day 1) also offers accommodations with continental breakfast.

Outside of Town

Amicalola Falls State Park, State 52 (706–265–2885, park; 706–265–8888, lodge), provides camping sites and has a modern lodge with a restaurant, gift shop, and conference facilities.

For More Information

Dahlonega–Lumpkin County Chamber of Commerce/Welcome Center, 13 South Park Street, Dahlonega, GA 30533. (706) 864–3711 or (800) 231–5543; www.dahlonega.org.

White County Chamber of Commerce, 122 North Main Street, Cleveland, GA 30528. (706) 865–5356 or (800) 892–8279; www.white countychamber.org.

Knoxville, Tennessee

World-Class Adventure / 2 Nights

This vibrant city, situated in a placid green valley near the Great Smoky Mountains National Park and surrounded by seven of the Tennessee Valley Authority's (TVA) "Great Lakes of the South," is ideal for a relaxed long weekend. Some cities are so overwhelming that if you try to see everything that's there in a few days, you come home so exhausted that you feel as if you need another vacation. Located only three-and-a-half to four hours north of Atlanta on I–75, Knoxville offers just the right balance between frenzy and boredom. Due to Knoxville's convenient location, you can easily spend a day in the mountains or buck the rapids on a white-water river and still be back in the city for dinner and a show.

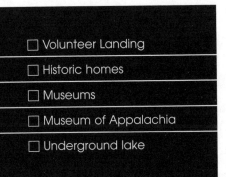

☐ Volunteer Landing
☐ Historic homes
☐ Museums
☐ Museum of Appalachia
☐ Underground lake

Knoxville is a very walkable city. Many of the hotels are situated conveniently close to World's Fair Park, the riverfront, attractions, restaurants, and shops. Several districts are beautified by streetscapes—blocks and blocks adorned with elegant lampposts, cheerful banners, sculpture, brick sidewalks and crosswalks, and planters bursting with flamboyant flowers.

The city was founded in 1786 by James White. The land he claimed, where the Holston and French Broad Rivers meet to form the mighty Tennessee River, was given to him for service in the American Revolution. Two years later, when William Blount was appointed governor of the territory south of the Ohio River, he decided to move the capital to a more centralized location and chose the area near James White's fort. Knoxville served as the capital of the newly formed state of Tennessee from 1796 to 1812. Tennessee was the last state to secede from the Union and the first to be readmitted. The state was strongly divided during the Civil War, with eastern Tennessee supporting the Union and the remainder

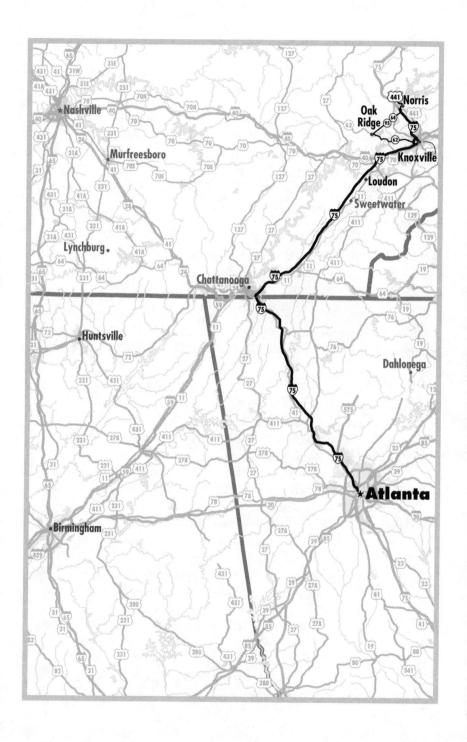

of the state supporting the Confederacy. The state ranks second to Virginia in the number of Civil War battles fought on its soil.

Day 1 / Morning

Leave Atlanta in the morning and take I–75 toward Knoxville. Stop in **Loudon,** Tennessee, to see the **Carmichael Inn Museum,** 501 Poplar Street on the Courthouse Square (865–458–1442). The 1820 log cabin, once used as a stagecoach inn, serves as a museum featuring local memorabilia. Pick up a brochure for the Downtown Loudon Walking Tour, a self-guided exploration of the antebellum and postbellum architecture, from the Chamber of Commerce, 318 Angel Row (865–458–2067).

Loudon boasts two wineries where you can take a tour and enjoy a tasting: **Loudon Valley Vineyards and Winery,** 130 Riesling Court (865–986–8736), and **Tennessee Valley Winery,** 15606 Hotchkiss Valley Road East (865–986–5147).

Continue north on I–75 to **Knoxville.**

LUNCH: **Chesapeake's,** 500 Henley Street (865–673–3433), features fresh seafood cooked using Maryland recipes. Also steaks, chicken, raw bar.

Afternoon

It makes sense to begin an exploration of this delightful city by stopping at three of its newest attractions: Volunteer Landing, the Gateway Regional Visitors Center, and the Women's Basketball Hall of Fame on the riverfront. **Volunteer Landing,** Neyland Drive to Hill Avenue (800–727–8045; www.volunteer-landing.com), is a multimillion-dollar project that encompasses 1 mile of riverfront with trails as well as attractive landscaping including waterfalls and native plantings. Two hundred years of Knoxville history as a river town—from Cherokee times and European settlement to the era of steamboats and the Civil War to the 1982 World's Fair—are explored through audio, text, and photographs.

The **Gateway Regional Visitors Center,** 900 Volunteer Landing Lane (865–971–4440 or 800–727–8045; www.knoxvillegateway.com), celebrates the diversity of the region with exhibits on the abundant natural resources of the Southern Highlands, the cultural resources of the area, and the technological resources of the Department of Energy's Oak Ridge Complex. The five national parks surrounding Knoxville are showcased in the Natural Atrium. Knoxville is highlighted in the Tennessee

Valley Overlook Theater. Scientific and technological assets are the focus of the Technology Gardens. This is also the place to get information about up-to-the-minute attractions, tours, restaurants, and lodgings.

A one-of-a-kind in the world, the **Women's Basketball Hall of Fame,** 700 Hall of Fame Drive (865–633–9000; www.wbhof.com), is also located near the river. The building is identified by the world's largest basketball on top of it. The hall of fame experience is a hands-on one with interactive exhibits as well as displays that chronicle the history of the collegiate, Olympic, and professional sport. In addition, the museum sports three indoor courts and an interactive locker room where you can hear a coach's half-time talk. The waterfront location permits visitors a panorama of the Smoky Mountains, Tennessee River, and downtown.

Before any of you railroad buffs leave Volunteer Landing, climb aboard the **Three Rivers Rambler,** Volunteer Landing (865–524–9411; www.threeriversrambler.com), and thrill to a ninety-minute vintage steam train ride to the Forks of the River, seeing some wonderful scenery and an engineering marvel along the way. The train operates weekends April through November except for days of football home games. The first three weekends in December, the train becomes the Christmas Express.

To understand the city's history, visit **James White's Fort,** 205 East Hill Avenue (865–525–6514), which was begun in 1786 by the city's founder. The original log house, surrounded by a stockade, contained two large rooms—one up and one down. The upstairs chamber, a dormitory-style bedroom, was the sleeping quarters for the parents and seven children. All other functions of daily living were carried out in the downstairs room. Because this was the only substantial building in the vicinity, it often served as a hotel for travelers as well. When the number of children made it impractical to accommodate guests, a guest house was added.

In addition to the detached kitchen and the guest house, several other authentic buildings have been moved to the site, affording the visitor a compact look at pioneer life. There's a loom house, blacksmith's shop, smokehouse, and small museum. Closed Sunday. January and February also closed Saturday.

Just down the street is **Blount Mansion,** 200 West Hill Avenue (865–525–2375 or 888–654–0016; www.blountmansion.org), built in 1792 as the home of the state's first territorial governor. It was the birthplace of the state of Tennessee. The word *mansion* is relative in terms of the log cabins that were the only other homes around. This was the first frame

Home of James White, founder of Knoxville

house built west of the Alleghenies. The story is that Mrs. Blount refused to move to the frontier unless she had a house similar to the one she was being asked to leave.

The original house—built high above and facing the river—contained only a great room, parlor, and one other room. The family was raised and the business of government was run from this simple beginning. Later a formal parlor was added and a separate office built for the governor. As with other houses of the day, the kitchen was in a separate building. Blount Mansion is furnished simply but elegantly, with pieces representative of the late 1700s, as well as a few originals. In fact, the pieces are considered to be one of the finest collections of late-eighteenth-century furnishings in the area. Colonial Revival gardens surround the house.

DINNER: An excellent way to get a good overview of the city and see the skyline against a gorgeous sunset is to cruise along the river aboard the **Star of Knoxville** paddle wheeler, 300 Neyland Drive (865–525–7827; www.tnriverboat.com). The boat offers several options, including sightseeing only or sightseeing along with lunch or dinner. The particularly romantic will enjoy the moonlight cruise. A roofed but open-air upper deck and an enclosed lower deck ensure that passengers are comfortable in any weather.

LODGING: Maple Grove Inn, 8800 Westland Drive (865–690–9565 or 800–645–0713; www.maplegroveinn.com), offers bed-and-breakfast accommodations in a lovely Georgian-style home built in 1799. Located on fifteen acres, the inn features a pool, tennis, some suites with Jacuzzis, a sauna, and private porches.

Day 2 / Morning

BREAKFAST: At the inn.

Visit the **Armstrong-Lockett House,** 2728 Kingston Pike (865–637–3163), which is called Crescent Bend. The gracious white house was built in 1834 by Drury Paine Armstrong and was last privately owned by William P. Toms, who donated it to the city. Inside, the mansion houses the Toms Memorial Collection of American and English furniture and decorative arts of the eighteenth century. Most outstanding is an entire room displaying English silver from 1640 to 1820, including works that represent an unusual number of female silversmiths.

It's outside, however, that you'll get the best surprise. The back of the house overlooks the steep descent to the river. What could have been an impassable cliff has been transformed into a seven-tiered formal Italianate garden. Known as the W. P. Toms Memorial Gardens, the grounds boast fountains and glorious plantings that change with the season. You can't even see the entire garden from the house or all of it from any point at any one time. The steep descent allows you to see only two or three levels at a time, so you're not overwhelmed by seeing it all at once. It's like opening a package with layers and layers of tissue paper that keep you guessing right to the bottom. Drive across the river sometime later, and you can get an overall view of the garden—although you can't see the floral displays as clearly from this vantage point. Closed January and February.

Ramsey House Plantation, 2614 Thorngrove Pike (865–546–0745), completed in 1797, was the first stone house in Knox County. It stands on one hundred acres that remain from the original plantation. Interesting architectural details of the pink marble house include blue limestone quoins and keystone arches over windows and doors and carvings in the consoles under the dentiled cornices. Open April through mid-December Tuesday through Sunday. Open the remainder of the year by appointment.

Marble Springs State Historic Farmstead, 1220 West Governor John Sevier Highway (865–573–5508), was the plantation home of Tennessee's first governor, John Sevier, who served six terms and went on to put in two terms as a U.S. representative. Poke around the six relocated cabins on the property. Call for hours.

The **Old City Historic District,** centered on Jackson and Central, is a quaint area of more than fifty antiques shops, art galleries, nightclubs, and restaurants located in restored nineteenth-century brick warehouses. Known as the Music Crossroads of East Tennessee, the district offers jazz, classic acoustic rock, country, dance, and a variety of popular live music nightly. Special activities in the Old City during the year include St. Patrick's Day, Mardi Gras, and Victorian Christmas in the Old City. Before you leave the Old City, drive through the **Old Gray Cemetery,** 543 North Broadway (865–522–1424)—not only a burial ground of who's who of Knoxville but also an ornate Victorian park. Adjacent to the cemetery is the **Knoxville National Cemetery,** burial place of Union casualties from the battle of Fort Sanders, one Confederate soldier, and veterans of later wars. Dog lovers and military veterans alike will be touched by the **War Dog Memorial Statue** on the grounds of the University of Tennessee Veterinary Hospital, 2407 River Drive. The likeness of a proud Doberman honors all dogs who served the military in World War II.

LUNCH: Regas Restaurant, 318 North Gay Street (865–637–9805), has been a Knoxville tradition since 1919, serving upscale surf and turf for lunch and dinner. Reservations recommended.

Afternoon

Choose from among several diverse museums for your afternoon's entertainment:

The **Volunteer State Veterans Hall of Honor,** 8030 Dodson Road (865–577–0757), contains more than 2,000 relics that pay tribute to those who have served in the armed services from the Revolutionary War to Desert Storm. One exhibit explains how Tennessee got its nickname, the Volunteer State, during the Mexican War. The Civil War display reflects the divided loyalties that affected Tennessee.

At the **Frank H. McClung Museum,** 1327 Circle Park Drive on the University of Tennessee campus (865–974–2144; http://mcclung museum.utk.edu), Tennessee's history, culture, art, and geology are interpreted from prehistoric to contemporary times. The museum has exhibits in the fields of anthropology, archaeology, decorative arts, natural history, and ancient Egypt.

A state-of-the-art architectural landmark, the **Knoxville Museum of Art,** 1050 World's Fair Park Drive (865–525–6101; www.knoxart.org), offers a permanent collection of contemporary art, art exhibitions from around the world, an exploratory gallery for children, and an outdoor sculpture garden.

A vast array of east Tennessee artifacts spanning the past 200 years fills the **East Tennessee Historical Society Museum,** 601 South Gay Street (865–215–8824 or 866–ETHC–911), now in impressive new quarters. Established in 1834, the society is one of the oldest cultural institutions in the state. The "East Tennesseans" permanent exhibit contains everything from Davy Crockett's first rifle and marriage license to an overcoat made by President Andrew Johnson to how World War II was decided in the secret city of Oak Ridge, where the first atomic bomb was made in 1945. For the kiddies, Davy's Attic is a kid-size log cabin with children's clothing such as that worn by Davy Crockett to try on, books to read, and puppets so tykes can make up their own show. Throughout the timeline exhibit, there are boxes with touchables. "Holiday Time in East Tennessee" is an annual favorite from early December through mid-January. Temporary exhibits bring fascinating perspectives to other aspects of east Tennessee history.

DINNER: The **Butcher Shop Steakhouse,** 806 World's Fair Park Drive (865–637–0204), serves top-quality, fresh-cut steak that you can cook yourself on the premises, or let the experienced chefs do it for you.

LODGING: Maple Grove Inn.

Day 3 / Morning

BREAKFAST: At the inn.

Located on TN 61 just 16 miles north of Knoxville off I–75 in **Norris** is the **Museum of Appalachia** (865–494–7680 or 865–494–0514; www.museumofappalachia.com), a living-history pioneer homestead that contains a huge collection—at 300,000 items, the world's largest accumulation—of early mountain artifacts. The seventy-acre museum contains more than thirty authentic log cabins and buildings, gardens surrounded by split-rail fences, numerous farm animals, and the Appalachian Hall of

Fame—a tribute to mountain people. Owner John Rice Irwin has achieved his goal of making the "dwellings appear as though the family had just strolled down to the spring to fetch the daily supply of water."

LUNCH: Light meals available at the museum.

Afternoon

Norris boasts several other attractions. **Norris Dam State Park,** 125 Village Green Circle, Lake City (865–426–7461; www.state.tn.us/ environment/parks/parks/NorrisDam), has overlooks on both sides of the Norris Dam, the first flood-control structure built by the TVA. A major attraction at the park is the **Lenoir Museum Complex** (865–494–9688), which includes the **Lenoir Pioneer Museum,** which has thousands of early American items; the 1798 **Rice Grist Mill,** a working corn-grinding mill; and the **Crosby Threshing Barn,** which retains its original machinery and old farm tools. Open Wednesday through Sunday May through December.

Take TN 64/95 to **Oak Ridge.** One of the world's largest science and energy museums is the **American Museum of Science and Energy,** 300 South Tulane Avenue (865–576–3200; www.amse.org). It contains 200 interactive displays, computer games, and live demonstrations that explain fossil fuels and alternative energy sources. The "Oak Ridge Story" exhibit chronicles the World War II Manhattan Project. Best of all, it's free. Closed Monday.

The **Graphite Reactor,** on the grounds of the Oak Ridge National Laboratory, One Bethel Valley Road, Oak Ridge (visitor information 865–574–7199), the world's oldest nuclear reactor, is a National Historic Landmark. Built during World War II as part of the Manhattan Project, it was later used for peacetime applications of nuclear energy. You must make arrangements prior to the day of your visit.

Take TN 62 back to I–75 in Knoxville to begin your homeward journey. If you have time on the way home, stop in Sweetwater, between Knoxville and Chattanooga, to explore the **Lost Sea,** 140 Lost Sea Road (423–337–6616; www.thelostsea.com). Not only is this an impressively large cavern with some of the widest and highest rooms of any cavern in the Southeast, but it also contains the world's largest underground lake— four and a half acres. You're led to the bottom of the cavern and then taken for a glass-bottomed-boat ride. You can just imagine the Phantom of the

Opera poling his boat across the mirror surface of this eerie lagoon.
Take I–75 back to Atlanta.

There's More

African-American culture. The Beck Cultural Exchange Center, 1927
Dandridge Avenue (865–524–8461), is dedicated to researching, preserving, and displaying the achievements of African Americans in Knoxville
from the early 1800s. The center contains books, photographs, newspapers,
recordings, biographies, and works of art. *Roots* author Alex Haley, who
was a native of Henning, Tennessee, spent the last fourteen years of his life
in east Tennessee near Knoxville. Alex Haley Heritage Square in
Morningside Park, which pays lasting tribute to the rich legacy left by the
storyteller, author, and humanitarian, contains a larger-than-life statue of a
casually dressed Haley holding his famous work. The statue is designed for
interaction and makes a great photo op.

Country music. Dolly Parton had her broadcast debut at the age of seven
at Knoxville's WIVK radio station. Other stars with some connection to
Knoxville are Hank Williams, the Everly Brothers, Roy Acuff, the Midday
Merry-Go-Round, and even Elvis Presley. The Cradle of Country Music
Walking Tour, which begins at the East Tennessee Historical Society
Museum, 600 Market Street (800–727–8045), downtown, has nineteen
stops highlighted by markers and photographs. You can also pick up a
brochure from the museum or the Knoxville Convention and Visitors
Bureau.

Tours. Knoxville Trolley Lines (865–637–3000), using antique trolleys and
vintage 1972 trolley buses, operates two free downtown routes with stops
at many important attractions from Monday through Friday every five to
ten minutes from early morning to dinnertime. The Knox County Tourist
Commission (865–523–7263 or 800–727–8045) has prepared several driving tours of the immediate vicinity. You can pick up brochures from the
Gateway Regional Visitors Center, 900 Volunteer Landing Lane
(865–971–4440 or 800–727–8045).

Zoo. Knoxville Zoological Gardens, 3500 Knoxville Zoo Drive, near exit
392 off I–40 (865–637–5331; www.knoxville-zoo.org), boasts one of the
largest chimpanzee exhibits in the country, Chimp Ridge. More than
1,000 animals from around the world inhabit the beautiful parklike setting.
The zoo features a bird show, camel rides, Gorilla Valley, Penguin Rock,

Pridelands African lion exhibit, and Prairie Dog Pass.

Special Events

Knoxville

April. Dogwood Arts Festival and Farragut Festival on the Green, the first weekend in April, presents art exhibits, crafts, shopping, music, sports, food, and more. (423) 637–4561.

November–December. Christmas in the City features music of the season, trees on downtown rooftops, thousands of lights, a lighted boat parade, whimsical window scenes, and dozens of other events. (865) 215–4248.

Norris

October. Tennessee Fall Homecoming, Museum of Appalachia, is a celebration of Appalachian culture and heritage, with more than 400 old-time musicians, singers, craftspeople, and artisans, as well as demonstrations of rural pioneer activities such as boiling molasses and making lye soap. (865) 494–7680.

December. Christmas in Old Appalachia, Museum of Appalachia, features pioneer Christmas decorations and traditions. (865) 494–7680.

Other Recommended Restaurants and Lodgings

The Captain's Retreat, 3534 Lakeside Drive, Lenoir City (865–986–4229), is a rustic, old-timey cabin with slick contemporary modifications and modern creature comforts. Guest rooms, though small, are nicely decorated in different themes and well appointed. Each boasts a whirlpool tub, and several have private screened porches. A rocker-filled front porch and a covered dock allow you to get even closer to nature, but probably the most popular outdoor diversions are the hammock and the hot tub.

Wayside Manor Bed and Breakfast, 4009 Old Knoxville Highway, Rockford (865–970–4823), offers fireplaces, Jacuzzi baths, a pool, a hot tub, a creek, and tennis.

The Whitestone Country Inn, 1200 Paint Rock Road, Kingston (865–376–0113 or 888–247–2464; www.whitestoneinn.com), is a grand resort on a hilly, tree-covered, 360-acre estate that affords sweeping vistas of Watts Bar Lake on the Tennessee River. Luxurious accommodations are available in the inn, conference center, barn, or little red schoolhouse. Many guest rooms feature a fireplace and/or a whirlpool tub. Amenities include two restaurants, wedding chapel, 8 miles of walking trails, and 8,000 feet of lake frontage with canoes, kayaks, and paddleboats. Other amenities at the resort include tennis courts, a regulation croquet court, and carriage rides.

Restaurants abound in Knoxville—the citizenry really likes to eat. Several passenger and freight railroad stations have been converted for use as restaurant complexes. One of our favorites:

Calhoun's on the River, 400 Neyland Drive (865–673–3355), is noted for barbecue—especially pork baby-back ribs, hickory smoked and slow roasted in their own sauce. Also steaks and prime rib.

For More Information

Knoxville Convention and Visitors Bureau, 601 West Summit Hill Drive, Suite 200B, Knoxville, TN 37902. (865) 523–7263 or (800) 727–8045; www.knoxville.org.

Oak Ridge Convention and Visitors Bureau, 302 South Tulane Avenue, Oak Ridge, TN 37830-6726. (865) 482–7821 or (800) 887–3429.

SOUTHBOUND
ESCAPES

SOUTHBOUND ESCAPE ONE

Columbus/Buena Vista, Georgia

Fountains, Fizz, and Fantasy / 2 Nights

Columbus, a real river city, sports several nicknames: Fountain City, inspired by its numerous fountains; Port City, because it is the northernmost navigable port on the Chattahoochee River; Soft Drink Capital, because the Coca-Cola, Royal Crown, and Nehi formulas were devised by local residents; and Georgia's West Coast, because the city borders

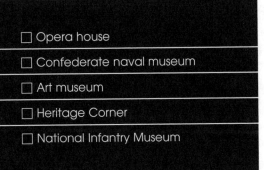

☐ Opera house

☐ Confederate naval museum

☐ Art museum

☐ Heritage Corner

☐ National Infantry Museum

Alabama not only with the Chattahoochee but also with several fabricated lakes. Columbus is noted for several specialty dishes: the Country Captain, a tomato and chicken dish; the Scramble Dog, a weiner on a bun heaped with onions, cheese, chili sauce, and oyster crackers; and the tradition of putting peanuts in your Coca-Cola (pronounced "Co Cola").

Buena Vista—self-billed as America's Front Porch—is the legatee of one of Georgia's most audacious folk artists, who left his colorful compound to the town.

Day 1 / *Afternoon*

Take I–85 south to I–185 to **Columbus.** (For information about Columbus, consult www.historiccolumbus.com and www.visitcolumbus ga.com.)

DINNER: The **Bludau's Goetchius House Restaurant,** 405 Broadway (706–324–4863; www.goetchiushouse.com), in the Historic District, serves magnificent continental cuisine in an 1839 New Orleans–style mansion furnished with Victorian and Empire antiques.

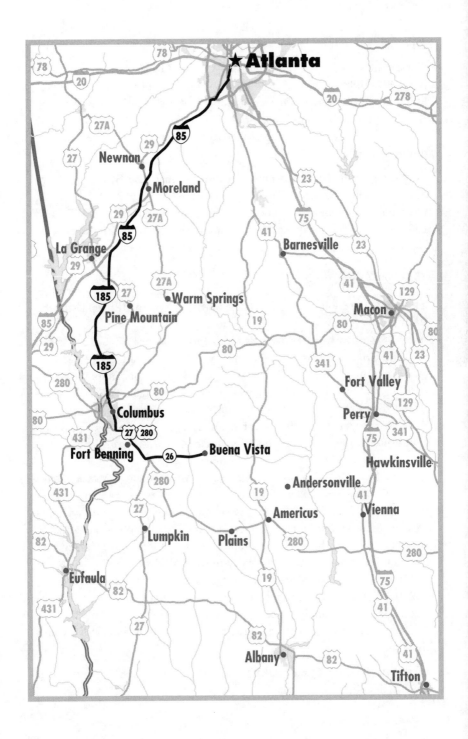

Evening

Try to attend a play at the **Springer Opera House,** 103 Tenth Street (706–327–3688 or 706–327–3869; www.springeroperahouse.org), established in 1871. The State Theater of Georgia, it has seen the likes of Edwin Booth, Oscar Wilde, John Philip Sousa, Will Rogers, and Irving Berlin. The season runs September through May. Tours by appointment except June through August. Call (706) 324–5714.

LODGING: 1870 Rothschild/Pound House B&B, 201 Seventh Street in the Historic District (706–322–4075 or 800–585–4075; www.poundhouseinn.com). Located in a Second Empire Victorian "Painted Lady," the bed-and-breakfast offers antiques-filled guest rooms, several with working fireplaces. Cocktails and hors d'oeuvres in the afternoon.

Day 2 / Morning

BREAKFAST: Fill up on a big, hot, Southern homemade breakfast at the B&B.

The **Columbus Ironworks,** 801 Front Avenue (706–327–4522), now the Convention and Trade Center, was a major producer of cast-iron products. During the Civil War it was a chief supplier of cannons and iron cladding and engines to Confederate gunboats and rams. After the war it settled down to make ice machines until 1965, after which it was abandoned for years before being restored and given a new identity. The South Hall houses an exhibit of products manufactured at the ironworks during the 1800s.

The **Port Columbus Civil War Naval Museum,** 1002 Victory Drive (706–327–9798; www.portcolumbus.com), the only such museum, contains the remains of the ironclad ram *Jackson* and the gunboat *Chattahoochee,* as well as prototypes of experimental vessels, other Confederate artifacts, weapons, ship models, and uniforms. There is also an interactive Confederate ironclad ship simulator. Open Monday through Friday.

The **Columbus Museum,** located at 1251 Wynnton Road (706–649–0713), is the second largest art museum in the state. Renowned for its permanent and changing fine-art exhibitions, it also offers a film, *The Chattahoochee Legacy;* a regional history gallery; and an interactive youth museum.

LUNCH: Rankin Quarter, 21 Tenth Street (706–322–8151), serves deli sandwiches with a local flair.

Afternoon

Let your lunch settle as you relax alongside **Riverwalk,** a 15-mile riverfront promenade with its gazebos, benches, and fountains. The spot is also popular with walkers and joggers. (For more information, call 706–322–1613 or 800–999–1613.)

Columbus is a treasure trove of architectural gems. Numerous structures and entire districts are included on the National Register of Historic Places or are National Historic Landmarks. Get a brochure for Original City Tours from the **Convention and Visitors Bureau,** 1000 Bay Avenue (706–322–1613; twenty-four-hour information, 706–322–3181; www.visitcolumbusga.com), but save the tour for tomorrow.

Heritage Corner is not only a walking tour of five historic 1820s to 1870s structures but a survey of architectural styles. The properties are located at Seventh Street and Broadway. One of those dwellings—an 1870 brick two-story Italianate structure, 700 Broadway (706–322–0756)—houses the Historic Columbus Foundation, where you can get tour tickets. Guided tours are at 2:00 P.M.

The Victorian cottage at 11 Seventh Street is the former **home of John Stith Pemberton**—the originator of the Coca-Cola formula. Pemberton became a pharmacist in 1850 and later established a wholesale-retail drug business. In his laboratory he tested agricultural chemicals for the state; however, he is most noted for the concoction of French Wine of Coca, a forerunner of Coca-Cola. Although 250 million Cokes are sold daily worldwide, it will amaze you to learn that Pemberton made only $1,500 from his elixir.

The **Walker-Peters-Langdon House,** at 716 Broadway, is a Federal cottage furnished with period pieces. Built in 1828, the year Columbus was founded, it is the oldest house in the city. One family owned the house from 1836 to 1966. Also on the grounds are an 1800s log cabin and an 1840 double-pen farmhouse.

DINNER: **Tavern on the Square,** 14 Eleventh Street (706–324–2238), offers deli dining in a pub atmosphere.

LODGING: 1870 Rothschild/Pound House B&B.

Day 3 / Morning

BREAKFAST: At the B&B.

Use the brochure you got yesterday for a walking/driving tour. It is divided into three tours: Uptown, High Uptown, and the Historic District. Uptown includes the restored Victorian Springer Opera House. High Uptown includes many opulent residences, such as the Rankin House, 1440 Second Avenue, which boasts the finest ornamental ironwork in Columbus. The Historic District encompasses Heritage Corner, the Chattahoochee Promenade along the river, the Columbus Ironworks Convention and Trade Center, the Port Columbus Civil War Naval Center, and such houses as the Folly, at 527 First Avenue, the nation's only antebellum double-octagonal house. This and most other homes are private and not open to the public.

LUNCH: Top Hat, 510 Ninth Street (706–322–2100), serves the hottest/spiciest chicken available.

Afternoon

South of Columbus on US 27/280 is **Fort Benning,** home of the U.S. Army's Infantry School, the world's largest and most modern military training center. Tour the **National Infantry Museum,** Building 396, Baltzell Avenue (706–545–2958; www.benning.army.mil), which has one of the largest and most complete collections of military and small arms in the country. The Hall of the U.S. Infantry traces the evolution of the foot soldier from the French and Indian Wars to the present with memorabilia from each of America's military involvements. The Hall of Flags displays military documents signed by all U.S. presidents, silver presentation pieces, military band instruments, and weapons. An exhibit honors Gen. Omar Bradley, who served at Fort Benning. Captured enemy military paraphernalia is displayed in the Axis Powers Exhibit.

From Fort Benning, take State 26 east toward Buena Vista. Turn off onto State 137W and take it to County 78 to **Pasaquan,** Eddie Martin Road (912–649–9444; www.pasaquan.com), one of the most unusual sights you'll ever see. The four-acre complex features brilliantly rendered and flamboyantly painted walls, pagodas, and outdoor sculptures by the late idiosyncratic visionary artist Eddie Owens Martin (1908–86), who dubbed himself St. EOM (his initials, pronounced as "home"), the self-proclaimed Wizard of Pasaquan.

Martin was born on July 4, 1908. By the time he was an adolescent, it became clear that the staid and proper life of a small southern town was not for him. He fled to New York, where he lived a bohemian life, study-

Pasaquan, Buena Vista

ing and taking on the characteristics of Greenwich Village artists, flashy hookers, Jazz Age musicians, and druggies. Martin visited some Far Eastern countries, where he became enthralled with mystic religions, the occult, lost civilizations, and yoga.

When his mother died in 1957, Martin returned to Buena Vista, but not to revert to a conventional lifestyle. He claimed that God had spoken directly to him and instructed him to create a place called *Pasaquan*— roughly translated to mean "bringing the past and future together." He transformed the family farm into a bizarre fantasyland of totem poles and temples, painting everything in sight to resemble a bad acid trip.

Eventually the world at large learned about Martin's artistry. He was even featured in *Smithsonian* magazine. Martin willed his paradise to the Marion County Historical Society. Open only by appointment, but it's worth the effort.

Leave Pasaquan and reenter the real world. Continue south into **Buena Vista** as your eyes adjust to everyday scenes. Go to the town square, where the graceful, late-nineteenth-century Italianate commercial buildings have been revitalized and offered a new life as shops and eateries.

Return to Columbus and retrace I–185 and I–85 to Atlanta.

There's More

Black heritage. Columbus contains a wealth of landmarks connected with Black history. A brochure is available from the Convention and Visitors Bureau, 1000 Bay Avenue (706–322–1613 or 800–999–1613), for a driving tour of twenty-four sites that include churches, cemeteries, a theater, businesses, and the homes of such prominent Black residents as famous jazz singer "Ma" Rainey and the first Black combat pilot, Eugene Bullard.

Special Events

April. Riverfest Weekend/Salisbury Fair, held along the Riverwalk by the Chattahoochee River in Columbus, is a family-oriented festival featuring arts and crafts, primitives, collectibles, artists at work, a children's carnival, pig racing, entertainment on three stages, and a barbecue cook-off. (706) 324–7417.

Other Recommended Restaurants and Lodgings

Wyndham Hotel, 800 Front Avenue, Columbus (706–324–1800), overlooking the river, includes suites in the 125-year-old Empire Mills section. Dine in Pemberton's Cafe, decorated with Coca-Cola memorabilia to honor Dr. J. S. Pemberton, creator of the soft drink, or relax in the sporting environment in Hunter's Lounge.

Columbus claims to have the highest concentration of barbecue restaurants anywhere. One of them is Country's, 3137 Mercury Drive (706–563–7604), which serves barbecue slow-cooked over hickory and oak, as well as other country cooking.

For More Information

Columbus Convention and Visitors Bureau, 1000 Bay Avenue, Columbus, GA 31902. (706) 322–1613 or (800) 999–1613.

SOUTHBOUND ESCAPE TWO

Callaway Gardens/ Pine Mountain, Georgia

Georgian ABCs—Azaleas, Butterflies, and Circuses / 2 Nights

Textile magnate Cason Callaway once said, "Every child ought to see something beautiful before he's six years old—something he will remember all his life." Mr. Callaway probably never envisioned that his gardens would provide a glimpse of splendor to an endless cavalcade of children of all ages. Familiar to and beloved by Georgians and other residents of the Southeast, **Callaway Gardens** (800–CALLAWAY; www .callawaygardens.com), with its year-round, 2,500-acre horticultural display gardens and 14,000-acre resort, is becoming world renowned.

☐ Gardens

☐ Butterflies

☐ Antiques

☐ Outdoor activities

☐ Animal safari

The focal point of the resort is, of course, the gardens, which include 2,500 acres of woodlands and lakes. Besides the gardens, the resort offers an inn with a variety of fine dining experiences, cottages, villas, golf, tennis, sailing, a gun club, bass and bream fishing, swimming, and a summer recreation program, which includes Florida State University's "Flying High" Circus. Thirteen lakes and more than 20 miles of roadways, hiking, and bicycling trails unveil the woodland and garden areas to visitors.

Conceived by Callaway, the facility began in the 1930s as his humble vacation retreat. Callaway's experimentation with reviving depleted cotton fields gradually developed into ever-expanding gardens. Opened to the public in 1952, the gardens contain trails dedicated to azaleas, wildflowers, rhododendrons, and hollies. In fact, the gardens feature more than 450 species of hollies—the world's largest public display. Of the 700 varieties of azaleas, the most notable is the reddish orange plumleaf, or prunifolia— a summer bloomer that is native only within a 100-mile region. The plum-

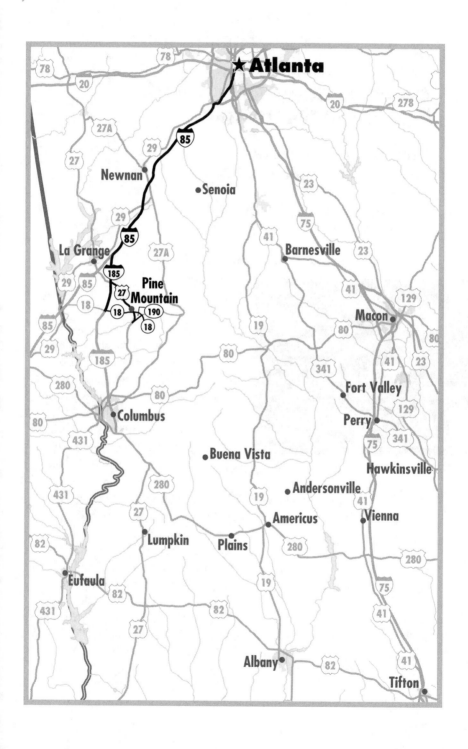

leaf azalea was in danger of extinction until the Callaways propagated it and planted it in the gardens.

Day 1 / Afternoon

Leave Atlanta in midafternoon. Take I–85 south to I–185, which you will take to US 27; then turn east to **Pine Mountain,** home of Callaway Gardens resort.

DINNER: The **Plantation Room** at the Callaway Gardens Inn is renowned for its Friday-night seafood buffet.

LODGING: The **Resort at Callaway's** accommodations include a motel-style inn with 349 rooms, 155 two-bedroom cottages, and 49 two-, three-, and four-bedroom villas. Both the cottages and the villas are complete with fireplaces, fully equipped kitchens, decks, and screened porches.

Day 2 / Morning

BREAKFAST: Order a hearty full southern breakfast at the **Callaway Country Kitchen** in the Callaway Country Store. Be sure to order some of Callaway Gardens's Speckled Heart Grits. They're called speckled heart because the unique flavor comes from the heart of the corn, which most processors remove to use for corn oil but which, when retained, leaves small black flecks. Callaway Gardens is also famous for its Georgia-cured bacon and its jams and jellies made from muscadine grapes harvested from the gardens' vines. You can purchase the bacon, grits, and muscadine products, as well as other Callaway specialties, from the facility's gift shops and the Callaway Gardens Country Store.

Explore the myriad of attractions in the gardens by car or bicycle. Begin at the **Virginia Hand Callaway Discovery Center** at the intersection of Highways 18 and 354. The new facility serves as the welcome center and offers an orientation film *Time and the Gardens* as well as special rotating interactive exhibits to encourage repeat visits. A Birds of Prey show is presented three times a day (once in winter) at the center's amphitheater. Your next stop will probably be the newly renovated **John A. Sibley Horticultural Center,** with its exceptional conservatory. Although most hothouses are merely giant glass greenhouses, this one is an environment where the indoors and outdoors merge almost imperceptibly. Both temperate and tropical plants are represented. Only one of the highlights of the center is a two-story waterfall you can walk behind.

Eighteen major floral displays are scheduled annually, of which the two most popular are the autumn mums and Christmas poinsettias. Changing, larger-than-life-size topiary exhibits have ranged from dinosaur themes to *Alice in Wonderland* characters.

The new **Callaway Brothers Azalea Bowl** is the world's largest azalea garden. This forty-acre site features more than 5,000 hybrid and native azaleas, as well as an array of plants to guarantee color throughout the year. Named in memory of brothers Ely Callaway Sr. and Fuller Callaway Sr., the latter the father of the garden's founder, the azalea garden also features beautiful architecture.

Nestled in the woods and situated so it reflects in the mirror surface of Falls Creek Lake is the stone, English Gothic–style **Ida Cason Callaway Memorial Chapel.** A shrine to Callaway's mother, it was constructed entirely of Georgia materials. Its unusual stained-glass windows represent the four seasons.

Living-history demonstrations of pioneer skills such as spinning are presented periodically at the rustic log cabin.

LUNCH: Within the gardens, the **Gardens Restaurant** serves salads and light meals overlooking Mountain Creek Lake.

Afternoon

The **Cecil B. Day Butterfly Center** is the largest glass-enclosed tropical butterfly exhibit in North America—a garden of rich hues in constant motion. More than 1,000 "flowers of the air" fly freely or rest on lush leaves as visitors ramble among them. Some of these bursts of living color may even come to rest on your shoulder. Among the tropical plants, mandarin ducks, bleeding heart doves, and other ground birds live in this paradise regained. G. Harold Northrop, former president of Callaway, called the butterfly center "the most significant environmental project, in terms of helping people understand the delicate balance of nature, that has been started in this country."

Mr. Cason's Vegetable Garden, seven-and-a-half acres of fruit, vegetables, herbs, and flowers, features a section used for the southern set of the PBS series *The Victory Garden.* An experimental area is devoted to flowers and plants that attract butterflies, an appropriate endeavor because of Callaway Gardens's butterfly center.

If you have any time or energy left over after spending a day in the gardens, you might want to swim at a pool or in the lake, play golf or tennis, or take fly-fishing lessons. The facility is laced with miles of bike and nature trails. Callaway Gardens has four golf courses, including the Mountain View course, which is ranked among the top U.S. courses by *Golf Digest* and *GOLF* magazines. The tennis center features clay and hard courts, racquetball courts, and a pro shop. Bicycle and boat rentals are available.

DINNER: The **Piedmont Dining Room** at the Southern Pine Conference Center offers an inviting setting surrounded by nature. Buffets and chef stations provide a tantalizing variety.

LODGING: Callaway Gardens Resort.

Day 3 / Morning

BREAKFAST: After yesterday's gastronomic orgy, perhaps a light breakfast at the inn is in order.

Dress in jeans and head for the **Roosevelt Riding Stables,** 1063 Group Camp Road, off Highway 190 (706–628–7463 or 877–696–4613; www.rooseveltstables.com), just outside Pine Mountain. Part of Franklin D. Roosevelt State Park, the stables offer guided horseback trail rides by the hour, half-day, full-day, or even City Slickers–like overnight rides that include campouts where you cook meals from a chuck wagon, tell stories around a campfire, and sleep under the stars. Moonlight rides are also popular in October. Open Tuesday through Sunday.

LUNCH: **Cricket's,** State 18 East (706–663–8136), specializes in Cajun and Creole cuisine and is well known for its gumbo. Located in a Bavarian chalet. Lunch and dinner daily except Monday.

Afternoon

In the historic **Village of Pine Mountain,** you'll find more than fifty gift and antiques shops, outlets, and restaurants. The **Kimbrough Brothers General Store,** 137 North Main Street (706–663–2528), has been in operation by a Kimbrough family member since 1892. More than sixty dealers participate in the **Pine Mountain Antique Mall,** 230 South Main Street (706–663–8165). Auctions are held the second and fourth Saturday of each month. **Anne Tutt's Gallery,** Chipley Village, US 27 (706–663–8032), offers Anne's unique jewelry designs and paintings by her husband, Alex Kalinin.

Historical records, photos, and local artifacts are displayed at **Chipley**

Historical Center, 146 North McDougald Avenue (706–663–4044).

Two miles north of Pine Mountain, at 1300 Oak Grove Road, is the **Pine Mountain Wild Animal Safari** (706–663–8744 or 800–367–2751), 500 acres where 200 to 300 animals wander freely. You can take a self-guided driving tour or (seasonally) a guided bus tour. Other attractions at the park include an authentic Old McDonald–type farm operation, serpentarium, monkey house, petting zoo, alligator pit, tropical birds, Baby Land USA, the Georgia Wildlife Museum, animal shows (daily in summer, weekends in the spring and fall), and gift shop.

Retrace State 18, I–185, and I–85 to Atlanta.

There's More

Hiking. The 23-mile Pine Mountain Trail follows Pine Mountain Ridge from the Callaway Country Store on US 27 to the WJSP-TV tower on State 85W in Warm Springs. Although the footpath crosses peaceful forests, splashing rivulets, tumbling waterfalls, and rocky promontories, there are a few steep, tiring grades. Panoramas of the valley below open up from several scenic overlooks.

Outdoor activities. Franklin D. Roosevelt State Park, State 190 (706–663–4858; www.gastateparks.org/info/fdr/), is a 10,000-acre park with twenty-one cabins, camping, a pool, two lakes, hiking, and horseback riding.

Summer family adventure program. Weeklong sessions at Callaway Gardens provide families staying at the cottages or villas with an all-day, every day schedule of activities for each member of the family three years old and older. The heart of the program is Florida State University's "Flying High" Circus. The performers do double duty as counselors for activities such as swimming, boating, arts and crafts, dancing, and ecology talks, and they perform magic shows and teach children simple circus acts. (800) CALLAWAY.

Special Events

Callaway Gardens

For all activities call (800) CALLAWAY.

There's never a dull moment at Callaway Gardens. In addition to major festivals, there are frequent seminars and special activities. The two premier events are the fall steeplechase and the Christmas lights extravaganza, "Fantasy in Lights."

May. Masters Water-Ski Championship.

September–October. The Sibley Horticultural Center is alive with thousands of brilliant hanging chrysanthemums cascading from the balconies.

November. The Steeplechase at Callaway is a glamorous annual event that benefits community arts groups in west-central Georgia. On a brisk fall afternoon, devotees congregate for one of the most handsome hunt meets in the country. Food is an essential element of the day. Other events include the Chase Ball and Jack Russell terrier races. The resort offers a weekend package that includes accommodations.

Friday before Thanksgiving through the Sunday after Christmas. (Check for exact dates.) For those to whom Christmas isn't Christmas without snow, the best opportunity to experience a hassle-free blizzard in Georgia is by touring Callaway Gardens's Christmas extravaganza, "Fantasy in Lights." In addition to snowflakes, visions of sugarplums dance before your eyes as you encounter them—in living color and more than life-size. The 5-mile, ride-through, sound-and-light odyssey winds through a dozen whimsical illuminated tableaux that resemble musical Christmas cards. The after-dark attraction claims to be the largest outdoor lighted exhibition in the nation. Advance purchase tickets are recommended. Times are reserved in fifteen-minute slots.

Other Recommended Restaurants and Lodgings

Sportsman's Grill, 5700 Highway 354, Chipley Village, Pine Mountain (706–663–8064), is a sports bar that serves outstanding onion rings.

For More Information

Pine Mountain Tourism Association, 101 East Broad Street, Pine Mountain, GA 31822. (706) 663–4000 or (800) 441–3502; www .pinemountain.org.

Resort at Callaway, US 27, Pine Mountain, GA 31822. (800) CALLAWAY; www.callawaygardens.com.

Barnesville/Hawkinsville/Perry/Fort Valley, Georgia

Horse and Buggy / 2 Nights

Graceful Standardbred horses, manes streaming, trot or pace smoothly around the red-clay oval track, towing charming sulkies piloted by drivers in brilliant silks. Is this the Red Mile Race Track in Lexington, Kentucky, or the Belmont in Saratoga, New York? No, it's Hawkinsville, Georgia—since 1894 the winter home and training ground of many of North America's best pacers and trotters.

- ☐ Buggy Capital of the World
- ☐ Trotters and pacers
- ☐ Peaches
- ☐ Pecans
- ☐ Camellias

Like many towns in Georgia, Hawkinsville's Golden Age was in the last decades of the nineteenth century and the early years of the twentieth century, when the profits from King Cotton made it possible to build opulent homes and businesses. About the same time, northern horse owners discovered that Hawkinsville's moderate climate and excellent track surface of high-quality Georgia red clay made the town an ideal spot to ensure year-round race training for their horses. That tradition continues today.

For the uninitiated, Standardbreds as a breed are only about 200 years old. The term *Standardbred* originated because early trotters were required to achieve a certain standard for the mile distance in order to be registered. Pacers and trotters have different gaits. Pacers move both legs on the right side of their body together, then both left legs. Until they learn the gait, horses often wear hobbles, leg loops that ensure the legs move in the correct rhythm. Trotters move the front right leg with the back left, then the front left with the back right. Both are incredibly smooth gaits that make the horses appear to glide above the surface of the track. In fact, we've

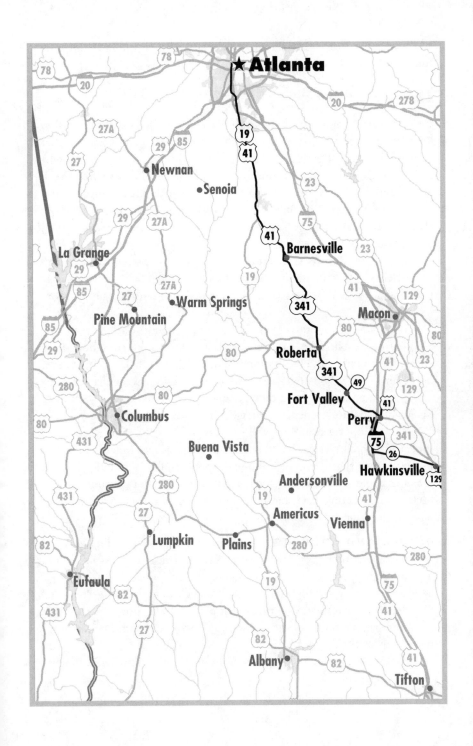

taken a picture that clearly shows all four feet off the ground at the same time (see page 83).

Day 1 / *Afternoon*

Leave Atlanta in midafternoon and head south on US 41 to **Barnesville,** "the Buggy Capital of the World" and scene of the annual September Barnesville Buggy Days. Get a brochure for a walking tour of the downtown area and neighborhoods of Victorian homes from the **Barnesville–Lamar County Chamber of Commerce,** 100 Commerce Place (770–358–2732; www.barnesville.org). In addition, Barnesville's **Main Street** features several antiques shops that specialize in a variety of styles and periods.

The **Confederate Cemetery,** on Greenwood Street, contains 150 Confederate graves, including that of "Uncle" George Schram. This sturdy Confederate veteran walked to all the Confederate reunions until he was in his eighties.

Take US 341 south to I–75, then go south one exit to the Hendersonville exit. Take State 26 west about a mile and turn right into the entrance of luxurious **Henderson Village,** 125 South Langston Circle, near Perry (478–988–8696 or 888–615–9722; www.hendersonvillage .com), a unique lodging and dining experience located in a collection of nineteenth-century homes and cottages on eighteen acres at what was once a stagecoach intersection. This will be your base for the remainder of this itinerary. If you arrive early enough, spend some quality time doing nothing in the formal gardens, take a dip in the pool, stroll the grounds, or watch the farm and exotic animals. Other activities include biking, guided horseback riding, sporting clays, and hunting in season. Carriage rides and massage can be arranged.

DINNER AND LODGING: At Henderson Village, sprawling verandas and white columns recall the beauty and romance of the Old South. Twenty-eight spacious guest rooms and suites, located in two turn-of-the-twentieth-century houses and six tenant cottages, are elegantly decorated to reflect the warmth and charm of that period. Today, however, the guest accommodations boast all the modern amenities and some boast a fireplace and/or a whirlpool bath. Enjoy a gourmet dinner in the Langston House Restaurant, where your taste buds will be tantalized with innovative Southern cuisine.

Hawkinsville Harness Festival

Day 2 / Morning

BREAKFAST: Savor a full breakfast at the Langston House or in the privacy of your room.

Take State 26 east to **Hawkinsville.**

Visitors are welcome at the **Lawrence L. Bennett Harness Horse Training Facility,** on US 129 south of town (478–892–9463; www.georgiaharnesshorsetrainingfacility.com). More than 350 horse owners and trainers accompany splendid steeds to Hawkinsville from October through April, contributing between $5 million and $6 million to the local economy. Early morning is when the horses are most likely to be out training on the 0.5- and 1-mile tracks.

The premier event in Hawkinsville is the **Hawkinsville Harness Festival** (478–783–1717), a weeklong event held in early April that provides an opportunity to see if the months of training and practice have paid off before the horses, trainers, and drivers head north for a season of pari-mutuel racing events. Other activities at the festival—which has been chosen as one of the "Top Twenty Festivals in the Southeast" by the

Southeast Tourism Society—include a barbecue cooking championship, arts and crafts, a beauty pageant, a confectionery bake-off, a golf tournament, a performance at the historic opera house, food, and musical entertainment. The forerunner of today's festival began in 1894 when the Wiregrass Exposition was organized so men could decide who had the best horse, women could show off their needlework, merchants could display their wares, and folks could come from miles around to watch the races and socialize.

LUNCH: The **Track Kitchen,** trackside (478–892–9463), serves short-order meals and is a great place to chat with owners, trainers, and drivers.

Afternoon

Back in town, the **Hawkinsville/Pulaski County Chamber of Commerce,** 100 Lumpkin Street (478–783–1717), provides an excellent map to guide you on a driving tour of some fifty historic buildings. One of the most significant homes you'll drive or walk by is plantation-style **Taylor Hall** on Kibbee Street. Built in 1824, it is the oldest home in Pulaski County. Another architecturally significant building is the 1907 **Historic Opera House,** corner of Broad and Lumpkin Streets, where cultural performances are held throughout the year. Its impressive stage curtain is heavy canvas hand painted with oils. Outside on the lawn is "Katie," built in 1833, one of the oldest steam pumper fire engines in the world.

Don't leave town without stopping at the **Butler Brown Gallery,** State 26 (478–892–9323). The well-known local artist's pastoral scenes and still-life paintings have hung in the governor's office at the state capitol in Atlanta and in the White House during Jimmy Carter's tenure. Despite his celebrity, Butler's paintings aren't astronomically priced.

Retrace State 26 to I–75 and go north to **Perry,** dubbed the Crossroads of Georgia because of its position at the geographic center of the state, where US 341/41 and the Golden Isles Parkway intersect with I–75. The small city was named after naval hero Comm. Oliver Hazard Perry.

The **Perry Local Welcome Center,** 101 Courtney Hodges Boulevard just off I–75 (478–988–8000), provides a brochure for two separate historic walking/driving tours. Tour A covers twenty-five sites in a 12-block area, including the Houston County Court House, several banks, churches, and historic homes. Tour B begins in front of the courthouse and covers twelve sites in a 12-block area.

Perry is the home of the **Georgia National Fairgrounds and Agricenter,** General Courtney Hodges Boulevard (478–987–3247), a mammoth exhibition facility that stages the Georgia National Fair, as well as horse shows, stock shows, and rodeos throughout the year.

Peach picking is a major activity around Perry. Several orchards invite you to pick your own or buy fresh peaches from roadside stands from mid-May to mid-August.

Retrace I–75 south to State 26, then turn west back to Henderson Village.

DINNER AND LODGING: Henderson Village.

Day 3 / Morning

BREAKFAST: A full breakfast at the Langston House or in the privacy of your room will get your day off to a good start.

Travel north on US 341 to **Fort Valley.**

Fort Valley, county seat of Peach County, is the top peach producer in the Peach State. It is the site of June's Peach Festival and four peach-packing plants that offer shopping and plant tours. One of those is **Lane Packing Company,** State 96 East (478–825–3592 or 800–27–PEACH; www.lanepacking.com), where during the harvest season, from Memorial Day through Labor Day, visitors can watch the entire peach-packing process from an elevated platform that overlooks the football-field-size plant. A four-generation family operation, Lane packs more than thirty varieties, including Redglobe, Harvester, Dixieland, and Sunbright. Hand picked by more than 400 workers, 300,000-plus peaches are individually weighed, counted, separated, and packed per hour. This is the only plant of its kind in the East, using computer-controlled equipment and soft-handling techniques. Visit the roadside market and gift shop and be sure to sample homemade peach ice cream or peach or blackberry cobbler.

In addition to peaches, pecans are an important Georgia product. Since 1924 the **Jolly Nut Company,** 100 Commercial Heights (478–825–7708 or 800–332–1505; www.jollynut.com), has sold pecans in many forms. Located next to the processing plant, the Pecan Store sells pecan products, gifts from Georgia, candy, antiques, and recipes.

LUNCH: Peppercorn Cafe, 301 South Camellia Boulevard (478–822–9696), serves soups, salads, sandwiches, and specialities such as smoked barbecue.

Afternoon

Between Fort Valley and Marshallville, off State 49, is the headquarters of the American Camellia Society, at **Massee Lane Gardens,** 1 Massee Lane (478–967–2358 or 967–2722; www.camellias-acs.com), a nine-acre garden dedicated to many varieties of the aromatic and colorful blossom. Camellias bloom between November and March, but the gardens are bright with other flowers no matter what time of year. An authentic Japanese garden, rose garden, environmental garden, an extensive library, a gift shop, and an impressive collection of Boehm porcelains, rivaling those of Mobile's Bellingrath Gardens, are additional attractions.

Return to US 341 and go north to **Roberta,** typical of railroad towns at the turn of the twentieth century. The Downtown Historic District, incorporated in 1910, includes the restored Georgia Post Building, a vintage general store, and the Benjamin Hawkins Monument.

Take US 41 back to Atlanta.

There's More

Water sports. The Ocmulgee River offers a public boat landing, fishing, waterskiing, and motorboating, as well as hunting.

Special Events

Barnesville

September. Barnesville Buggy Days commemorates the days of surrey tops and spoke wheels with buggy races and a parade with buggies, bands, floats, 250 horses, and more, as well as arts and crafts and antiques. Call the Barnesville–Lamar County Chamber of Commerce (770) 358–2732 (www.barnesville.org/buggy.html).

Fort Valley

June. Georgia Peach Festival, a salute to the lifeblood of the region, features arts and crafts, entertainment, and food—some of it containing the all-important peach. (478) 825–4002.

Hawkinsville

April. Festivities at the Hawkinsville Harness Festival include, in addition to the two days of pacing and trotting races, a week's worth of activities: a beauty pageant, a golf tournament, a flea market, arts and crafts, tours of some of Hawkinsville's stately homes, a Confection Bake-off, and the Spring Pig Ribbin' Cookoff. Call the Hawkinsville–Pulaski County Chamber of Commerce at (478) 783–1717.

Perry

April and October. On the third weekend of April and October, the Mossy Creek Barnyard Festival, on State 96, provides an opportunity to glimpse "the way it used to be." In addition to pioneer demonstrations, music and food enhance the celebration. Call the Perry Area CVB at (478) 988–8000.

October. The Georgia National Fair is a week of family-oriented activities that revolve around traditional agricultural livestock and horse shows, home and fine-arts competitions, concerts, a carnival, the shops of McGill Marketplace, food, and fireworks. (478) 987–3247.

Other Recommended Restaurants and Lodgings

Barnesville

Pastime Grill, 208 Main Street (770–358–1637), for lunch and dinner.

Fort Valley

China House, 103 North Camellia Boulevard (478–825–1473), for lunch and dinner.

Evans-Cantrell House, a bed-and-breakfast at 300 College Street (478–825–0611), is an Italian Renaissance Revival mansion built in 1916 by A. J. Evans, well known as the Peach King because of his numerous orchards and packing operations.

Hawkinsville

The Steak House Restaurant, 101 Buchan Drive (478–892–3383), specializes in charbroiled flavor. Noon buffet daily. Seafood buffet Friday evenings.

Perry

Angelina's, 1500 Sam Nunn Boulevard (478–987–9494), serves Italian fare.

For More Information

Barnesville–Lamar County Chamber of Commerce, 100 Commerce Place, Barnesville, GA 30204. (770) 358–2732; www.barnesville.org.

Hawkinsville–Pulaski County Chamber of Commerce, 100 Lumpkin Street, Hawkinsville, GA 31036. (478) 783–1717.

Peach County Chamber of Commerce, 201 Oakland Heights Parkway, Fort Valley, GA 31030. (478) 825–3733.

Perry Area Chamber of Commerce, 1105 Washington Street, Perry, GA 31069. (478) 987–1234.

Perry Area Convention and Visitors Bureau, 101 General Courtney Hodges Boulevard, Perry, GA 31069. (478) 988–8000; www.perryga.com.

SOUTHBOUND ESCAPE FOUR

Macon/Juliette, Georgia

White Columns and Fried Green Tomatoes / 2 Nights

Macon—"the city of white columns and cherry blossoms"—got its nickname from its bountiful antebellum structures and its profusion of pink springtime blooms. With 180,000 Yoshino cherry trees, Macon boasts more cherry trees than Washington, D.C. The blooming city is at its most flamboyant during the March Cherry Blossom Festival.

Forward-thinking city founders laid out the ample parks and broad boulevards you see today. In the years prior to the Civil War, affluent planters and prosperous businessmen used the bounty of their labors to build opulent mansions in town. Various stories circulate about why the city was spared during the Civil War, but the result is that most of those structures survive to this day to captivate resident and visitor alike.

- ☐ Whistle Stop Cafe
- ☐ Cherry trees
- ☐ Stunning architecture
- ☐ Black heritage
- ☐ Native American history

Macon is located on Georgia's fall line. Millions of years ago this area was on the shores of a Paleozoic sea. When the water receded, the area was left with one of the world's largest kaolin deposits, in which it's not unusual to find sand dollars and sharks' teeth. Early Native American tribes lived here 10,000 to 12,000 years ago. Priests in de Soto's 1540 expedition baptized two Native Americans—the first recorded Christian baptisms on the new continent.

Tiny Juliette's claim to fame is that it was the site used for shooting the movie *Fried Green Tomatoes*.

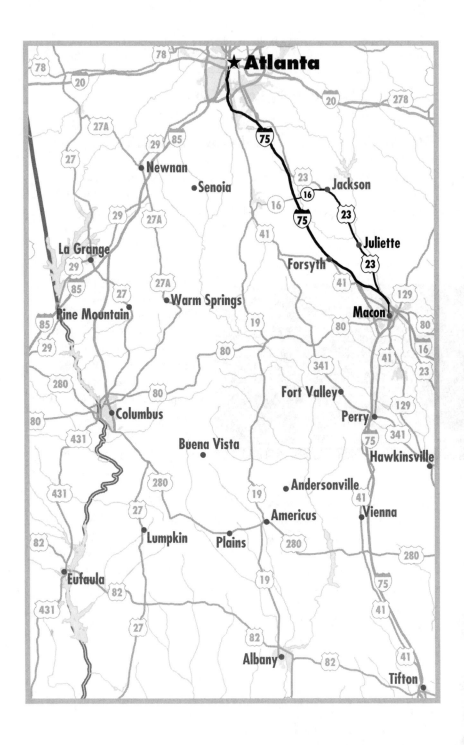

Day 1 / *Morning*

Leave Atlanta on Friday morning and take I–75 south to State 16, where you will go east. At Jackson take US 23 south to **Juliette.** Make sure to be there in time for lunch at the **Whistle Stop Cafe.** Although the 1991 movie, based on Fannie Flagg's book, is set in Alabama, it was actually filmed in diminutive Juliette, a site chosen by Flagg herself. In its prime Juliette was a busy textile and railroad town. Its mill was once the world's largest powered by water. When the mill closed in 1957, the town began to decline—stores were boarded up, houses abandoned. The old deserted mill drooped dejectedly beside the railroad tracks. The hamlet eventually became a ghost town, but an almost-overnight metamorphosis occurred with the coming of the movie. The big event of the year is the Green Tomato Festival in October.

LUNCH: The heart of the quaint country crossroads village is the Whistle Stop Cafe, 443 McCrackin Street (478–992–8886; www.thewhistlestop cafe.com). Step inside, and you'll be transported back fifty years by the furniture and memorabilia left from the movie set. Of course, fried green tomatoes lead the menu items, but you can also order other rib-sticking southern specialties. The cafe is open Wednesday through Saturday from 11:00 A.M. to 7:00 P.M., Tuesday and Sunday from 11:00 A.M. to 4:00 P.M. on a first-come, first-served basis. Just sign your name on the list hanging on the screen door, and you'll be called when it's your turn. Lines are long, but you can while away your wait in one of the rocking chairs on the porch.

Afternoon

After lunch, explore the historic buildings along **McCrackin Street.** The bank, courthouse, depot, drugstore, and old dry goods store have been transformed into antiques and crafts shops as well as quaint boutiques such as Towanda's. You'll even see Idgie Threadgoode's gaily painted mailbox. Stop in at the tiny wooden courthouse to sign the guest book. On the day we visited, tourists from Germany, the Netherlands, England, and Canada had preceded us.

Turn right off McCrackin Street onto Juliette Road, go 4 miles, and turn right again. Follow the signs for 3.5 miles—part on gravel road, most on dirt road—to **Jarrell Plantation Historic Site** (478–986–5172; www.gastateparks.org/info/jarrell/), operated by the State Parks Department. The self-contained site portrays rugged Georgia farm life

Whistle Stop Cafe, Juliette

from the 1840s to the 1940s. This is not the romantic plantation of *Gone with the Wind;* it is a primitive farm of twenty historic buildings. Several original rustic homes contain looms, spinning wheels, a quilting frame, cobbler's bench, wood-burning stove, and simple original furnishings. The farm structures include a cotton gin, sawmill, carpenter shop, blacksmith shop, three-story barn, beehives, well, shingle mill, cane furnace, cane mill and planer, smokehouses, and wheat houses. Other artifacts include engines and tools. Farm animals, gardens, and a grape arbor lend an air of authenticity.

Generations of the Jarrell family made their home here for one hundred years. The buildings and artifacts they willed to the state encompass one of the most sizable and complete collections of original family relics in Georgia. Special events and exhibits are held at the plantation throughout the year.

Continue south on US 23 to **Macon.**

DINNER: A favorite after-work gathering spot for Maconites is the **Downtown Grill,** 562 Mulberry Street Lane (478–742–5999), which serves steaks and pastas.

LODGING: In keeping with the antebellum character of Macon, you might like to stay in a historic bed-and-breakfast. The sumptuous **1842 Inn,** 353 College Street (478–741–1842 or 877–452–6599; www.1842inn.com), offers luxurious accommodations in the grand ante-bellum Greek Revival mansion or in its adjoining Victorian cottage. Some guest rooms feature working fireplaces and/or Jacuzzis.

Day 2 / Morning

BREAKFAST: A substantial continental breakfast will be served to you in your room on a silver tray, complete with fresh flowers and a newspaper.

You could spend days on foot just wandering the streets of Macon's six historic districts. The diversity of the city's architectural styles is a pho-tographer's heaven. Begin at the Macon-Bibb County CVB's Downtown Welcome Center, housed in **Terminal Station,** 200 Cherry Street (478–743–3401 or 800–768–3401; www.maconga.org), once the railroad center of the Southeast. Built in 1916, the 520-foot-long station saw one hundred passenger trains a day. Get an overview of the city with Sidney's Historic Tours, which leaves from the terminal, or get brochures for sev-eral themed, self-guided excursions.

Spend the morning visiting three historically and architecturally sig-nificant homes. One of Macon's most extravagant historic mansions is the **Hay House,** 934 Georgia Avenue (478–742–8155; www.hayhouse.org), built in the 1850s by William Butler Johnston, keeper of the Confederate treasury. Occupied by only two families, the mansion, which is a National Historic Landmark, is owned and operated by the Georgia Trust for Historic Preservation. Built in the Italian Renaissance style, the grand, 18,000-square-foot, redbrick villa contains twenty-four antiques-filled rooms; when built, it incorporated such then-unheard-of conveniences as indoor plumbing, an enormous attic water tank, walk-in closets, an eleva-tor, an intercom, and the best ventilation system ever designed for an American home up to that time.

Superior workmanship resulted in 12-foot-high, 500-pound front doors; 16- and 30-foot ceilings; carved marble mantels; elaborately embossed cornices, medallions, and moldings; and intricate trompe l'oeil wall and ceiling paintings only now rediscovered after years of being cov-ered by layers of paint and wallpaper. The painted ornamentation in the main hall has been documented as the finest-quality marbleizing in this country. The dining room contains a European-made arched and curved stained-glass window called *Four Seasons of a Vineyard.* A stained-glass rosette soars over the center of the room. The mansion is overflowing with sumptuous furnishings and museum-quality objets d'art.

The **Cannonball House and Museum,** 856 Mulberry Street (478–745–5982; www.cannonballhouse.org), was the only building in Macon actually struck during a Union attack in 1864. A cannonball smashed through a column of the Greek Revival home, landed in the parlor, and rolled to a stop in the central hall, where it remains today. Two rooms of the house are furnished as replicas of chambers at old Wesleyan College, the first woman's college in the country and home of the first national sororities. The detached brick kitchen and servants' quarters serve as a small museum. Open Monday through Saturday.

Georgia's revered poet Sidney Lanier was born in Macon in 1842 at his grandparents' home, an 1840 Victorian cottage. A linguist, mathematician, and lawyer, Lanier had a natural ability to play any instrument and would have preferred to be remembered as a musician. He served in the Confederate Army and was captured while commanding a blockade runner. Although Lanier lost his health while he was imprisoned and died at thirty-nine, he left behind a beloved body of work, including his two most famous poems, "The Marshes of Glynn" and "Song of the Chattahoochee." Memorabilia from his life and period furnishings are displayed at **Sidney Lanier Cottage,** 935 High Street (478–743–3851). Open Monday through Saturday.

LUNCH: Len Berg's, 240 Post Office Alley (478–742–9255), serves southern home cooking. Specialties include fresh vegetables, homemade rolls, fried oysters, and macaroon pie. Named one of *Georgia Trend*'s "Top 50 Georgia Restaurants." Open Monday through Saturday, but don't wait too late to eat, because the restaurant closes at 3:00 P.M. No credit cards.

Afternoon

Named in honor of Harriet Tubman, mastermind of the Civil War Underground Railroad that spirited slaves north, the **Tubman African-American Museum,** 340 Walnut Street (478–743–8544), displays art and artifacts about African-American life. An arresting mural records the 400-year journey and achievements of Blacks from Africa to contemporary America.

At the **Museum of Arts and Sciences,** 4182 Forsyth Road (478–477–3232; www.masmacon.com), you can see art and science exhibits, an important gem and mineral collection, and the three-story

Discovery House and Backyard. The Discovery House features an artist's garret, humanist's study, and scientist's workshops—each filled with fascinating interactives. The Backyard features live animals in natural habitats. The complex also includes a planetarium, nature trails, Mary's Garden, and the Kingfisher Cabin—the former dwelling and workshop of author Harry Stillwell Edwards.

Macon's and Georgia's musical heritage are celebrated at the **Georgia Music Hall of Fame,** 200 Martin Luther King Jr. Boulevard and Mulberry Street (478–750–8555 or 888–GA–ROCKS; www.gamusic hall.com), a perpetual music fest. You're sure to find whatever turns you on: rock, jazz, rhythm and blues, gospel, country, or classical. A visit here is good foot-stomping, hand-clapping fun. Located adjacent to Terminal Station, the hall of fame focuses on Georgia's diverse musical legacy through the tunes and memorabilia of Macon artists such as "Little Richard" Penniman, Otis Redding, Lena Horne, and the Allman Brothers Band; as well as other Georgia greats such as Augusta's James Brown and Jessye Norman; Athens's R.E.M., the B-52s, and Widespread Panic; Columbus's "Mother o the Blues," Gertrude "Ma" Rainey; Monticello's Trisha Yearwood; and other homegrown musicians. Georgia's music makers are so varied that every one in your band—whether musically challenged or a budding rock star or classical artist—can find something to enjoy. Vintage listening rooms filled with memorabilia, instruments, costumes, photos, and other artifacts, each devoted to a different style of music, provide a feast for the ears. For serious aficionados, audio programs intermix music, artists' interviews, and historical context. The grand finale, in the Gretsch Theater, is guaranteed to get everyone's fingers snapping. In this interactive theater audience members vote to choose three videos from various genres.

Play ball at the **Georgia Sports Hall of Fame,** 301 Cherry Street (478–752–1585; www.gshf.org), to learn about Georgia's storied athletic heritage, which is showcased at this museum. Exhibits honor heroes from the state's top high school, collegiate, amateur, and professional teams as well as individual athletes such as Hank Aaron, Herschel Walker, Fran Tarkenton, Bill Elliott, Edwin Moses, Jackie Robinson, and others. Budding sports superstars will love the interactive displays such as a NASCAR simulator or those that allow wannabe jocks to kick field goals, shoot hoops, or be a wheelchair paralympian. The state-of-the-art theater designed after ballparks of yesteryear is sure to bring back nostalgic memories for the older generation.

DINNER: Upscale, sophisticated Southern cuisine is served at the **Tic Toc Room,** 408 Martin Luther King Jr. Boulevard (478–744–0123). The restaurant boasts elaborate wine and martini lists, has a piano bar, and offers live entertainment Friday and Saturday nights from 9:00 P.M. to 12:20 A.M. Closed Sunday and Monday.

EVENING: The rich variety of Macon's architectural treasures creates a photographer's paradise, but the opportunities to sightsee don't go down with the sun. Residents of one historic neighborhood are participating in a special lighting project called **Lights on Macon,** which bathes these stately homes in the warm glow of spotlights during evening hours—making them appear even more spectacular. After a heavy dinner you may need to walk off your repast. Get a walking tour brochure from the welcome center so you can follow the route and read about the various houses.

LODGING: 1842 Inn.

Day 3 / Morning

BREAKFAST: At the inn.

Just north of I–16 and east of downtown off State 57 is the **Ocmulgee National Monument and Indian Mounds Visitor Center Museum,** 1207 Emory Highway (478–752–8257; www.nps .gov/ocmu/), where you can see several Native American temple and burial mounds, North America's only reconstructed prehistoric ceremonial earth lodge, exhibits of artifacts from the six distinct Native American groups who occupied the site, and a movie that traces the Native American history of the area back 12,000 years. The earth lodge was a ceremonial building that was a meeting place for political and religious leaders. A fire preserved evidence of many features, which gave archaeologists a firm basis for the reconstruction. The clay floor is about 1,000 years old. A Cornfield Mound yields signs of a cultivated field that was located unusually close to the village site. Prehistoric trenches may have been defensive or may have been borrow pits from which earth was dug to create the mounds. Excavations of an old trading post yielded axes, clay pipes, beads, knives, swords, bullets, flints, pistols, and muskets. The 683-acre park also contains the Opelofa Nature Trail, which winds through the lowlands of Walnut Creek.

LUNCH: H&H Restaurant, 807 Forsyth Street (478–742–9810), serves enough meat, vegetables, bread, and a beverage to fill even the most ravenous appetites for a fixed price. Just to give you an idea: when Macon's Allman Brothers Band was just getting started, members used to buy one gargantuan plate, and they'd all eat off of it. Later, when they became famous and got a hankering for soul food, they'd fly owner Mama Louise out to California to cook for them.

Afternoon

Make a stop at the **City Auditorium,** 415 First Street (478–751–9152), built in 1925 with the world's largest copper dome. A painting depicting the leading citizens in the city's history spans the 10-foot-wide and 60-foot-long proscenium. Murals by George Beattie in the **U.S. Federal Building/Post Office,** 451 College Street (478–752–8400), trace Macon's history.

In the twentieth century, Macon has had a rich Black musical tradition. **Pleasant Hill Historic District,** one of the first Black neighborhoods listed on the National Register of Historic Places, was the childhood home of "Little Richard" Penniman. Otis Redding and Lena Horne also called Macon home. Macon's WIBB-AM is where James Brown got his recording break, and the restored **Historic Douglass Theatre,** 355 Martin Luther King Jr. Boulevard (478–742–2000), once a segregated music hall for African Americans, hosted Bessie Smith, Cab Calloway, and Count Basie, among others. Otis Redding was discovered there. Today the theater is the site of live performances and trendy entertainments such as laser shows and IMAX films.

If you're fond of antiques, Macon is an antiques lover's heaven, with plenty of shops and antiques malls. Downtown contains several shops, while **Ingleside Village,** Ingleside Avenue between Rogers and Corbin Avenues, is becoming known as Antique Alley, with its collection of quaint shops for gifts, clothing, and art, as well as antiques. Wander through even more shops in the Forsyth Road/Bass Road/Riverside Drive area. Bolingbroke sports another four shops.

Take I–75 to Atlanta.

There's More

Jackson

Outdoor activities. High Falls State Park, 76 High Falls Park Drive off I–75 at exit 65 (478–993–3053; www.gastateparks.org/info/highfall/), located on the Piedmont Fall Line, is the site of Georgia's southernmost waterfall. The park, with a 650-acre lake, offers camping and water sports.

The Dauset Trails Nature Center, 360 Mount Vernon Church Road off State 42 (770–775–6798), consists of 1,000 acres that feature 6 miles of hiking trails, as well as plant identification and ecology programs.

Water sports. Jackson Lake, with 4,700 acres and a 135-mile shoreline, offers all water sports.

Macon

Water sports. West of town between State 74 and US 80 is Lake Tobesofkee, which offers three beaches, numerous water sports, camping, picnicking, and tennis, as well as the Arrowhead Arts and Crafts Festival, held the last weekend of October. Tobesofkee Recreation Area, 600 Moseley Dixon Road (478–474–8770).

Special Events

Macon

March. Cherry Blossom Festival, the city's premier springtime event, features more than 400 activities. (478) 751–7429 or (800) 768–3401; www.cherryblossom.com.

September. Sweet Georgia Jam, a celebration of the state's musical heritage, includes daily and nightly concerts in a variety of historic venues representing every genre of music.

December. White Columns and Holly is a monthlong Christmas celebration featuring concerts, theater, and tours of the Hay House, Lanier Cottage, and several private homes, all of which are lavishly decorated and have Christmas baked goods, crafts, and gifts for sale. Contact the Macon–Bibb County CVB at (800) 768–3401.

Other Recommended Restaurants and Lodgings

Juliette

Jarrell 1920 House, 715 Jarrell Plantation Road (478–986–3972 or 888–574–5434; www.jarrellhouse.com), was the largest of the family homes at what is now the Jarrell Plantation State Historic Site. Retained by the family when they donated the plantation to the state, the large, rambling house offers guests a perfect history lesson as well as bed-and-breakfast accommodations.

Macon

Crowne Plaza Macon, 108 First Street (478–746–1461 or 800–227–6963), is a high-rise hotel located in the heart of the historic district. It offers a concierge level, pool, sauna, Paul's Restaurant, a cafe, bar, and lounge.

Michael's on Mulberry, 588 Mulberry Street (478–743–3997) offers fine dining with indoor and outdoor seating. Closed Sunday.

Nu-Way Weiners, 430 Cotton Avenue (478–743–1368; www.nu-way weiners.com), has been an institution in this location with the same neon sign since 1916. Famous for its private-label weiners and secret-recipe chili sauce, the fast-food restaurant also serves burgers and sandwiches. Open Monday through Friday 6:00 A.M. to 7:00 P.M., Saturday 7:00 A.M. to 6:00 P.M.; closed Sunday. Pull up the Web site—you'll enjoy the music and can create your own Nu-Way Weiner.

For More Information

Macon–Bibb County Convention and Visitors Bureau, Terminal Station, 200 Cherry Street. (478) 743–3401 or (800) 768–3401; www.macon ga.org.

SOUTHBOUND ESCAPE FIVE

Americus, Georgia, to Eufaula, Alabama

Pigs, Peanuts, Presidents, and Painted Ladies / 2 Nights

South Georgia is the "Pecan Capital of the World," known far and wide for not only the nut itself but also pies, cookies, candies, and other treats made from it. Two presidents of the United States have made this region home. Franklin D. Roosevelt spent time at his Little White House in Warm Springs, and Jimmy Carter still resides in Plains.

The "Classic Mansion" region of the Chattahoochee Trace area of Georgia/Alabama, centered on Eufaula, Alabama, is noted for its unusual array of outstanding antebellum and postbellum structures. You don't have to go all the way to Natchez or Vicksburg or even to Savannah or Charleston for a spring pilgrimage of spectacular southern homes when Eufaula is so close. Numerous structures and entire districts, all built with cotton profits, are included on the National Register of Historic Places or are National Historic Landmarks. The Seth Lore and Irwinton Historic District alone has more than 700 historic and architecturally significant structures, including an imposing collection of mid- to late-nineteenth-century small-town commercial buildings.

- ☐ Victorian historic districts
- ☐ Lindbergh Memorial
- ☐ Jimmy Carter's hometown
- ☐ Living-history village
- ☐ Civil War cemetery

Day 1 / Morning

Leave Atlanta in the morning and head south on I–75. You might want to stop off in Macon, which is described in the "White Columns and Fried Green Tomatoes" escape, page 89, or in Perry, which is detailed on page 84 in the "Horse and Buggy" escape.

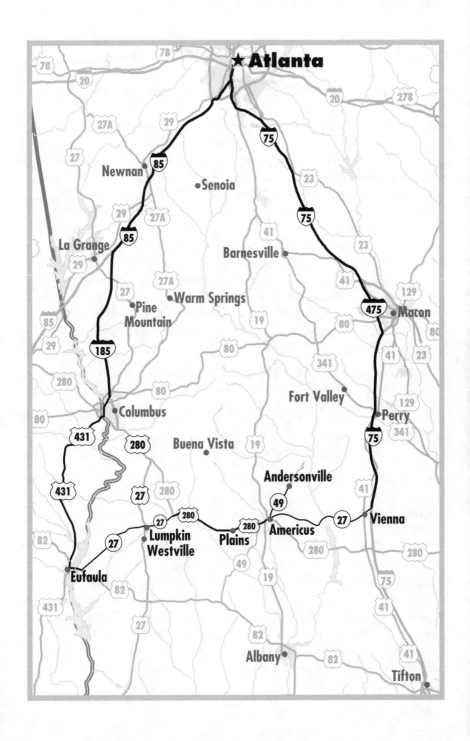

When you reach **Vienna** (pronounced VIE-enna), get a brochure for a driving tour of sixty historic sites from the **Dooly County Chamber of Commerce,** 117 East Union Street (229–268–8275). Poke your head into the many antiques and crafts shops that line Union Street and fan out on Second and Third Streets.

Native son Walter F. George was a renowned Georgia politician who served as a U.S. senator for more than thirty-five years. He is best known as the framer of the North Atlantic Treaty Organization. The **Walter F. George Law Office and Museum,** which preserves memorabilia from the statesman's career, is located on State 215 in George Busbee Park, named for a recent Georgia governor who also came from Vienna.

Curator Margaret Hegidio can tell you every cotton pickin' thing you ever wanted to know about growing cotton in Dooly County as well as a lot of other things about cotton at the **Cotton Museum,** 1321 East Union Street (no phone). Dooly County is the highest cotton producing county in the state, so what more natural place than Vienna for a museum to King Cotton? Inside the rustic old one-room school, you'll find antique tools and cotton by-products as well as photographs and a video about the harvest process.

LUNCH: Get some fabulous take-out barbecue from **Mamie Bryant's BBQ Pit,** 308 Eighth Street (229–268–4179), and then go to George Busbee Park for a picnic.

Afternoon

Take State 27 west to **Americus,** which boasts a large historic district of antebellum and Victorian architecture that dates from 1800. Brochures for walking and driving tours are available from the **Americus/Sumter County Chamber of Commerce,** 400 West Lamar Street (229–924–2646; www.americus-online.com).

You may not know that Americus is the home of Habitat for Humanity's International Headquarters, 322 West Lamar Street (229–924–6935 or 800–HABITAT; www.habitat.org), where you can see a video and view exhibits about this organization's work to provide adequate housing for people around the world. Nearby is the **Global Village and Discovery Center,** West Church Street (866–924–5823; www.habitat.org/gvdc/), a six-acre site where you can walk through a Living in Poverty Area and then tour examples of Habitat houses from fifteen countries around the world, learn how to make bricks and tiles, and see other exhibits.

DINNER AND LODGING: Americus is endowed with several outstanding choices in accommodations. The most impressive is the restored 1892 **Windsor Hotel,** 125 West Lamar Street (229–924–1555). An architectural masterpiece, it is one of only five Georgia hotels listed in the National Trust for Historic Preservation's Historic Hotels of America. The Italianate-style, castlelike hotel, adorned with a Flemish stepped roof and a Romanesque tower, features the Bridal Suite and the Carter Presidential Suite. Have dinner in the elegant Grand Dining Room and enjoy the musical entertainment in the cocktail lounge, Floyd's Pub. Daily lunch buffet and Sunday brunch.

Evening

Check to see if there is a performance at historic **Rylander Theatre,** 310 West Lamar Street (229–931–0001; www.rylander.org).

Day 2 / Morning

BREAKFAST: Have a continental or full breakfast at the hotel.

Take State 49 north toward **Andersonville** (www.andersonville georgia.com). On the way, stop at the **Lindbergh Memorial** at Souther Airfield, which commemorates Charles Lindbergh's visit in 1923 to purchase and test the single-engine Jenny four years before his historic solo flight across the Atlantic.

Andersonville is a Civil War village and home of the **Andersonville National Historic Site,** 406 Cemetery Road (229–924–0343; www.nps.gov/ande/). Camp Sumter, as it was officially known, was the largest Civil War military prison in the Confederacy, placed where officials believed there would be greater safety and more abundant food. Although the prison was built to handle 10,000 prisoners at a time, at one point it held 32,000. During its brief operation more than 45,000 Union soldiers were confined there, of whom almost one-third died from disease, malnutrition, overcrowding, or exposure.

After the war, Clara Barton was sent to Andersonville to establish the whereabouts of missing Union soldiers. She was able to locate and mark the graves of all but 460 of the men who died there.

In 1890 the land was purchased by the Department of the Grand

Living history at Andersonville National Historic Site

Army of the Republic (GAR), a Union veterans' organization, which then sold it to the Women's Relief Corps, the national auxiliary of the GAR. The ladies were responsible for seeing that trees were planted and monuments erected. They donated the memorial park to the people of the United States in 1910, and it was made a National Historic Site in 1970.

The visitor center houses a museum that contains exhibits about Andersonville and Civil War prisons in general. A brochure and audiotape are available for a self-guided tour. Wayside exhibits along the tour route re-create the harsh conditions that existed. Sometimes costumed guides demonstrate the brutal methods that were used to control prisoners. The Prisoner of War Museum chronicles American wars with a film, *Echoes of Captivity,* and exhibits. Guided tours are given at 11:00 A.M. and 2:00 P.M. The most poignant event is the annual Memorial Day celebration, when the cemetery is a sea of 16,000 fluttering American flags.

The nearby restored Civil War village of Andersonville itself is a tiny, sleepy hamlet, although it was a bustling place during the Civil War. Prisoners arrived there by rail and were marched to the prison, so the town became the supply center. Andersonville's **Welcome Center and Drummer Boy Civil War Museum,** 114 Church Street (229–924–2558), housed in the old railway depot and an adjacent rail car, display authentic documents, guns, swords, flags, two drummer boy uniforms, Union and Confederate uniforms, and other Civil War relics. Open Thursday through Sunday.

LUNCH: Granny's Kitchen, 280 Hillcrest Grange Drive (229–924–0028), serves all-around good home cooking, especially vegetables and desserts.

Afternoon

From Americus go west on US 280 toward **Plains,** home of former President Jimmy Carter, now the **Jimmy Carter National Historic Site,** 300 North Bond Street (229–824–4104; www.nps.gov/jica). Just outside of town, stop at the Georgia Visitor Center and pick up a brochure for a self-guided tour that describes twenty-seven sites in Plains and the surrounding area. Now, we're talking a one-horse town here (population 716). There are no stores other than a couple of places that sell souvenirs or antiques and a couple of restaurants and bed-and-breakfasts. Standing by the depot, you can see almost everything there is to see.

Start your tour at the visitor center located in the old Plains High School on North Bond Street. You'll see an orientation film and view exhibits about Carter's life and career. You can purchase a tour book that will guide you through all the Carter-related sites in and around Plains.

Next stop should be Carter's first campaign headquarters, housed in the **Depot Museum,** Main Street and M. L. Hudson Street, in the center of town. Pictures and memorabilia about the campaign are exhibited.

Other points of interest to drive by include Plains Methodist Church, where the Carters reputedly got engaged and were later married; and the public housing apartment the young couple lived in after he got out of the Navy.

While you're in Plains, keep your eyes open. You might even see the unassuming former president out jogging early in the morning or bicycling through town with Mrs. Carter. Several times a month Carter teaches Sunday school at Maranatha Baptist Church. You can find a schedule of former President Carter's teaching dates on the Web site www.nps.gov/jica.

The highlight of a trip to the National Historic Site is a visit to the **Carter Boyhood Farm** in nearby Archery. There are various ways to get there—you could walk the 10-mile round-trip like Carter did as a boy, you can drive, or you can take the Southwest Georgia Excursion Train. (More about it later.)

The boyhood home is a simple farm, restored to reflect the pre-electricity 1930s era when the Carter family lived there. Inside the farmhouse, you'll see Jimmy's austere room and hear the former President's recorded commentary about his life at the farm. Outside you'll see a simple dirt tennis court (the family's one luxury), barn, blacksmith shop, pump house, general store, and the cabin of a Black family who lived there.

The **Southeast Georgia Excursion Train** (headquarters in Cordele; 229–276–2371 or 800–864–7275) runs 35 miles between Archery and Cordele with stops at Plains, Americus, Leslie, and Georgia Veterans State Park. Affectionately known as the SAM Shortline because it was once part of the Savannah, Americus, and Montgomery Railroad, the train offers coach and first-class seats in restored 1940s-era cars. You can get off at any of the stops to sightsee and get back on any return train, even spending the night and returning another day.

DINNER AND LODGING: The Windsor Hotel.

Day 3 / Morning

BREAKFAST: At the hotel.

Take US 280/State 27 to **Lumpkin.**

On the square, presided over by an impressive courthouse, is the restored **Bedingfield Inn** (229–838–6419), once a stagecoach inn and family residence built by Lumpkin's first doctor. Today it is a museum furnished as it would have been when it operated as a frontier inn. While you're at the inn, pick up a brochure for the Stagecoach Trail, a driving tour past twenty-three pre-1850 homes.

Also on the square is the **Hatchett Drug Store Museum,** which is fully furnished and equipped as it was as a turn-of-the-twentieth-century apothecary. Some of the memorabilia date back to the Civil War.

Just south of town on US 27/State 1 is **Westville,** "where it's always 1850." Westville (229–838–6310 or 888–733–1850; www.westville.org) is a working living-history village in the tradition of Williamsburg, although not on such a grand scale. Westville never existed as a real town, but by restoring and relocating original buildings from around Georgia, a village has been re-created that vividly portrays the state's preindustrial life and the culture of the 1850s.

The village is not complete but is developing just as a town would have in the 1850s. Essential buildings such as homes and blacksmith shops were constructed first. Less essential structures such as government buildings and churches came next. Currently, several styles of homes, from primitive cabins to simple farmhouses to elegant town houses, are represented, as are a church, school, shops, blacksmith shop, cotton gin, whiskey still, and a cane mill and syrup kettle. Vegetable gardens and farm animals lend an air of authenticity.

Guides garbed in period costumes dispense history, while craftspeople demonstrate shoemaking, candle dipping, rake making, and other skills of the period. If you're lucky, you'll be there when the tempting scent of baking gingerbread or country biscuits will lead you to taste a sample. The works of local craftspeople are for sale at the country store.

Continue west on State 27 across the Chattahoochee River to **Eufaula,** Alabama.

LUNCH: **Creek Restaurant,** 3301 South Eufaula Avenue (334–687–0083), features catfish and shrimp.

Afternoon

Begin your tour of Eufaula by visiting **Shorter Mansion,** 340 North Eufaula Avenue (334–687–3793), which serves as the city's visitor center. Magnificently restored, the mansion features Confederate relics, antiques, and memorabilia that depicts the lives of six Alabama governors. Pick up a brochure for the driving tour through the Seth Lore and Irwinton Historic District here or from the Eufaula-Barbour Chamber of Commerce, 333 East Broad (334–687–6664).

Hart House, 211 North Eufaula Avenue (334–687–9755), a one-story Greek Revival house built in 1850, is the visitor information center for the Historic Chattahoochee Commission, which promotes tourism in both the Georgia and Alabama counties that border the Chattahoochee River. Some of the furnishings are original.

Owned by the Alabama Historical Commission, the Italianate-style **Fendall Hall,** 917 West Barbour Street (334–687–8469), was built in 1860. Waterford chandeliers, hand-stenciled walls, and murals attest to the elegance of the era.

Several significant private homes you should walk or drive by include Sheppard Cottage, 504 East Barbour Street, considered to be the oldest residence in Eufaula, and the 1905 Victorian Dogwood Inn, 214 North

Eufaula Avenue, which is distinguished by a stylized dragon that crowns the peak of the front porch gable. The Tavern, Front Street, considered to be Eufaula's oldest frame structure, was originally an 1830s inn for Chattahoochee River travelers, then served as a Confederate hospital. More history can be found at **Fairview Cemetery,** North Orange Avenue, enclosed by an iron fence that once surrounded the old Union Female College. It contains European settlers' graves, slave burial grounds, Confederate graves, and an old Jewish section.

There's More

Lumpkin, Georgia

Outdoor activities. Providence Canyon State Conservation Park, State 39C west of Lumpkin (229–838–6202), known as Georgia's Little Grand Canyon, is one of Georgia's Seven Wonders. Chasms, crevices, and canyons are awesome witness to nature's unrelenting destructive assault of wind and rain. The result of one hundred years of erosion, multitinted canyon walls create a stunning natural painting, with orange, salmon, and red predominant, but with hints of white, gray, and purple delighting the eye. In addition to dramatic vistas, the park has the highest concentration of rainbow-colored wildflowers in Georgia. In a state known for its wide variety of azaleas, this area boasts a large number of the rare orange plumleaf azalea—found only within a 100-mile region. The park includes an interpretive center, picnic areas, hiking and backpacking trails, pioneer camps, and a group shelter.

Water sports. Florence Marina State Park, State 39C (229–838–4244; www.gastateparks.org/info/flormarin/), is at the northern end of Lake Walter F. George on the Georgia/Alabama border. The Kirbo Interpretive Center explains the rich cultural history of Stewart County through artifacts from the prehistoric Paleo-Indian period through the early twentieth century. The park offers water sports, camping, swimming, tennis, a marina, and rental cottages.

Special Events

Andersonville, Georgia

May. Andersonville Antiques Fair, held Memorial Day weekend, features 150 dealers in antiques, Civil War artifacts, and old-time crafts. Activities include marching, drilling, and skirmishing by Civil War reenactors, as well as performances of country and gospel music. (229) 924–2558.

First weekend of October. The Andersonville Historic Fair features a Civil War encampment and skirmish between Confederate and Union troops; demonstrations from old-time craftspeople such as blacksmiths, potters, glassblowers, and quilters; and performances by square dancers, cloggers, and military bands. A large flea market draws bargain hunters from miles around to shop for furniture, glassware, china, dolls, silver, coins, Civil War artifacts, Native American artifacts, World Wars I and II military items, and high-quality arts and crafts. (229) 924–2558.

Eufaula, Alabama

April. Pilgrimage of Historic Homes and Gardens, Alabama's oldest pilgrimage, is a three-day event that includes access to houses and gardens not usually open to the public, art exhibits, garden teas, musical concerts, a needlework show, an antiques show, and candlelight and chamber music at Shorter Mansion. One special activity is "Tales from the Tomb," when citizens portray famous and not-so-famous residents of Fairview Cemetery who share the dramas and scandals of the aristocratic river town and recount the chilling arrival of Yankee troops. The Living Black History Exhibition features artisans and craftspeople practicing and demonstrating blacksmithing, shaped-note singing, quilting, caning, and other skills. Contact the Eufaula Heritage Association at (334) 687–3793 or (888) EUFAULA.

Lumpkin, Georgia

For all events at Westville, call (229) 838–6310 or (888) 733–1850, or log on to www.westville.org.

October/November. Westville's Harvest Festival runs three weeks in October and the first week in November. Modeled after the old agricultural fairs of pre–Civil War days, the fall event highlights harvest activities such as cane grinding and syrup making. The last remaining antebellum animal-powered cotton gin operates during the fair.

December. During December, Westville displays period decorations and numerous festivities such as a yule log ceremony, a Christmas tree lighting, and the burning of the greens to celebrate the season.

Vienna, Georgia

October. The Big Pig Jig, Georgia's official Barbecue Cooking Championship, draws about 120 teams, competing in ribs, shoulder, whole hog, and Brunswick Stew categories. Winners advance to the national competition. (229) 268–8275 or (229) 268–4554; www.bigpigjig.com.

Other Recommended Restaurants and Lodgings

Americus, Georgia

1906 Pathway Inn, 501 South Lee Street (229–928–2078 or 800–889–1466; www.1906pathwayinn.com), offers quiet comfort surrounded by luxury and elegance in a stunning Beaux Arts home in a historic district. The inn has been voted the Best Bed and Breakfast in the Presidential Pathways Area by the *Georgia Journal* magazine and one of the most romantic places to celebrate Valentine's Day by Albany's Channel 10 TV.

Americus Garden Inn, 504 Rees Park (229–931–0122 or 888–758–4749; www.americusgardeninn.com), is an elegant bed-and-breakfast located in an 1847 mansion in a historic district on Rees Park.

Forsyth 1889 Bar and Grill, 126 West Forsyth Street (229–924–8193), serves great, juicy all-American hamburgers in a casual dining atmosphere.

Eufaula, Alabama

Lakepoint Resort State Park, off US 431 (334–687–8011), features a resort inn with a restaurant and gift shop, cottages, improved and primitive campsites, camp store, golf course, swimming, tennis, and marina.

Plains, Georgia

Hugh Carter, with the help of his cousins Jimmy and Rosalynn Carter, rehabilitated a historic building downtown into the Historic Plains Inn and Antiques, Main Street (229–824–4517; www.plainsgeorgia.com /Plains_Inn.htm). Each of the seven spacious period rooms, which are located upstairs, is decorated to represent a decade in the former President's life from 1920 to 1980. Complimentary breakfast is included. Downstairs the space is divided into twenty-five booths for various antiques dealers.

Michele's Restaurant, 109 Main Street, just off the square (229–838–9991), features hearty helpings of Southern home cooking served cafeteria-style. Save room for a piece of one of the luscious pies.

Across the street from the Carter campaign headquarters is the delightful pink Victorian Plains Bed & Breakfast Inn, 100 West Church Street (229–824–7252). Carter's mother, Miss Lillian, roomed there as a single woman and shortly after her marriage when she was carrying the future president.

For More Information

Americus/Sumter County Chamber of Commerce, 400 West Lamar Street, Americus, GA 31709. (229) 924–2646; www.americus-online.com.

Andersonville Trail Association, 113 Church Street, Andersonville, GA 31711. (229) 928–2303.

Dooly County Chamber of Commerce, 117 East Union Street, Vienna, GA 31092. (912) 268–8275; www.doolychamber.org.

Eufaula Heritage Association, 340 North Eufaula Avenue, Eufaula, AL 36072. (334) 687–3793.

Georgia Visitors Information Center, 1763 US 280 West, Plains, GA 31780. (229) 824–7477.

Historic Chattahoochee Commission, 211 North Eufaula Avenue, Eufaula, AL 36072-0033. (334) 687–9755.

Helpful Web site: www.cityofvienna.org.

SOUTHBOUND ESCAPE SIX

Thomasville, Georgia, and Havana/Quincy, Florida

Arts and Roses / 3 Nights

In the waning years of the nineteenth century, south Georgia and parts of the Florida panhandle enjoyed a golden age as wealthy northerners discovered that the area made an attractive place to winter. In addition to the mild climate, the privileged classes were particularly drawn by the abundance of wild game, and they believed that the pine-scented air had therapeutic properties and that the area was free of lowland marshes that bred disease-carrying mosquitoes. Soon large resort hotels appeared, which were visited by presidents, royalty, business tycoons, and famous actors. Although the extension of the railroads farther south into Florida eventually decreed that the region lost out to more trendy destinations, there is still much to offer. Today the area between Thomasville and Tallahassee has the largest concentration of working plantations in the country. Although most aren't open to the public, you can visit one and stay at several others, which operate as inns, bed-and-breakfasts, or resorts. The small Florida panhandle towns of Havana and Quincy, which resemble south Georgia much more than stereotypical Florida, are stops on the North Florida Art Trail, which stretches from Havana to Chattahoochee and also includes Gretna, Midway, and Greensboro.

☐ Rose Garden

☐ Southern plantations

☐ Art and antiques

Day 1 / Morning

Leave Atlanta via I–75 and drive south to Tifton. From there take US 319 southwest to **Thomasville.** Although most of the South suffered after the Civil War, Thomasville experienced unprecedented growth fueled by timber and agriculture, and the extensions of the railroads brought in new people and commerce.

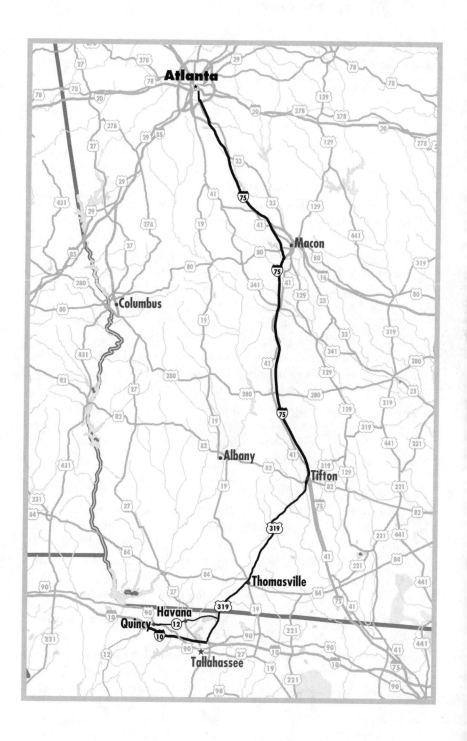

LUNCH: **Neel House Restaurant,** 502 South Broad Street (229–227–6300), offers a buffet or sandwiches, salads, pastas, and soups, served in the Victorian setting of a neoclassical mansion.

Afternoon

Known as the Rose City, Thomasville boasts more roses than people, and although the grand turn-of-the-twentieth-century hotels are long gone, the town retains much of the charm of the era. Every form of nineteenth-century architecture is said to exist in the seven historic districts. Guided tours depart from the **Destination Thomasville Tourism Authority Welcome Center,** 401 South Broad Street (912–227–7099; www.thomas villega.com), or go on your own.

One of the first winter cottages in Thomasville was the Queen Anne Victorian–style **Lapham-Patterson House Historic Site,** 626 North Dawson Street (229–225–4004; www.gastateparks.org/info/lapham/). Built in 1885, it boasted a gas-lighting system, hot and cold running water, and built-in closets. It also features a ground floor where none of the rooms is rectangular or square.

Enjoy fascinating tales about the wealthy who visited during the winter resort era and examine memorabilia from the great hotel era of the late 1800s at the **Thomas County Historical Museum,** 725 North Dawson Street (229–226–7664; www.rose.net/~history), where you can view artifacts from the area's many plantations and several antique automobiles. On the grounds are examples of pioneer cabins and other dwellings as well as a Victorian bowling alley.

Thomasville's **Rose Garden,** Smith Avenue and Covington Drive near Cherokee Lake (800–704–2350), is a showcase for more than 250 species represented by 500 plants. In addition to its roses, Thomasville's pride and joy is the 300-plus-year-old **Big Oak** at the corner of East Monroe and Crawford. You'll be astounded at the tree's mind-boggling 162-foot limb spread (wider than Niagara Falls is deep), 66-foot height, and 24-foot trunk circumference. It is the largest live oak east of the Mississippi. In order to preserve the tree, the city has restricted what can be driven under it.

DINNER AND LODGING: **Melhana, The Grand Plantation Resort,** 301 Showboat Lane (229–226–2290 or 888–920–3030), is a place where everyday cares melt away. Luxurious bed-and-breakfast accommodations are offered in the graceful 1825 mansion, and cottages and other outbuildings have been converted into guest rooms and suites. Each guest chamber has its own distinct personality, but each is appointed with lovely antiques and/or period reproductions and every possible amenity: king- or queen-size beds, plush bathrobes, televisions, and custom-made duvets or down comforters. Some are further enhanced with a fireplace and/or whirlpool bath. A heated indoor pool, clay tennis court, croquet lawn, fitness facility, and gourmet dining in the Chapin Dining Room round out the amenities.

Evening

Although there's nothing more pleasant after your elegant feast than strolling around Melhana's grounds or rocking on the veranda, check to see if there's an exhibit or performance at the **Thomasville Cultural Center,** 600 East Washington Street (229–226–0588; www.tccarts.org). The center offers exhibits, plays, and musical performances. Check with **Thomasville On Stage and Company** (229–226–0863) for other performances.

Day 2 / Morning

BREAKFAST: In the Chapin Dining Room at Melhana.

Continuing south on US 319, transport yourself back to the opulent times enjoyed by Thomasville's turn-of-the-twentieth-century winter visitors by visiting **Pebble Hill Plantation,** US 319 South (229–226–2344; www.pebblehill.com). The forty-room mansion is filled with antique furnishings, sporting art, and an extensive collection of Native American artifacts. Tour the magnificent stables and the kennels, school, infirmary, and other structures important to running a plantation. You'll particularly enjoy the garage filled with vintage cars and carriages. Please note that children younger than six are not admitted to the house and the estate is closed in September.

Continue south on US 319. After you cross the state line into Florida, take County Road 12 to State 12, then proceed south to **Havana,** the Art and Antique Center of North Florida. Havana, founded as a railroad town at the turn of the twentieth century, was named for the Cuban capital because of the town's association with cigars. Havana has been devastated twice—once by fire and once by the decline of the tobacco industry, but tobacco barns and redbrick warehouses survive. The town rebounded in 1984, when local merchants reclaimed the abandoned tobacco warehouses and created a thriving community of shops, galleries, and studios. Pick up a guide to the North Florida Art Trail at any of the numerous shops.

LUNCH: Southern Delights, Planters Exchange Co-op Building, 204 Second Street (850–539–2285), serves homemade soups, quiches, and assorted sandwiches. Before or after your meal, wander through the treasures offered by sixty antiques dealers.

Afternoon

Shops and galleries abound. The **Florida Art Center and Gallery,** 208 First Street Northwest (850–539–1770), owned by renowned watercolorist Lee Mainella, showcases the works of a number of artists in a variety of media and offers a full-service art school and workshops. Fine art and crafts can be found at the **Planters' Exchange,** a renovated tobacco warehouse that now houses the **Art Trail Studios and Shoppes.** A don't-miss shop is **Traditions at Main Street,** which features local products, unique designs, and antiques.

Take FL 12 toward Quincy, stopping along the way for dinner.

DINNER: Enjoy an enormous dinner at the **Nicholson Farmhouse Restaurant,** 200 Coca Cola Avenue off FL 12 (850–539–5931; www.nicholsonfarmhouse.com), housed in the oldest farmhouse in the area. Hearty steaks are the specialty. Choices include the house special sweetheart steak for two (two rib eyes in the shape of a heart), T-bones, Delmonicos, New York strips, sirloins, and tenderloins as well as grilled chicken and pork chops, fresh fish of the day, and shrimp farmhouse-style. Alcoholic beverages aren't served, but you can bring your own. Before or after dinner, wander the grounds and examine the farm outbuildings and other historic buildings moved to the farm, and stop in at Time Created Heirlooms, and Patrick's Store, two on-site gift shops.

Continue southwest on FL 12 to beautiful **Quincy.** As the cigar business prospered and grew, Quincy became the second largest Florida city in 1854. Although the industry was devastated by the Civil War, at the turn of the twentieth century the development of shade tobacco brought a renaissance of a tobacco economy that dominated the area for more than eighty years—earning it the title Shade Tobacco Capital of the World. Quincy has been known for decades as the Coca-Cola town because so many citizens were early investors in the company and became fabulously wealthy. At one time, 68 percent of all Coca-Cola stock was owned by Quincy residents, who continue to hold 10 percent of the company's stock. Various warehouses, packing houses, and opulent homes are the result of tobacco or

Coca-Cola wealth. The entire downtown, 36 square blocks, is designated as a National Historic District and is listed on the National Register of Historic Places. Pick up a brochure for a walking/driving tour of the area from the Gadsden County Chamber of Commerce, 221 North Madison Street (850–627–9231 or 800–627–9231).

Evening

Check ahead to see if there is a performance of a traveling Broadway musical or other show at the **Quincy Music Theatre,** 118 East Washington Street (850–875–9444; www.qmtonline.com), located in the restored art deco–style Leaf Theater. The largest community theater in the region, it is the only one dedicated to the production of major musicals. In addition, special concerts, comedy acts, and children's shows are performed throughout the year.

LODGING: McFarlin House Bed and Breakfast Inn, 305 East King Street (850–875–2526; www.mcfarlinhouse.com), is housed in a magnificent century-old Queen Anne Victorian–style mansion in the historic district. Nine charmingly different guest rooms are amply supplied with all the modern conveniences—some boast a gas-log fireplace and/or a two-person whirlpool tub.

Day 3 / Morning

BREAKFAST: Enjoy a full breakfast at the inn.

Use your brochure for a walking/driving tour of town. Stop by **Gadsden Arts,** 13 North Madison Street (850–875–4866; www.gadsden arts.com), an artists' co-op in the historic Bell and Bates Hardware Building that shows the works of local commissioned artists several times a year. Among the works for sale at the gallery are the watercolors of Joel Sampson, who favors historic local buildings as subjects.

From Quincy take I–10 east to US 319 at Tallahassee back to Tifton, where you will pick up I–75 back to Atlanta.

There's More

Havana/Quincy, Florida

Outdoor activities. The vast waterways of Gadsden County—the Apalachicola and Ochlockonee Rivers and Lakes Talquin and Seminole—

provide unlimited recreation for anglers (a freshwater fishing license is required), boaters, waterskiers, swimmers, and sailboarders. Camping, hiking, biking, and fossil hunting are popular pastimes at Lake Talquin State Forest.

Thomasville, Georgia

Hunting and shooting sports. Hunters flock to Thomas County almost as frequently as the quail, duck, and dove. Several plantations and hunt clubs are open to the public. Myrtlewood Plantation, Campbell Street (229–228–6232), offers quail and white-tailed deer hunting in season and sporting clays year-round.

Nature study. Birdsong Nature Center, 2106 Meridian Road (229–377–4408), originally Birdsong Plantation, is where you can observe birds up close and listen to a symphony of bird calls, frogs, alligators, and other sounds of nature. The center also features a butterfly garden and 10 miles of nature trails.

Special Events

Havana/Quincy, Florida

October. Havana Bead Festival, a juried art show, is the South's largest gathering of beadworkers and jewelers. More than one hundred of the nation's best artists, designers, and manufacturers participate. (800) 627–9231.

Thomasville, Georgia

April. The annual Rose Show and Festival offers a rose exhibit and competition, parade, theater productions, beauty pageant, country fair, sports and culinary events, and much, much more. Call (229) 227–3310 or check the Web site www.downtownthomasville.com/RoseFest.html.

November. Plantation Wildlife Arts Festival showcases the finest in paintings, sculpture, carvings, and photography by noted wildlife artists.

December. Thomasville is well known for its Victorian Christmas celebration, with horse-and-carriage rides, strolling costumed carolers, seasonal decorations, and refreshments. Call (229) 227–7020. Also enjoy one of the Pebble Hill Plantation Candlelight Tours. Call (229) 226–2344.

Other Recommended Restaurants and Lodgings

Quincy, Florida

Allison House Inn, 215 North Madison Street (850–875–2511 or 888–904–2511), offers English-style bed-and-breakfast accommodations in a home in the historic district. Built in 1843, it is one of the oldest homes in the area.

Quincefield Inn, 121 North Jackson Street (850–627–2196), is located in a stately 1892 home. Themed rooms include Audubon, Garden, Classical, Victorian, and the Nest.

Thomasville, Georgia

Thomasville boasts at least ten historic bed-and-breakfasts. Here are just a few:

1884 Paxton House, 445 Remington Avenue (229–226–5197), offers elegant bed-and-breakfast accommodations in a grand Victorian Gothic mansion and several cottages. Indoor lap pool and hot tub.

Evans House Bed and Breakfast, 725 South Hansell Street (229–226–1343 or 229–226–9174), occupies a historic home.

Serendipity Cottage, 339 East Jefferson Street (229–226–8111 or 800–383–7377), provides comfortable bed-and-breakfast rooms in an upper-middle-class turn-of-the-twentieth-century home with gracious public spaces and individually decorated guest rooms.

For More Information

Destination Thomasville Tourism Authority, 135 North Broad Street, Thomasville, GA 31792. (229) 227–7099 or (800) 704–2350.

Gadsden County Chamber of Commerce, 208 North Madison Street, Quincy, FL 32351. (850) 627–9231 or (800) 927–6231; www.gadsden cc.com.

Thomasville–Thomas County Historic Plantations Convention and Visitors Bureau, 401 South Broad Street, Thomasville, GA 31799. (299) 228–7977 or (866) 577–3600.

EASTBOUND
ESCAPES

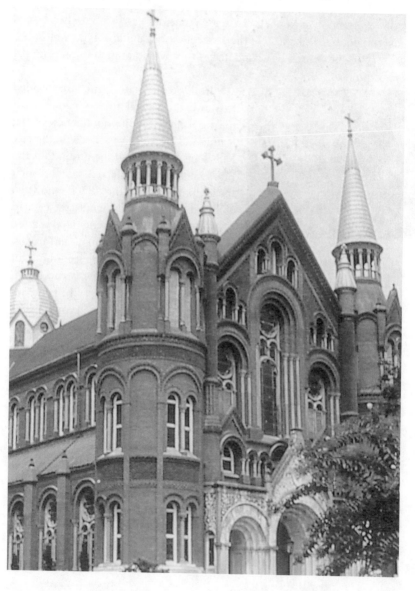

Columbia, South Carolina

A Capital Place / 2 Nights

Columbia, a vibrant Sunbelt city with a gracious past, is not only a seat of government but also a hub of the arts, education, and history, as well as the gateway to the central heartland, Lake Murray, and numerous recreational opportunities.

☐ Museums

☐ Historic homes

☐ Galleries

☐ Artists' studios

In 1786 the state legislature decided to move the capital from Charleston to the midlands near the confluence of the Saluda and Broad Rivers. Because the city had to be created from the ground up, the first session of the General Assembly didn't meet until 1790. In the 1820s renowned architect Robert Mills, who later created the Washington Monument, designed courthouses, public buildings, and canals. The Columbia Canal, which linked Columbia and Charleston, brought prosperity to the area by spawning numerous mills along the Broad River. By the time of the Civil War, Columbia was a flourishing city. In February 1865, just two months before the end of the war, Sherman's army burned Columbia back to the ground. The city recovered quickly during Reconstruction, however, and keeps on growing.

Day 1 / Afternoon

Take I–20 from Atlanta to **Columbia.** You might want to stop off and visit some of the sites in Augusta, Georgia; North Augusta, South Carolina; or Aiken, South Carolina (consult the "A City You Can Cotton To" and "Where the North Meets the South" escapes, pages 132 and 160). Otherwise, drive straight through to Columbia and plan to arrive in the early to middle afternoon, so you can begin with the visitor center and then visit some sites that are not open on weekends.

At the **Columbia Metropolitan Visitors Information Center,** 900 Assembly Street (803–545–0000 or 800–264–4884, ext. 1), you can

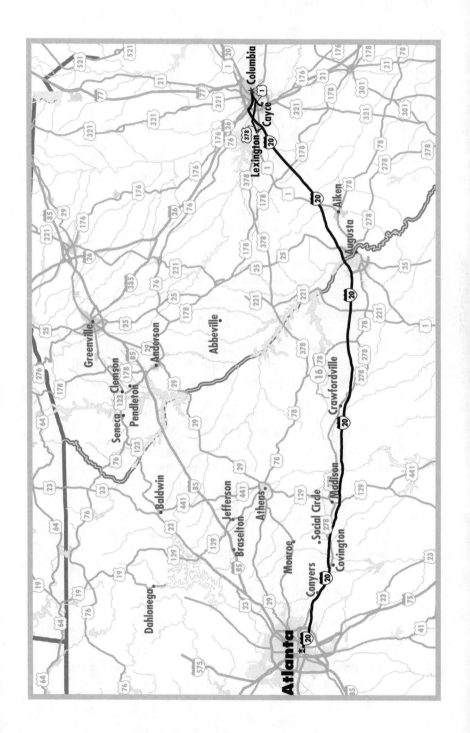

see the award-winning orientation film *The Spirit of Columbia,* pick up brochures, get recommendations on places to stay or eat, and purchase Columbia souvenirs.

Brochures for walking/driving tours are also available from the **Historic Columbia Foundation,** 1601 Richland Street (803–252–1770). The historic district is broken down into three tours, each 1 mile or less.

Take in the **South Carolina Confederate Relic Room and Museum,** Columbia Mills Building, 301 Gervais Street (803–737–8095; www.state.sc.us/crr/). Although displays span the time period from the Revolutionary War to the space age, emphasis is on the Civil War era. Exhibits include clothing, flags, newspapers, photographs, money, and other artifacts.

The historic **State House,** Main and Gervais Streets (803–734–2430), was still under construction as the Civil War wound down. Just months before Lee surrendered to Grant, Union general William T. Sherman's army pillaged and destroyed Columbia on its way north. The State House survived, however, with minimal damage. Notice the bronze stars that identify pockmarks from Union cannonballs. Tours of the home of the General Assembly and the governor's office are available, and you can watch the proceedings of the state legislature from the brass-railed visitors' galleries.

Sometime while you're in town, drive by *Tunnelvision,* Taylor and Marion Streets, an optical illusion painting by artist Blue Sky of a tunnel on the side of the AgFirst Farm Credit Bank.

In Memorial Park, at Hampton and Gadsden Streets, is a **Vietnam Memorial,** the largest monument of its type outside Washington, D.C. The park also contains several other monuments dedicated to South Carolinians who have lost their lives in other wars.

Enjoy the city center without ever getting in your car by riding Columbia's trolley—a convenient, nostalgic, and scenic way to get around. The trolley runs from 11:20 A.M. to 2:30 P.M. Monday through Friday, except major holidays, and serves the Main Street and Congaree Vista area.

DINNER: Blue Marlin, 1200 Lincoln Street (803–799–3838), features fresh seafood and low-country specialties.

Evening

Wander around the antiques shops, trendy boutiques, artists' studios, and galleries of the **Congaree Vista District/West Gervais Street**

Historic District, an area of converted warehouses that has become the heart of the arts and antiques community in Columbia as well as home to numerous restaurants and nightspots. **Trustus Theatre,** 520 Lady Street (803–254–9732), offers a regular show nightly and a Friday late-night happening.

LODGING: Claussens Inn, 2003 Greene Street (803–765–0440 or 800–622–3382; www.claussensinn.com), a delightful small bed-and-breakfast inn located in a converted bakery, is in the heart of the Five Points area near USC and the capitol. Turndown service; complimentary wine.

Day 2 / Morning

BREAKFAST: A continental breakfast is delivered to your room at the inn.

Spend the morning visiting Columbia's historic homes and the afternoon at the city's museums. You can tour the homes on your own or take a guided tour with **Columbia Historic Homes Tour,** operated by the Richland County Historic Preservation Commission (803–252–1770). Tours depart from the Robert Mills House and Gardens. Combination tickets can be purchased that include all four of the following houses.

The **Robert Mills House and Park,** 1616 Blanding Street (803–252–1770; www.historiccolumbia.org/houses/robertmills.htm), was the home of Robert Mills, one of America's most noted architects. Mills was the first to be named federal architect of the United States, was designer of the Washington Monument, and was creator of many of Columbia's public buildings and residences. The house, which he designed and built in 1823, features his trademark Ionic portico and curved walls and is sumptuously furnished with period antiques.

The **Hampton-Preston Mansion and Gardens,** 1615 Blanding Street (803–252–1770; www.historiccolumbia.org/houses/hampton.htm), was the imposing town home of Confederate leader Gen. Wade Hampton, who later went on to become governor. The house, built in 1818, was occupied by Union officers in 1865.

Woodrow Wilson Family Home, 1705 Hampton Street (803–252–1770; www.historiccolumbia.org/houses/woodrow/htm), was the home of the future president when his father was teaching at the Columbia Theological Seminary. Some family furniture is displayed, including the bed in which Wilson was born. Beautiful mature magnolias were planted by Wilson's mother more than one hundred years ago.

Mann-Simons Cottage, 1403 Richland Street (803–252–1770; www.historiccolumbia.org/houses/mann-simons.htm), built in the early 1800s, became the home of Celia Mann, a slave who bought her own freedom and walked from Charleston to Columbia to start a new life. It now serves as the Museum of African-American Culture.

Significant homes you can drive by include **Chestnut Cottage,** 1718 Hampton Street, home of Confederate general James Chestnut and his wife, Mary, who is well known for her Civil War diary; the 1820 **DeBruhl-Marshall House,** 1401 Laurel Street; the 1874 **Guignard House,** home of Jane Guignard, Columbia's first female doctor; and the 1840s **Lorick House,** 1727 Hampton Street, a Gothic Revival with gingerbread trim and cornices over the windows. **Governor's Green,** 800 Richland Street (803–737–3000), is a nine-acre complex consisting of the 1855 Governor's Mansion, the 1854 Lace House (named for its ornate ironwork), and the 1830 Caldwell-Boylston House.

While you're out and about, drive by the former **Big Apple Night Club,** 1000 Hampton Street, where the "Big Apple" national dance craze got started during the 1930s and where the "Carolina Shag" got its start. It is open only for special events.

LUNCH: Gourmet Shop, 724 Saluda Avenue (803–799–3705), is a specialty food and wine store and cafe with indoor and outdoor seating.

Afternoon

An eclectic collection that ranges from contemporary art to old masters fills the **Columbia Museum of Art,** Main and Hampton Streets (803–799–2810; www.colmusart.org). The museum's Kress Collection is one of the largest accumulations of Baroque and Renaissance art in the Southeast. There's also a children's gallery. Free admission on Saturday.

McKissick Museum of the University of South Carolina, USC Horseshoe, Sumter Street (803–777–7251; www.cla.sc.edu/MCKS/), is actually a collection of museums that houses art exhibits and geologic and gemstone displays, including fluorescent minerals and gemstones, and statesman Bernard Baruch's silver collection. The historic Horseshoe area of USC is the original campus of South Carolina College, which was established in 1801. The buildings, which have been restored to their earliest appearance, served as hospitals for both sides during the Civil War.

Art, history, natural history, science, and technology are covered at the **South Carolina Museum,** 301 Gervais Street (803–898–4921;

Museum of African-American Culture/Mann-Simons Cottage

www.museum.state.sc.us/). The state's largest museum and one of the largest in the Southeast, it is housed in a renovated 1896 textile mill that was the first one in the world to be electrified. This is one museum that lives up to its claim that it has something for everyone and even has a children's museum. Exhibits include "Space Science," artifacts used by South Carolina's five astronauts; "Native Americans"; "Civil War Arms," muskets, swords, sidearms, a cannon used in a futile attempt to protect Columbia from Sherman's army, and a replica of the Civil War submarine *Hunley;* contributions of slaves and their descendants; and the state's ecosystems. A display that depicts the state's love affair with the automobile includes a 1914 Model T, a 1934 Rolls-Royce, and a 1922 Anderson. Centerpieces of the exhibit on the state's prehistoric past are a life-size replica of a mastodon and a prehistoric giant white shark that is 43 feet long and weighs 6,000 pounds.

DINNER: Motor Supply Co. Bistro, 920 Gervais Street (803–256–6687), changes its menu every day but features regional cuisine.

Evening

Columbia boasts eleven theater groups, including the **Town Theatre,** 1012 Sumter Street (803–799–2510). The oldest continuously operating community theater in the country, it has presented performances since 1924. You can also enjoy the **Sizzlin' Summer Concert Series** (803–343–8750), a fifteen-week series at Finley Park that features jazz, country, rhythm and blues, and bluegrass.

LODGING: Claussens Inn.

Day 3 / Morning

BREAKFAST: At the inn.

Ranked among the top ten zoos in the country, **Riverbanks Zoo and Garden,** 500 Wildlife Parkway off I–126 at the Greystone Riverbanks exit (803–779–8717; www.riverbanks.org), replicates microcosmic rain forest, desert, undersea, and southern farm environments for its 2,000 animals. Water and light give the illusion of privacy and wild, unlimited space. Special programs include feeding the sea lions, a tropical rainstorm in the birdhouse, and scuba-diving demonstrations in the aquarium/reptile complex. Riverbanks Farm is a working farm with sheep, pigs, cows, and horses. Watch milking demonstrations each morning. The garden features seventy acres devoted to woodlands, various formal gardens, including a spectacular walled garden, peaceful river views, and awesome valley overlooks.

LUNCH: At the zoo. Options include an on-site Burger King and several concession wagons. Just outside the gates are an Applebee's and a Morrison's Cafeteria.

Afternoon

North of Columbia off I–20 at Jackson Boulevard is **Fort Jackson Museum,** 2179 Sumter Street, Fort Jackson (803–751–7419), named for President Andrew Jackson, who was a South Carolina native. Exhibits in the museum cover 200 years of military history with emphasis on Fort Jackson's role in training and educating new American soldiers. Another display recounts Jackson's life. Fort Jackson is the U.S. Army's largest and most active initial entry training facility, processing 50 percent of the men and women who enter the service each year. Also at the Fort is the **U.S. Army Chaplain Museum** (803–751–8827) and the **U.S. Army Finance Corps Museum** (803–751–3771).

Take US 1 south to **Cayce,** which sits on the site of Fort Granby, one of the earliest inland villages in South Carolina and the scene of two Revolutionary War battles. Make an appointment in advance to visit the **Cayce Historical Museum,** 1800 Twelfth Street Extension (803–796–9020, ext. 3030), housed in a replica of the old Cayce House, a mid-eighteenth-century trading post. Also on the grounds are an authentic kitchen house, smokehouse, and dairy.

Take US 378 to **Lexington,** formed in 1785 and named for the first battle of the Revolutionary War. Visit the **Lexington County Museum Complex,** 231 Fox Street (803–359–8369), which consists of several antebellum buildings that include cabins, homes, a post office, and a barn housing decorative art of the period, tools of self-sufficiency, handmade furniture, textiles, and toys.

Lexington's Old Mill, 711 East Main Street (803–356–6931), which produced mattress ticking and red fabric for prison uniforms at the turn of the twentieth century, now houses a festive marketplace, family-oriented restaurants, shopping, and the Patchwork Players (803–333–0372; www.patchworkplayhouse.com), a nationally known dance and dinner theater group.

Take SC 6 south to I–20 and return to Atlanta.

There's More

Biking/walking. Columbia Riverfront Park and Historic Columbia Canal, Laurel Street (803–733–8331), at the city's original 1906 waterworks and hydroelectric plant, is a tranquil setting for strolling, cycling, and jogging.

Canoeing/hiking. Congaree Swamp National Monument, 200 Caroline Sims Road off SC 48 (803–776–4396; www.nps.gov/cosw/), a dark-water wonderland known for its biological diversity and record-size trees, features self-guided canoe trails as well as a boardwalk and 18 miles of hiking trails.

Guided canoe trips on several of South Carolina's rivers are operated by Adventure Carolina, 1107 State Street, Cayce (803–796–4505). The organization also offers kayaking, sea kayaking, backpacking, camping, and rock-climbing trips, as well as clinics, workshops, and classes.

River Runner Outdoor Center, 905 Gervais Street (803–771–0353), provides guided trips on the Saluda and Congaree Rivers.

Nature study. Peachtree Rock Nature Preserve, off SC 6 near Edmund (call the South Carolina Nature Conservancy at 803–254–9049), has a curiously diverse set of ecosystems, from desert to mountain.

Ruins. Although Gen. Wade Hampton's town house survived the Civil War, his Millwood Plantation did not. Tours of the ruins, off Garners Ferry Road (803–252–1770), are conducted, by reservation, the last Sunday of the month from March through November.

Special Events

October. The ten-day South Carolina State Fair offers spectacular grandstand entertainment, agricultural exhibits, and a thrilling midway. (803) 799–3387; www.scstatefair.org.

December. Carolina Carillon is the state's premier holiday parade. Call the South Carolina Action Council at (803) 343–8750.

Other Recommended Restaurants and Lodgings

Chestnut Cottage Bed and Breakfast, 1718 Hampton Street (803–256–1718), is a Federal-style cottage that was the Civil War home of Mary Boykin Chestnut.

Dreher Island State Park, SC 571 on Lake Murray (803–364–3530), has two- and three-bedroom, fully equipped villas on the shoreline. Boat dock, store/tackle shop, fuel, boat ramps.

Richland Street Bed and Breakfast, 1425 Richland Street (803–779–7001), offers accommodations in a Victorian-style home in the downtown historic area.

For More Information

Capital City/Lake Murray Tourism and Recreation Association and Lake Murray Country Visitors Center, 2184 North Lake Drive (State 6), Irmo, SC 29063. (803) 781–5940 or (800) 951–4008.

Columbia Metropolitan Convention and Visitors Bureau, 1200 Main Street, Columbia, SC 29202. (803) 545–0000 or (800) 264–4884; www.columbiacvb.com.

Lexington Chamber of Commerce, 321 South Lake Drive, Lexington, SC 29072. (803) 359–6113.

EASTBOUND ESCAPE TWO

Augusta, Georgia

A City You Can Cotton To / 2 Nights

Even if you don't play golf, if you can spell it, you must know about Augusta's Masters Golf Tournament, held at the exclusive Augusta National Golf Club each spring. Only a lucky few can get admittance during the first three days of practice rounds, however. The rest of the year, the club is private and closed to visitors.

□ Augusta Canal

□ Riverwalk

□ Historic homes

What few would-be travelers know is that Augusta is Georgia's second oldest city and that it has many other appealing attractions and numerous exciting events. Located at the Piedmont Fall Line, Augusta was on the seashore several million years ago. In 1983 a prehistoric whale was unearthed, and you can still find ocean fossils. During the French and Indian Wars, Augusta was the most exposed frontier settlement. The British used Augusta as a communications center linking Pensacola and Detroit during the Revolution. When Light-Horse Harry Lee captured Augusta in 1781, the British relinquished their claim to Georgia. Augusta served as the capital of Georgia for ten years.

The Savannah River was the city's commercial lifeline. Heavily traveled by barges and johnboats, the waterway carried cotton, tobacco, and other products to the coast. To serve the transportation center, the first U.S. iron steamboat, the *John Randolph,* was constructed for the Augusta-Savannah run.

The Augusta Canal, a National Historic Landmark used by hikers, bikers, canoers, anglers, and environmentalists, was designated as one of eighteen National Heritage Areas by Congress in 1996. Years ago the canal was employed during the week for transporting people, materials, and cotton, and on weekends it was used as a recreational waterway for picnics, social events, and escape from the city. Today events are held at

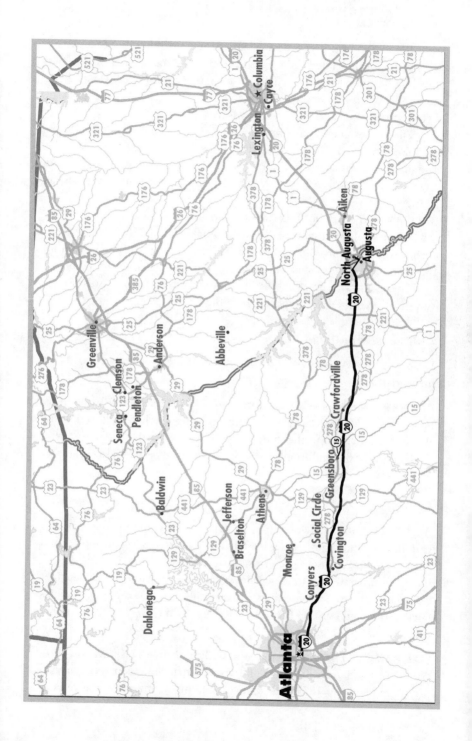

the dance pavilion, barbecue pit, and picnic shelter. The old towpath where the mules hauled the barges up and down the canal provides hiking, biking, and nature walks. The Clearing is a landing for bikers, hikers, and canoers and is popular for picnics. There's also a canoe portage between the canal and the Savannah River.

The city was considered up-country by coastal colonists and has been a cool escape for 200 years. In addition, for many years Augusta was the end of the line for the railroads from the North and was a successful resort town until railroad tycoon Henry Flagler extended the railroads to Florida.

Only two to three hours away from metro Atlanta (depending on where you live), Augusta is perfect for a quick getaway. The small city has such a wealth of intriguing places to stay that it's hard to choose among them, and its eating establishments range from the casual to the sublime.

There's always something exciting going on in Augusta, so it's time you discovered the Best-Kept Secret in the South.

Day 1 / Afternoon

Head east from Atlanta via I–20 and get off at the Washington Road exit in **Augusta.**

DINNER: Michael's Restaurant and Piano Bar, 2860 Washington Road (706–733–2860), is upscale without being overly formal and stuffy. We can confirm that the movers and shakers of the city eat there. Godfather of Soul and Augusta native James Brown—a regular—came in while we were there.

Evening

Augusta has an award-winning opera, ballet, and symphony that perform year-round. The Augusta Lynx Ice Hockey team scores big during fall and winter, and the Augusta Green Jackets baseball team entertains crowds during the summer. Check to see what performances or games are on tap during your visit. Even on evenings when nothing special is going on, folks flock to the Soul Bar, 984 Broad Street, downtown (706–724–8880), to listen to jazz.

LODGING: The entrancing **Partridge Inn,** 2110 Walton Way (706–737–8888 or 800–476–6888; www.partridgeinn.com), began as a private residence in 1879 and was expanded many times over the years. It served as Augusta's "grande dame" hostelry during the height of the city's resort trade, 1889 to 1930.

Authentically restored and elegantly furnished, the five-story inn, with 156 rooms, suites, and studios, boasts 0.25 mile of porches and private balconies. What could be more southern than relaxing in a wicker rocker on one of these verandas with a cool drink in hand? Other amenities include two restaurants, a lounge, pool, and exercise facility. The Partridge Inn is one of only five historic hostelries in Georgia that are members of the National Trust for Historic Preservation's Historic Hotels of America.

Day 2 / Morning

BREAKFAST: A complimentary light breakfast buffet is served each morning in the lounge of the Partridge Inn.

Begin your tour of Augusta at the **Visitor Information Center** (706–724–4067), located inside the **Augusta Museum of History,** 560 Reynolds Street (706–722–8454; www.augustamuseum.org).

After you get brochures and advice from the friendly staff at the Visitor Information Center, stay a while to tour the museum, which takes visitors on a 12,000-year journey into Augusta's past. The museum's 15,000 artifacts pertain to the city and the surrounding area from the Paleo-Indian period to the present, concentrating on Augusta's transformation from a trading post to an industrial and commercial center. The Confederate collection features uniforms, flags, and weaponry. Closed Monday and major holidays.

Across from the museum and information center, courtyard—paved with bricks embossed with AUGUSTA—leads to the Riverwalk. A fountain erupting from the courtyard paving like Old Faithful is a tantalizing temptation for children of all ages to run through during hot spells. Along this courtyard old cotton warehouses have been rejuvenated and transformed into trendy boutiques and restaurants.

Akin to San Antonio's River Walk but on a smaller scale, Augusta's **Riverwalk,** on Reynolds Street between Seventh and Tenth, is a gigantic park created from a flood-prevention levee. The top of the levee is paved, and landscaped lawns slope down on both the land and the river sides. Granite markers embedded in the brick walls indicate the height of some of Augusta's most devastating floods. Overlooks and benches invite visitors to muse on the languorous course of the Savannah River and Augusta Canal. **Takarazuka,** a unique waterfall and miniature garden display on the lower level between Eighth and Ninth Streets, was a gift to the city from Japan. Concerts and other entertainment events frequently occur at the amphitheater overlooking the river. Spectators can even come by boat and enjoy the revelry from the water.

A few new buildings are tastefully appearing among the converted cotton warehouses. Port Royal on the Savannah is a mixed-use high-rise containing condominiums and the **National Science Center Fort Discovery,** 1 Seventh Street (706–821–0200; www.nscdiscovery.org). An interactive science museum for all ages, the museum boasts more than 250 interactive exhibits ranging from an indoor lightning display to a high-wire bicycle, an interactive theater, learning labs, a gift shop, and more.

Toward the north end of Riverwalk, both the Radisson Riverfront Hotel Augusta, 2 Tenth Street (706–722–8900), and the **Morris Museum of Art,** 1 Tenth Street (706–724–7501; www.themorris.org), blend beautifully with the red-and-gray brick of the old warehouses. The museum is the repository of the William Moore collection of southern, Civil War, and Black art. Free on Sunday; closed Monday.

LUNCH: The **Boll Weevil Cafe at the Riverwalk,** 10 Ninth Street Plaza (706–722–7772), serves a variety of southern and southwestern cuisine as well as wings and pizzas and has an astounding dessert menu.

Afternoon

The town where the Masters is played is the perfect spot for a garden dedicated to the sport. **Augusta Golf and Gardens,** 1 Eleventh Street (706–724–4443 or 888–874–4443; www.gghf.org), comprises seventeen acres near the banks of the Savannah River. Eight acres are devoted to beautifully landscaped and meticulously maintained display gardens dotted with ponds, fountains, waterfalls, and life-size sculptures of several golf greats: Ben Hogan, Bobby Jones, Ray Floyd, Byron Nelson, Jack Nicklaus, and Arnold Palmer. In the future the site will be the home of the Georgia Golf Hall of Fame.

Augusta also has several historic sites you shouldn't miss. **Sacred Heart Cultural Arts Center,** 1301 Greene Street (706–826–4700; www.sacredheartaugusta.org), was once a magnificent Romanesque Revival Catholic church and is identified by twin tin-roofed spires and characterized by the fifteen ornate patterns in the brickwork on the facade. Imported stained-glass windows cast jewel tones on the carved white

Italian marble interior. Saved and restored by concerned citizens, the structure now serves as the hub for the arts in Augusta. Although the offices of the ballet, symphony, theater, and other cultural groups as well as a gift shop are housed here, visitors are welcome to browse through the building, admiring the opulent stained-glass windows, marble, columns, and intricate carvings.

Tucked away near Thirteenth Street and Walton Way but worth searching out is **Meadow Garden,** 1320 Independence Drive (706–724–4174), the former home of George Walton—one of Georgia's three signers of the Declaration of Independence. Walton was, at twenty-six, the youngest of all the signers. Later he served in the army, the Georgia legislature, and the courts, and eventually he became governor. Built in two stages beginning in 1794, the house and its furnishings are simple colonial style. Meadow Garden was the first structure in Georgia preserved for historic reasons and is the oldest documented house in Augusta. Open Monday through Friday; Saturday by appointment.

Another house museum is the **Ezekiel Harris Home,** 1840 Broad Street (706–724–0436). Built in 1797, the house is furnished with eighteenth-century antiques. The **Lucy Craft Laney Museum of Black History,** 1116 Phillips Street (706–724–3576; www.lucycraftlaney museum.com), was built at the turn of the twentieth century. Laney, born into slavery, later graduated from Atlanta University, became a famous educator, and established her own school. She started Augusta's first Black kindergarten, nurse's training class, and the Haines Institute, educating thousands of Black students in her lifetime. Open daily.

Woodrow Wilson spent twelve of his boyhood years in Augusta when his father was the pastor of the First Presbyterian Church. The church was designed by Robert Mills, who designed the Washington Monument and the U.S. Treasury Building. Wilson lived across the street in the Presbyterian Manse, which is now open as the **Woodrow Wilson Childhood Home,** 419 Seventh Street (706–722–9828; www.wilson boyhoodhome.org). Thomas "Tommy" Woodrow Wilson, the twenty-eighth president of the United States, lived in this stately brick house from 1860 to 1870. Furnished as it would have been when the Wilsons lived there, the house contains some original pieces. After touring the house, visit the Carriage House/Stable. It was here at a secret meeting place in the hayloft that Tommy and some of his friends formed the Light Foot Base Ball Club. When Wilson visited the house while he was president, he reminisced about one of his earliest memories being hearing about Lincoln being elected and that there would be a war.

DINNER: Enjoy a casually elegant southern meal at the plantation-style **Dining Room at the Partridge Inn.**

LODGING: The Partridge Inn.

Day 3 / Morning

BREAKFAST: Sleep in, then have breakfast at the Partridge Inn.

Light traffic makes Sunday morning an excellent time for riding around, and the area near the Partridge Inn makes a good place to start. During the late 1800s and through the turn of the twentieth century, Augusta prospered and attracted residents and tourists to the cool heights of Walton Way. A drive through the **Summerville/Gould's Corner neighborhoods** is like entering a time warp, as Greek Revival mansions vie for attention with Italian Renaissance Victorians.

The **Olde Town Pinch Gut Historic District** is an in-town residential neighborhood that features many architectural styles popular at the turn of the twentieth century. Look for the fine millwork on the porches and the interesting roof lines. The neighborhood got its unkind name from the corsets with which ladies cinched themselves a century ago.

The life of the Augusta Canal is traced at August's newest attraction, the **Augusta Canal Interpretive Center,** 1450 Greene Street, Suite 400 (706–823–7089; www.augustacanal.com), which is located in the old Enterprise Mill. Begin with the film *The Power of the Canal* and then make you way through the numerous exhibits, many of which are interactive. Guided canal boat tours are available in season.

LUNCH: Mally's Bagels-n-Grits, 2742 Washington Road (706–736–0770), serves homemade soups of the day, hot sandwiches such as the New Yorker (sliced roast beef, mushrooms, and grilled onions with au jus), salads, and great wraps. It's also a well-known place to head for a breakfast of grits Benedict or sun-dried tomato bagels, baked on the premises. Their slogan is "Where North Meets South in Perfect Hominy."

Afternoon

After lunch drive by the **Gertrude Herbert Institute of Art,** 506 Telfair Street (706–722–5495), situated in a Federal-style house. Built in 1818 for

Augusta mayor Nicholas Ware at what was then the outrageous price of $40,000, the mansion was nicknamed Ware's Folly. Lafayette danced the minuet at a ball given here in his honor in 1825. Outstanding interior architectural details include an elliptical staircase ascending three stories, the dining room fanlight, and the Adam-style mantles.

Cross the Savannah River to **North Augusta,** South Carolina. The town began in 1833 as the terminus of the Charleston-Hamburg Railroad, at the time the longest steam-powered railroad in the world. At the turn of the twentieth century, North Augusta became a winter resort frequented by the very wealthy. Drive around the neighborhoods of magnificent Victorian mansions and cottages that remind us of that era.

Return to Atlanta via I–20.

There's More

Shopping. All along Broad Street, in the heart of historic downtown, you'll find quaint shops that specialize in collectibles and delectables. Watch numerous artists at work at Artists' Row between Tenth and Eleventh Streets, a thriving art community that spans more than a block of unique art galleries and studios. Demonstrations, artists' chats, and receptions take place monthly during the celebrated First Friday gatherings, when gallery hours are extended. Surrey Center is an upscale shopping center with four restaurants that range from a French bistro to an Italian grill, two nightclubs and bars, and a coffeehouse.

A visit to Fat Man's Forest, 1545 Laney Walker Boulevard (706–722–0796), is a must. Although Fat Man's has been a traditional stop for Christmas decorations for more than forty years, the emporium has branched out and now carries decorations for all holidays and has a costume shop and a florist. Open year-round.

Special Events

Year-round. Various fairs, festivals, concerts, and other activities occur at Riverwalk. The best source of information on river activities is Riverwalk Special Events, 15 Eighth Street (706–821–1754).

Augusta is known as the Water Sports Capital of the South because of the boating events held on the river.

January. Excluding the Masters, the city's premier event is the Augusta Futurity—the largest cutting-horse tournament east of the Mississippi and one of the top ten in the world. The fast-paced, intense event brings the country's foremost professional riders, trainers, owners, and horses to compete for hundreds of thousands of dollars in prizes. Call the Augusta Futurity office at (706) 724–0851.

April. Although tickets to the Masters Golf Tournament are unattainable for most people, practice-round tickets are available through a lottery system. Attending one of these rounds is a once-in-a-lifetime opportunity to visit the private club, which is abloom with azaleas and dogwoods, and to watch some great golf. Call (706) 667–6000 for a practice-round application.

Spring/summer. The river comes to a boil with River Race Augusta, the premier event of the International Outboard Grand Prix Series. Up to eighty boats compete in three outboard-powered classes. Tunnel boats reach 140 miles per hour. Call the Convention and Visitors Bureau at (706) 823–6600 or (800) 726–0243.

July. Augusta Southern Nationals Dragboat Racing is a weekend of supercharged engines on sleek fiberglass hydroplane or flat-bottomed boats competing in nine classes for $100,000 in prizes. In the eleven Pro Racing classes, top speeds exceed 230 miles per hour. Contact the Convention and Visitors Bureau at (706) 823–6600 or (800) 726–0243.

Other Recommended Restaurants and Lodgings

Augusta, Georgia

The Azalea Inn, 312 Greene Street (706–724–3454), is a charming bed-and-breakfast facility contained in two adjoining historic homes.

French Market Grill, 425 Highland Avenue (706–737–4865), voted the best restaurant in Augusta for seven consecutive years, serves Louisiana cuisine. American wines, beers from around the world, oyster bar.

La Maison on Telfair, 404 Telfair Street (706–722–4805), is an elegant restaurant located in an old Victorian home in historic downtown. Specialties such as wild game and seafood are prepared and served with the freshest and finest ingredients.

Radisson Riverfront Hotel Augusta, 2 Tenth Street (706–722–8900), features a conference center with a ballroom, riverside pool, restaurant, and lounge.

North Augusta, South Carolina

Rosemary Hall and Lookaway Hall, 804 Carolina Avenue (803–278–6222 or 800–531–5578), twin Greek Revival mansions built by two brothers at the turn of the twentieth century, operate as a European-style inn.

For More Information

Augusta Metropolitan Convention and Visitors Bureau, 1450 Greene Street, Suite 110, Augusta, GA 30901. (706) 823–6600 or (800) 726–0243; www.augusta.org.

EASTBOUND ESCAPE THREE

Anderson/Pendleton/Seneca/Clemson, South Carolina

Follow the Tiger Paws / *2 Nights*

Central to this escape is Lake Hartwell, which straddles the Georgia/South Carolina border. One of the South's largest and most popular public recreation lakes, it was built by the U.S. Army Corps of Engineers between 1955 and 1963 as a flood control and hydroelectric project on the Savannah, Tugaloo, and Seneca Rivers. With 56,000 acres of water and 962 miles of shoreline, Hartwell is one of the top three most visited lakes in the country. Not only does the lake provide just about every water sport imaginable, but the area is rich in historical lore handed down from the Cherokee Indians and the early Scottish-Irish settlers.

☐ One of the nation's largest historic districts

☐ Clemson University

Clemson University, the centerpiece of the town of Clemson, owes its existence to the son-in-law of statesman John C. Calhoun. In addition to Clemson, small towns that border the northern end of the lake include Anderson, Pendleton, and Seneca.

Day 1 / *Afternoon*

Take I–85 northeast from Atlanta, allowing for enough daylight hours at your destination to take in a few sights. After crossing the state line, stop at the **Fair Play Welcome Center,** 100 Welcome Center Place (864–972–3731), to pick up some tour information. Continue north on I–85 and turn south onto US 76 to **Anderson.**

In addition to wandering around the 16-block area listed on the National Register of Historic Places, admire the work of local, regional, and national artists at the **Anderson County Arts Center,** housed in the historic Carnegie Library at 405 North Main Street (864–224–8811).

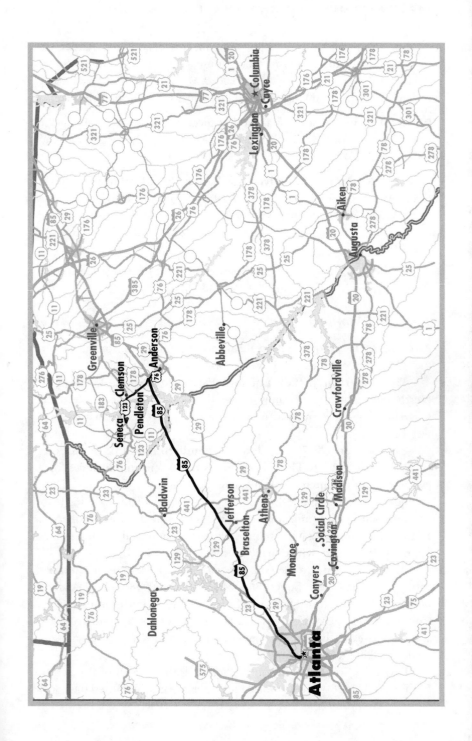

See the local history exhibits and memorabilia at the **Anderson County Museum** in the courthouse, 101 South Main Street (864–260–4737). Open Tuesday 10:00 A.M. to 7:00 P.M., Wednesday through Saturday 10:00 A.M. to 4:00 P.M. Closed Sunday and Monday.

DINNER: Dine on seafood and other specialties while overlooking the waterfront at the **Galley,** Portman Marina, 1629 Marina Road (864–287–3215).

LODGING: Anderson's River Inn Bed & Breakfast, 612 East River Street, Anderson (864–226–1431), is a 1914, two-story, Federal-style home that features three bedrooms with private baths.

Evening

Check ahead to see if there are any performances at the **Civic Center of Anderson,** 3027 Mall Road (864–260–4800).

Day 2 / Morning

BREAKFAST: Enjoy a full breakfast in the dining room or outside on the side porch at Anderson's River Inn Bed & Breakfast.

The **Anderson Jockey Lot and Farmer's Market,** 4530 US 29 North (864–224–2027), claims to be the South's largest flea market. Covering sixty-five acres and leasing space to 1,500 dealers, it may very well be.

Go north on US 76, past I–85, to **Pendleton,** one of the nation's largest historic districts. The district covers 6,316 acres and includes forty points of historic interest. Many of its buildings date from the 1700s. Antiques shops, art and gift shops, excellent restaurants, and charming bed-and-breakfasts make Pendleton one of the most visited places in America. Begin at the **Square,** a lively business district of shops and restaurants facing the village green, where many special events are held.

Although it's usually open only on weekdays, check to see if **Hunter's Store,** 125 East Queen Street (864–646–3782 or 800–862–1795), which houses the Pendleton District Historical, Recreational, and Tourism Commission, is open. It features an arts-and-crafts store, bookstore, exhibit area, and research library and provides a self-guided tape tour or self-guided walking tour brochure of town.

Farmers' Society Hall, on the Square, is the nucleus of Pendleton. It was built in 1826 as a courthouse, but when the district moved the court elsewhere, farmers took over the building and have used it ever since. The building is the oldest farmers' hall in the country.

LUNCH: Farmers' Hall Restaurant, on the Square (864–646–8161), serves a wide variety of items in a colonial atmosphere. Outdoor dining on the patio.

Afternoon

After lunch you can see Cherokee artifacts; pre-1925 farm equipment, including a cotton gin that predates Eli Whitney's; and tools at the **Pendleton District Agricultural Museum,** US 76 (864–646–3782), which is open by appointment.

Two gorgeous sister plantations nearby recall the early 1800s when wealthy low-country planters built homes in the up-country and moved to its more healthful climate. Both are open on Sunday afternoon April through October or by appointment, so call ahead. **Ashtabula Plantation,** SC 88 (864–646–7249), built in the 1820s by a family from Charleston, has been restored and furnished with period items. (Ashtabula is also open on Tuesday.) **Woodburn Plantation,** located on US 76 (864–646–7249), was the stately four-story mansion of Charles Cotesworth Pinckney, lieutenant governor of South Carolina between 1832 and 1834. (Woodburn is also open on Thursday.)

Continue north on SC 76, bypassing Clemson for the time being, and turn west at US 123, then south on SC 130 to **Seneca,** a town created at the junction of two rail lines linking Charlotte and Atlanta.

Lunney Museum, 211 South First Street (864–882–4811), housed in a California-style bungalow, exhibits an outstanding collection of Victorian furnishings, vintage costumes, and Oconee County memorabilia. Open Thursday through Sunday or by appointment.

Switch gears to the modern era at **Duke Power's World of Energy,** 7812 Rochester Highway/SC 130 (864–885–4600 or 800–777–1004). On Lake Keowee beside the Oconee Nuclear Plant, the museum has animated displays and computer games that demonstrate how natural resources are used to make electricity. Get a behind-the-scenes look at operators training on a nuclear control-room simulator. In addition, there are a nature trail and views of Lake Keowee and the Keowee Valley.

Retrace US 123 and US 76 to **Clemson.**

DINNER: Nick's Tavern and Deli, 107–2 Sloan Street (no phone), is downtown Clemson's oldest tavern and deli. The eclectic atmosphere features several collections: beer bottles and beer memorabilia, postcards, and auto-racing relics. The eatery, which is in walking distance of the campus, offers extensive appetizer, deli, and beer menus.

Evening

See if there is a performance by the **Clemson Little Theater,** Pendleton Playhouse, 214 South Mechanic Street (864–646–8100), which produces three plays a year.

LODGING: Clemson Suites, 106 Liberty Drive (864–654–4605), contains forty-four suites—all with full kitchens and two double beds.

Day 3 / Morning

BREAKFAST: At the hotel.

Most of the significant sites in this lovely southern town, home of Clemson University, are on the campus or connected with the college. Begin at the University Visitors Center in Tillman Hall (864–656–4789).

The 250-acre **South Carolina Botanical Garden,** 102 Garden Trail (864–656–3405), includes the former Horticultural Gardens and Forestry Arboretum. Several thousand varieties of native and introduced ornamental plants are arranged in trails or gardens: the Azalea and Camellia Trails, the Miller Dwarf Conifer Garden, the Flower and Turf Display Garden, and the Pioneer, Wildflower, and Bog Gardens. The Pioneer Garden is marked in braille. In addition to strolling, bird-watching, or jogging in the gardens, educational and cultural events draw visitors all year. Relocated to the gardens is **Hanover House,** built in 1716 by a low-country Huguenot family. It is furnished to represent the 1700s. New additions to the garden include the **Fran Hanson Discovery Center,** which serves as the visitor center and has a Garden Exploration Room as well as a gift shop and snack shop, and the **Bob Campbell Geologic Museum,** which showcases fossils, meteorites, and the like.

LUNCH: At the Fran Hanson Discovery Center at the garden.

Afternoon

Fort Hill, also known as the John C. Calhoun Museum, in the center of the campus (864–656–2475), was the orator's plantation home. One of the South's most noted statesmen, Calhoun served as vice president under both Andrew Jackson and John Quincy Adams and as a U.S. senator. Later

Fort Hill, Clemson

Fort Hill became the home of Calhoun's daughter Anna and her husband, Thomas Green Clemson, who willed it to the state in 1888 for the purpose of establishing a land-grant college. Now a National Historic Landmark, the museum contains memorabilia that belonged to Calhoun and Clemson.

Visit the **Rudolph E. Lee Gallery** on the campus, R. E. Lee Hall (864–656–3883), to see the most current trends in architectural design and construction. Before you leave for Atlanta, poke your head in at the Hendricks Center or the Student Union to taste and buy some of the university's famous ice cream. Take some home with you. For information on these two attractions, call the Clemson University Visitors Center at (864) 656–4789.

On the way out of town on US 76S, stop at the **Old Stone Church.** Damaged by fire years ago, the church is no longer in use, but its cemetery is the resting place of many area pioneers, including Revolutionary War hero Gen. Andrew Pickens, who helped build the church in 1797.

Return to I–85 and Atlanta.

There's More

Outdoor activities. Lake Hartwell State Park, 19138-A South Highway 11 off I–85 at Fair Play (864–972–3352), is a 680-acre park with numerous activities.

Water sports. Big Water Marina, 320 Big Water Road, Starr (864–226–3339), is a full-service marina on Lake Hartwell that offers boat rentals, gasoline, slip spaces, and boat repair and has a ship's store.

Portman Marina, 1629 Marina Road, Anderson (864–287–3211), is the largest full-service marina in South Carolina and offers the above services as well as wet and dry boat storage, a campground, and a lakefront restaurant.

White-water rafting. Forty miles of the tumultuous Chattooga National Wild and Scenic River separate Georgia and South Carolina. For rafting, canoeing, or kayaking tours, contact Wildwater, Ltd., Box 100, Long Creek, SC 29658 (800–451–9972), or Nantahala Outdoor Center, 851–A Chattooga Ridge Road, Mountain Rest, SC 29664 (800–232–7238).

Special Events

Clemson

March. Daffodil Festival at the South Carolina Botanical Garden blends art with nature using music, dance, storytelling, theater, nature walks, live animals, and more. (864) 656–3405.

May. Concourse Botanique is a conservation festival featuring music, storytelling, dance, and arts and crafts representing cultures from around the world. (864) 656–3405.

Pendleton

April. Historic Pendleton Spring Jubilee features entertainment, museum exhibits, house tours, arts and crafts, antiques, and great food. (864) 646–3782.

December. Holiday in the Village, the first weekend, includes carolers in period costumes, a lights display, a theater production, and other activities.

Other Recommended Restaurants and Lodgings

Country Kettle, 129 Mechanic Street across from the Village Green, Pendleton (864–646–3301), serves cafeteria-style and specializes in fresh vegetables and pies. Lunch.

Granny Zuercher's Bakery, 504 South Mechanic Street, Pendleton (864–646–3907), dispenses all kinds of breads and desserts.

Liberty Hall Inn and Cafe Leisure, 621 South Mechanic Street, Pendleton (864–646–7500), is a country inn built in the 1840s.

Mountain Lakes Vacation Rentals, 15298 Scenic Highway 11, Fair Play (864–972–0463), features lakefront homes by the week or weekend, as well as overnight rentals in town houses and bed-and-breakfasts.

For More Information

Anderson Area Chamber of Commerce, 706 East Greenville Street, Anderson, SC 29621. (864) 226–3454.

Clemson Area Chamber of Commerce, 1105 Tiger Boulevard, Clemson, SC 29633. (864) 654–1200.

Greater Seneca Chamber of Commerce, 236 Main Street, Seneca, SC 29678. (864) 882–2097.

Pendleton District, Historical, Recreational, and Tourism Commission, 125 East Queen Street, Pendleton, SC 29670. (864) 646–3782.

EASTBOUND ESCAPE FOUR

Athens/Monroe, Georgia

How 'Bout Them Dawgs? / 2 *Nights*

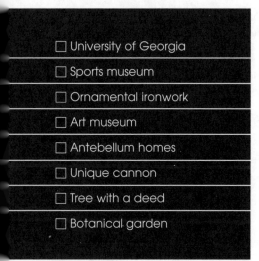

☐ University of Georgia

☐ Sports museum

☐ Ornamental ironwork

☐ Art museum

☐ Antebellum homes

☐ Unique cannon

☐ Tree with a deed

☐ Botanical garden

The "Classic City"—named for its predecessor in Greece—is not only the home of the University of Georgia, the nation's first state-chartered university, but also the site of America's first garden club. Moreover, the city boasts abundant reminders of antebellum grandeur, where majestic mansions are encircled by imposing columns and magnolia-shaded formal gardens. Athens was founded in 1801 simultaneously with the university and was spared during the Civil War. Union troops under the command of Gen. George Stoneman were ordered to destroy the rail lines, but they were ambushed by Confederate troops and imprisoned in Athens before being sent to Andersonville prison. After Atlanta's fall Sherman's troops moved southeast toward Milledgeville and bypassed Athens. Today the city centers on the university and is the home of the State Art Museum and the State Botanical Garden.

This escape is best taken during the week or at least to include a Friday because many of the attractions are closed on weekends.

Day 1 / *Afternoon*

Leave Atlanta in the early afternoon and take I–85 north to US 129 east. Stop in **Jefferson** at the **Crawford W. Long Museum,** 28 College Street (706–367–5307 or 706–367–5444; www.crawfordlong.org), site of the first painless surgery. The museum contains some personal items of Dr. Long, who is credited with the development of modern anesthesia. Closed Sunday and Monday.

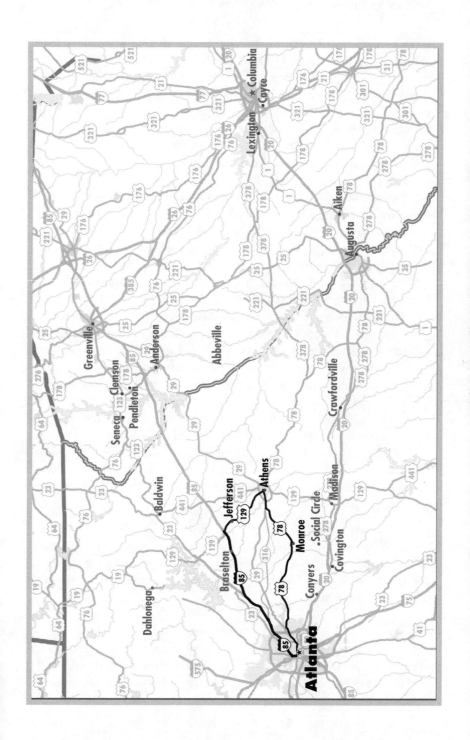

Continue on US 129 to **Athens.** Begin your tour at the Athens Welcome Center, located in the **Church-Waddel-Brumby House,** a restored Federal-period house at 280 East Dougherty Street (706–353–1820). Built in 1820 by Alonzo Church, who later became president of the university, it is considered to be the oldest residence in Athens. Pick up information for a self-guided tour of more than fifty important sites. Classic City Tours (706–208–TOUR) depart from here daily at 2:00 P.M. Reservations are recommended but not required.

Because they are open only during the week, there are two attractions you should visit this afternoon. The **Butts–Mehre Heritage Hall Sports Museum,** Lumpkin and Pinecrest Streets (706–542–9094), near the university, is a strikingly modern building of red granite and black glass. The museum showcases the dazzling athletic accomplishments of UGA students. Two Heisman Trophies are on display: those earned by Herschel Walker and Frankie Sinkwich. The museum is open Monday through Friday and during home football games.

The **U.S. Navy Supply Corps Museum,** 1425 Prince Avenue (706–354–7349; www.nscs.com, then click on "Services" and "Museum"), is located on the campus of the U.S. Navy Supply Corps School. The school trains business managers to administer the complex system of distributing supplies and materials to fleet units and shore stations throughout the world. Its museum depicts the development and growth of the Navy Supply Corps School through exhibits of ship models, historic uniforms, navigational equipment, galley gear, naval art, and personal memorabilia. The Archives Room houses photos, official records, and cruise books. Open Monday through Friday. Also on the campus is Winnie Davis Memorial Hall, dedicated to the daughter of Confederate president Jefferson Davis.

DINNER: **East–West Bistro,** 351 East Broad Street (706–546–9378), is actually two restaurants in one. The downstairs restaurant, which is moderately priced, serves Japanese-American fusion. The more upscale upstairs restaurant, which serves Northern Italian cuisine, is considered by many to be the best in Athens.

Evening

Your evening can come alive with a performance at the spectacular **University of Georgia Performing Arts Center,** 230 River Road (706–542–4400 or the box office, 888–289–8497). With magnificent

1,100-seat Hogdson Hall and 360-seat Ramsey Hall, the center is home to an outstanding lineup of award-winning acts. Last-minute tickets are frequently available.

LODGING: High-class bed-and-breakfast accommodations are available at the **Magnolia Terrace Guesthouse,** 227 Hill Street (706–548–3860), a lovely Classic Revival home built in 1903. Located in the Cobbham Historic District, the bed-and-breakfast is convenient to downtown and the university. Beveled glass, hardwood floors, high ceilings, decorative fireplace mantels, and ornamental moldings are reminders of the opulent age in which the house was built. Some rooms feature a working fireplace or a whirlpool tub. The large wicker-filled front porch supported by fourteen columns is a dandy spot to relax.

Day 2 / Morning

BREAKFAST: Enjoy a continental-plus breakfast at the B&B.

Begin a **tour of the university** by stopping in at the **UGA Visitors Center,** Four Towers Building, College Station Road (706–542–0842), located in a restored dairy barn at the East Campus. The visitor center provides not only assistance and information about the university but displays exhibits about campus life, distinguished alumni, university history, and more. From the visitor center you can take a formal guided tour (reservations required) of the campus to see the famous iron arch, museums, gardens, the stadium, and coliseum, or take a self-guided tour.

A good place to start a self-guided tour of the university is at the cast-iron **Arch** on the historic North University Campus, East Broad Street. Nothing represents the University of Georgia more than its Arch. A prominent illustration of graceful ironwork, the Arch serves as a gateway to the campus. Its three columns symbolize wisdom, justice, and moderation. The Arch and associated fence were originally erected in 1858 to keep freely wandering livestock and other domestic animals off the campus.

The Classic City is endowed with a plethora of well-preserved ornamental ironwork—an elaborate vestige of the nineteenth century. Much of what you see around town was manufactured locally at the Athens Foundry. Although the company has moved to Elberton, its original site is now part of the Foundry Park Inn and Spa.

Some other examples of ironwork on campus include the garden benches, stairways, and balcony balustrades in the Old North Campus Historic District, the lighting standards on the Broad Street Quadrangle, and the porch balustrade, which features cast medallions with portraits of famous poets and statesmen at the School of Law.

Also on the historic North University Campus is the **Founders Memorial Garden** (www.uga.edu/gardenclub/Founder.html), a small formal garden that commemorates the first garden club in America. The early 1800s house, which serves as a centerpiece for the garden, was once used as the headquarters of the Garden Club of Georgia, but it's now used by the School of Environmental Design. The headquarters of the Garden Club of Georgia has relocated to a grand new building located on the grounds of the State Botanical Garden of Georgia (see page 157).

Next go to the East Campus to visit the **Georgia Museum of Art**, 90 Carlton Street, Performing and Visual Arts Complex (706–542–4662). The Official State Art Museum houses a permanent collection of 5,000 works, including nineteenth- and twentieth-century American paintings, the Kress collection of Italian Renaissance paintings, and a significant collection of European, American, and Oriental prints.

LUNCH: Harry Bissett's New Orleans Cafe, 279 East Broad Street (706–353–7065), across the street from the Arch, is a favorite upscale hangout that specializes in Cajun and Creole cuisine. Designed with a classical motif, the building itself was constructed in the mid-1800s to house a drugstore.

Afternoon

College Square and the adjacent streets bordering the original quadrangle offer a variety of shopping, eating, and entertainment opportunities. Downtown is an exciting melting pot of students, faculty, businesspeople, and visitors.

Tour the 1845 Greek Revival **Taylor-Grady House,** 634 Prince Avenue (706–549–8688). The stately mansion is ringed by thirteen Doric columns—representing the thirteen colonies—connected by delicate ironwork. Henry W. Grady, noted southern journalist, orator, and editor of the *Atlanta Constitution,* lived in the house while he was a student at the university. He was instrumental in reuniting the North and the South after the Civil War and coined the phrase "New South." Open Monday through Thursday.

Among the many superb examples of ornate residential ironwork you can drive by is that found on the **University President's Home,** 570 Prince Avenue. "Welcoming arms," delicate ironwork stair rails on the double-curved stairway, draw the eye up to the Greek Revival mansion surrounded by fourteen Corinthian columns. Other notable examples include the Hunnicut House, 325 Milledge Avenue, now doctors' offices; the Hamilton House, 150 South Milledge Avenue, the home of Alpha Delta Pi Sorority; the Segrest House, 250 South Milledge Avenue, now home of Phi Mu Sorority; the Lucy Cobb Institute, corner of Milledge Avenue and Hancock, a former girls' school; the E. K. Lumpkin House, 937 Prince Avenue; the Sledge-Cobb House, 749 Cobb Street; the Camak House, 279 Meigs Street; and the Lyndon House, 293 Hoyt Street.

The most treasured Civil War artifact in Athens is the **double-barreled cannon,** situated in Cannon Park on the City Hall lawn, Hancock Street. The hypothesis behind the design of this one-of-a-kind weapon was that each barrel would be loaded with a cannonball connected to the other by a chain. When fired, the balls and chain would tear across the battlefield, mowing down wide swaths of the enemy.

Unfortunately, when it was tested, an observer reported that the cannonballs "plowed up an acre of ground, tore up a cornfield, mowed down saplings, and the chain broke, the balls going in opposite directions, one of the balls killed a cow in a distant field, while the other knocked down the chimney from a log cabin. The observers scattered as though the entire Yankee army had turned loose in that vicinity."

Although the "superweapon" failed, it is a testimonial to the creativity of its inventor—Athenian house builder John Gilleland. The cannon is situated so that it faces north—"just in case."

Athens is the only place we know of with a **Tree That Owns Itself.** Professor W. H. Jackson deeded the tree 8 feet of land on all sides at the corner of Dearing and Finley Streets because he enjoyed its shade so much.

Fire Station Number Two, 489 Prince Avenue (706–353–1801), is a triangular, 1901, two-story Victorian firehouse that contains a gallery and the headquarters of the Athens-Clark Heritage Foundation.

DINNER: Last Resort Grill, 184 West Clayton Street (706–549–0810), serves nouvelle southern cuisine for lunch and dinner. The restaurant used to be a nightclub and was where famous Athens groups R.E.M. and the B-52s got their start. Year-round patio. Exhibits of local artists' work.

Evening

A grand showplace, the **Classic Center Theatre,** 300 North Thomas Street (706–357–4555), is the venue for national Broadway touring shows,

Double-barreled cannon, Athens

the Athens Symphony, and other community-based programs.

The **Morton Theatre,** 199 West Washington Street (706–613–3770), financed by M. B. Morton—at one time considered the most influential Black politician and businessman in the state—is one of only four Black vaudeville theaters that exist in the nation. For the events calendar call (706) 613–3771. Tours are available by appointment. Although the **Georgia Theater,** 215 North Lumpkin Street (706–353–3405), was built in 1889, extensive renovations in 1935 resulted in the art deco facade. The theater is used for a variety of purposes, such as dollar movies and area band performances.

LODGING: Return for another restful night at the Magnolia Terrace Guesthouse.

Day 3 / Morning

BREAKFAST: Sleep in, then stoke up for another busy day before leaving the Magnolia Terrace Guesthouse.

Five miles of trails, lush gardens, and a 10,000-square-foot conservatory filled with tropical and semitropical plants await exploration at the **State Botanical Garden of Georgia,** 2450 South Milledgeville Avenue (706–542–1244; www.uga.edu/~botgarden/). Located on 313 forested acres along the Middle Oconee River, the grounds feature dramatic gorge-like ravines and spring-fed streams. Natural geologic disturbances caused by cotton farming, livestock grazing, and fire have made their mark on the land. A 125-year-old grove of beeches and other older hardwoods stand undisturbed on slopes that were too steep for terracing.

Special collections include magnolias; native and adapted trees and shrubs, including shade and ornamental trees; poisonous and medicinal plants; and herbaceous flower gardens. In the District Garden, plants represent the Garden Club of Georgia's seven districts: azalea, camellia, dogwood, laurel, magnolia, redbud, and viburnum. The Dunson Native Flora Garden is a collection of 300 species native to the southeastern United States.

LUNCH: Have a light meal in the **Garden Room Cafe** (706–542–6359) at the gardens. Located in the conservatory, the casual restaurant is light and airy and affords a beautiful view of the outdoors. Monthly art exhibits are held in the conservatory complex.

Afternoon

Take US 78 west from Athens to **Monroe.** Colonists first settled what is now Walton County in the late 1700s. Though growing, the area retains a quiet charm, with gently rolling hills and plenty of wide-open spaces. Eight former governors have called Walton County home. The enchanting town of Monroe boasts nine historic districts listed on the National Register of Historic Places. Admire the magnificent Walton County Courthouse, the Italianate Old Jail, and the rustic Harris Homestead. Several homes have a significant historical interest in addition to their architectural beauty.

The **McDaniel-Tichenor House,** 319 McDaniel Street (770–267–5602; www.georgiatrust.org/historic_sites/mcdaniel_tichenor .htm), was built in 1887 as the retirement home of Governor Henry McDaniel. He chose the Italianate Villa style so popular at the time. Upon McDaniel's and his wife's deaths, the house passed to their daughter Gypsy Tichenor, who had the house remodeled in 1930 to the Neoclassical Revival house you see today. The bracketed eaves were removed, as was the tower, which was replaced by a two-story gabled portico with four massive Temple of the Winds columns. Family members lived in the house until 1990, when it was bequeathed to the Georgia Trust for Historic Preservation. Refurbished, it is furnished with many original family pieces. The Walker House, across the street from the McDaniel-Tichenor House, was the home of another former governor, but it isn't open for tours.

Return to US 78 and continue west to Atlanta.

There's More

Athens

Outdoor activities. The various tracks and fields associated with the university make excellent places for walking, jogging, and sometimes bicycling. The Sandy Creek Nature Center, 205 Old Commerce Road (706–613–3615), consists of more than 225 acres of woodland, fields, and marshland that support a variety of wildlife, as well as 4 miles of trails and exhibit facilities. The newest addition to the center is ENSAT (Environment, Natural Science, and Appropriate Technology) Center, a state-of-the-art learning laboratory.

Special Events

Athens

May. Annual Twilight Jazz and Legacy Festival is highlighted by the Twilight Criterium and Tour de Georgia, a 60-kilometer professional race in which 125 cyclists vie for $10,000 in prize money. In addition there are other bicycle races, in-line skating, foot races, and jazz musicians. (706) 549–3070; www.athenstwilight.com.

October. Dawgfest is a celebration of UGA's homecoming with a parade and pep rally as well as a performance sponsored by the University Union. Call Student Activities at (706) 542–7774.

November–December. Christmas is celebrated in a big way in Athens. Just imagine the magnificent antebellum and Victorian mansions opulently bedecked for the festive season. The historic houses are often open for Christmas tours—sometimes by candlelight. All the live trees downtown are covered with tiny white lights. Christmas in Athens is a compilation of holiday festivities headlined by events occurring throughout November and December, including the Downtown Athens Christmas Parade of Lights, Classic City Christmas Weekend, and Festival of Trees. (706) 357–4430 or (800) 653–0603.

Other Recommended Restaurants and Lodgings

The Basil Press, 104 East Washington Street, Athens (706–227–8926), serves upscale American and French cuisine.

Other recommended Athens eateries include Athens Sushi Bar, 440 East Clayton Street (706–227–9339); DePalma's Italian Cafe, 401 East Broad Street (706–354–6966); Five Star Day Cafe, 229 East Broad Street (706–543–8552); and Bluebird Cafe, 493 East Clayton Street (706–549–3663).

The Foundry Park Inn and Spa, 295 East Dougherty Street (706–549–7020 or 866–9ATHENS; www.foundryparkinn.com), is Athens's only boutique inn. Built on the site of a historic foundry, it is centrally located downtown. The inn's restaurant, which serves dinner Tuesday through Saturday and Sunday brunch, occupies the historic 1829 Nathan Hoyt House. The Day Spa (706–425–9700) showcases a wide variety of treatments.

Nicholson House Historic Inn, 6295 Jefferson Road, Athens (706–353–2200; www.bbonline.com/ga/nicholson), is a magnificent historic 1820 Classic Revival home surrounded by thirty-four acres of open meadows and rolling hills dotted with magnolias and wild azaleas—all backed by heavy woods. Six of the beautifully appointed guest rooms are in the main house; two are in the converted carriage house.

For More Information

Athens Convention and Visitors Bureau, 300 North Thomas Street, Athens GA 30601. (706) 357–4430 or (800) 653–0603; www.visitathensga.com.

Walton County Chamber of Commerce, 323 Spring Street, Monroe, GA 30655. (770) 267–6594.

Crawfordville, Georgia, and Aiken/Abbeville, South Carolina

Where the North Meets the South / 2 Nights

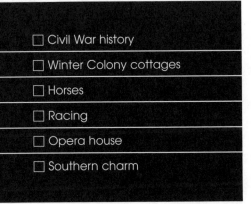

- ☐ Civil War history
- ☐ Winter Colony cottages
- ☐ Horses
- ☐ Racing
- ☐ Opera house
- ☐ Southern charm

Many towns claim to be representative of horse country, but we know of no other town than Aiken where roads and streets retain their sand surface so as not to injure the horses' feet. It only seems that every house has a horse trailer parked outside instead of an RV or boat. There are traffic signal change buttons located at a height where a mounted horseman or carriage driver can reach them without dismounting. Within the city limits Aiken boasts 2,000-acre Hitchcock Woods—the largest urban forest in the country—as well as a sand course for flat racing, a grass course for steeplechasing, a clay course for harness racing, and several polo fields.

Aiken was long a retreat for lowlanders from the Carolina coast who came to escape the oppressive coastal heat and humidity during the summer months. The town came to prominence, however, in the 1800s, when wealthy northerners discovered that the area was a perfect place to winter with their horses. The Winter Colony that soon developed supported several grand hotels until the visitors built their own cottages—gargantuan mansions on vast grounds. Although those glory days are over, Aiken continues to attract some of the nation's most promising horses, trainers, and horse enthusiasts, whether as visitors or permanent residents. As many as 900 polo, steeplechasing, trotting, and riding horses winter here. Polo matches and fox hunting are still very much part of the yearly calendar.

Visiting Aiken at any time is a treat, but a visit during one or more of the spring Triple Crown events is a special indulgence. The Triple Crown

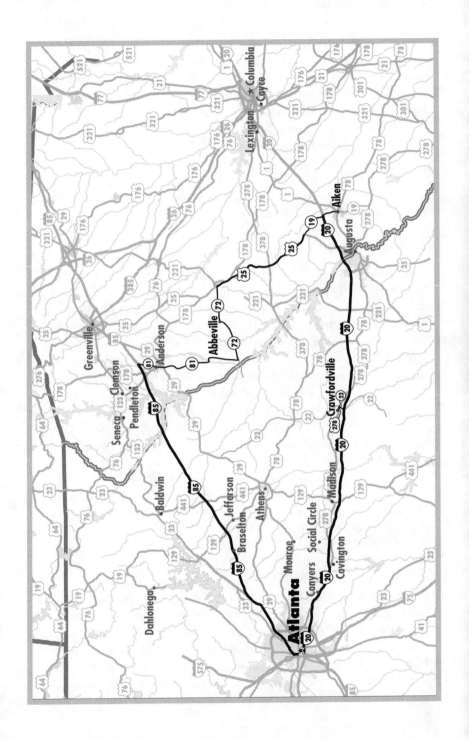

activities—the Aiken Trails, a flat race; the Aiken Steeplechase; and harness racing by pacers and trotters—occur three weekends in a row, usually in March. These races are so well attended that you should make your hotel reservations well in advance. Nationally recognized dressage, hunter and jumper, and combined training shows are among Aiken's other major annual events, as is a cutting-horse show.

Abbeville, known as the Birthplace and Deathbed of the Confederacy, is a charming small town acclaimed for the performances at its opulent opera house.

This is an escape best taken during the week or over a Friday/Saturday, because so many of the attractions are closed on Sunday.

Day 1 / Afternoon

Leave Atlanta in midafternoon and go east on I–20. Take a short detour to **Crawfordville,** Georgia, by taking exit 55 onto GA 22. Go north 2 miles, turn east onto US 278, and go 1 mile into Crawfordville, the site of **A. H. Stephens Historic Park,** Park Street (706–456–2602; www.gastateparks.org/info/ahsteph), one of Georgia's undiscovered treasures. The centerpiece of the park is the **A. H. Stephens Home,** which the nineteenth-century statesman called Liberty Hall. Although he was a tiny, sickly man who weighed less than one hundred pounds for most of his life, Stephens was called the Little Giant because he was a man of such high principle. Stephens, who served as the vice president of the Confederate States of America, had been both a representative and a senator in the U.S. Congress before secession. Although he was imprisoned for five months after the war because of his role in the Confederacy, he eventually returned to the Senate and later became governor of Georgia. He died in office and is buried in the front yard of the house, where a large tombstone and a statue honor him.

Stephens bought the house in 1834 and added the current rear veranda and a library-bedroom wing in 1858. In 1875 he tore down the main structure and built the present house. Stephens is said to have called the estate Liberty Hall because he felt at liberty to do anything he wanted there and because anyone, even a complete stranger, was at liberty to spend the night. In fact, Stephens set aside a bedroom to house travelers and called it the Tramp's Room. Many of the South's greatest leaders, such as Herschel V. Johnson, Joseph E. Brown, and Robert Toombs, were entertained there. Toombs came so often that a bedroom was set aside for his use. Today Liberty Hall is restored to reflect the 1875 period. Most of the beautiful antique furniture and much of the memorabilia are original to the house. Stephens's bedroom looks just as it did when he died in 1883.

Behind the house are several outbuildings, some of which are original, others of which have been reconstructed. They include a kitchen building and a slave house.

Also on the property is a fine **Civil War museum,** considered to be one of the best in the state. Exhibits include several scenes that depict a family sending their sons off to war, soldiers in a camp setting, and women at home supporting the war effort. Memorabilia include uniforms, weapons, medical equipment, documents, letters, diaries, and a collection of Civil War reunion souvenirs. Rather than simply enumerating what is in each display, the exhibits are accompanied by priceless quotations from the time. Be sure to take time to read them. The house and museum are closed Monday.

The A. H. Stephens Historic Park has two lakes, campsites, picnic pavilions, and hiking trails, including the 6-mile Beaver Lodge Trail.

Go back to I–20 and continue east across the Georgia/South Carolina line to SC 19, which you will take south to **Aiken.**

DINNER AND LODGING: The elegant **Seeger's Dining Room at The Willcox,** 100 Colleton Avenue (803–648–1898 or 877–648–2200). The Willcox, built in 1898, after the period of the large hotels that had once peppered Aiken, is an intimate thirty-room inn. Over the years it has seen its share of famous visitors—Franklin D. Roosevelt, Winston Churchill, and Count Bernadotte of Sweden, to name a few. Legend has it that at one time, the doormen would admit only gentlemen whose shoes were properly polished. Today the atmosphere is much more relaxed. Take advantage of the cozy lobby with several fireplaces and the intimate, club-like bar. Rooms and suites in the hotel, on the National Register of Historic Places, are filled with period antiques and reproductions, and some have soaking tubs. In addition, the hotel boasts a spa. The price includes all three meals plus afternoon tea.

Day 2 / Morning

BREAKFAST: Enjoy a hearty breakfast at The Willcox.

The best way to get an overview of Aiken and pick up some juicy tidbits of local history is to take a town tour with **Aiken Tours,** sponsored by the Aiken Chamber of Commerce (803–641–1111). It is best to make a reservation but is not absolutely necessary. Tours meet at the Aiken

Chamber of Commerce/Visitors Center, 121 Richland Avenue East, at 10:00 A.M. on Saturday morning. The ninety-minute tour showcases the historic Winter Colony neighborhoods, passes the three racetracks, points out the Rye Patch estate and the exclusive Palmetto Country Club, and makes a brief stop at **Hopelands Garden.** (For more information see Day 2, Afternoon.)

LUNCH: Dine at a sidewalk table or inside at the **New Moon Cafe,** 116 Laurens Street Northwest (803–643–7088), where there is an extensive menu of soups, salads, and sandwiches.

After lunch return to the **Aiken County Historical Museum,** 433 Newberry Street (803–642–2015), because on weekends it is open only from 2:00 to 5:00 P.M. Housed in a huge, rambling, 1931 mansion on the Banksia estate, the collections are astounding—especially for a small town. Room after room is crammed to overflowing with local memorabilia representing almost every facet of life in eighteenth- and nineteenth-century South Carolina. In addition to a parlor and kitchen, another room is set up with the complete contents of a post office. Yet another contains an old-fashioned drugstore with a soda fountain from the former town of Dunbarton. One room is devoted to the Polidor and Schreadley Miniature Circus collection—the country's largest and most comprehensive collection of miniature circus tents, parade wagons, animals, and more. An 1890 one-room China Springs schoolhouse and the Ergle log cabin from the early nineteenth century—both appropriately furnished—have been moved to the grounds.

Afternoon

Return to Hopelands Garden, Whiskey Road (803–642–7630), and stroll around the fourteen acres of landscaped grounds; then visit the **Thoroughbred Racing Hall of Fame,** located in the old carriage house and stables. For a horse to be inducted, it must have been trained in Aiken, and all are national champions. Photos, racing silks, trophies, and other memorabilia from these champions are displayed, as are changing exhibits of equine art. Outdoor concerts and theatrical productions are performed on the grounds during the summer months.

If you have time, visit the galleries of the **Aiken Center for the Arts,** 122 Laurens Street (803–641–9094), and then explore the quaint shops in the Alley and those on Laurens and Newberry Streets. For tasteful Aiken souvenirs visit the **Screenprint Factory,** 157 Laurens Street

Northwest (803–649–7552). **Plum Pudding,** 101 Laurens Street (803–644–4600), has a wide range of gifts, gourmet and international items, as well as a coffee and cappuccino bar. **Tea Garden Gifts,** 112 Laurens Street Northwest (803–648–6124), features a gallery of wonderful items including Crabtree and Evelyn products and stationery. The **Curiosity Shop,** 158 Laurens Street Northwest (803–644–0004), sells Irish and British items.

Leave Aiken and go north on SC 19, which becomes US 25/US 178, to Greenwood, then turn west on SC 72 to **Abbeville,** a centerpiece of the Old 96 District.

DINNER AND LODGING: The **Belmont Inn,** 104 East Pickens Street (864–456–9625 or 877–459–8118; www.BelmontInn.net), is perfect for theatergoers. Located just across the street from the Abbeville Opera House, the inn offers not only theater/accommodations packages but also light refreshments at intermission and after the show. The charm and elegance of the early twentieth century are reflected in the large but cozy rooms, high ceilings, fireplaces, and sweeping veranda.

Evening

Take in a play at the **Abbeville Opera House** (864–459–2157), which presides over the Town Square like a dowager duchess, and then have drinks or snacks at the Belmont Inn's **Curtain Call Lounge.**

Day 3 / Morning

BREAKFAST: The Heritage Dining Room at the Belmont Inn serves a complimentary continental breakfast to guests.

Abbeville holds a unique place in Confederate history. The first organized secession meeting met there in 1860. It is claimed that the last Confederate cabinet meeting was held there in 1865. Thus, the Civil War began and ended in this small South Carolina town. (Georgians claim that the last cabinet meeting occurred in Washington, Georgia, just before Jefferson Davis was captured in Irwinton, Georgia, but let's not split hairs.)

Famed American statesman John C. Calhoun launched his public career in Abbeville. Other famous former residents include nineteenth-century Black leader Bishop Henry McNeal Turner, one of the founders of the African Methodist Church, and Thomas D. Howie, a World War II hero known as St. Lo.

Recognizing that Abbeville is one of the few places left that offers a simple rural life, eighty Mennonites have moved to the area within the past few years. Enjoy the home cooking of one of several Mennonite restaurants in town. (See "Other Recommended Restaurants and Lodgings.")

Abbeville's downtown, graced by more than 300 antebellum and postbellum homes, commercial buildings, and stately churches, is on the National Register of Historic Places. The historic area is easily explored on your own, but guided walking and driving tours are available. The **Greater Abbeville Chamber of Commerce,** 107 Court Square (864–366–4600 or 800–333–6262), which also serves as the Abbeville Welcome Center, offers a video presentation followed by a tour, Monday through Friday. Located in the historic Old Bank Building, the center also contains five historic paintings by William Kurtz that depict life in Abbeville from 1756 through Reconstruction.

LUNCH: Rough House Billiards, Court Square (864–366–1932), is an old-fashioned soda fountain/cafe/pool hall that looks like nothing has been changed—or dusted—for at least fifty years. They serve great hot dogs.

Afternoon

The neat-as-a-pin town square is flanked by nineteenth-century buildings. If you didn't attend a performance at the opera house last night, you'll want to tour the performance hall. Completed in 1908, the opera house provides seating for 350 on the main floor and has a balcony and four elegant boxes, as well as office space for the city government. The structure is considered to be an opera house rather than a theater because the stage space equals or exceeds the audience seating space. Backstage are three floors of dressing rooms with a window from each hallway opening onto the stage so performers can follow the action and not miss their cues. The back wall stands more than 100 feet tall. Four bricks thick without restraining rods, it is the tallest freestanding brick wall in the Western Hemisphere. In earlier times entertainers such as Fanny Brice, Jimmy Durante, and Groucho Marx graced the stage; however, when movies became popular, especially "talkies," the theater closed and slumbered like Rip Van Winkle for years.

Completely restored to its turn-of-the-twentieth-century appearance with the exception of the addition of air-conditioning and rocking chair seats, the opera house reopened in May 1968. The same hemp-rope-pulled rigging system for changing sets makes the opera house the only remaining "hemp house" in South Carolina. Since the theater reopened, the increase in tourism to the region has permitted the theater organization to expand from solely a winter season to a community-theater winter season and a repertory-company summer season that together provide thirty-six weeks of live theater yearly.

Visit the **Burt-Stark House,** North Main and Greenville Streets (864–459–4297), where Davis's cabinet meeting took place. The Greek Revival mansion was built in the 1830s and is furnished in period antiques, including two pieces of original furniture that remain: one a desk used by Burt; the other, the bed in which Jefferson Davis slept after his ill-fated cabinet meeting. Open Friday and Saturday. Otherwise by appointment.

Trinity Episcopal Church, 103 Church Street (864–459–5186), built in 1859–60, is the oldest church in Abbeville. It is noted for its Tracker Organ and for its stained-glass windows, both of which came from England and had to run the blockade of Charleston during the Civil War. The cemetery has graves that date from 1859.

Abbeville County Library, 1 South Main Street (864–459–4009), displays Abbeville native Dr. Samuel Poliakoff's collection of western art.

If you love antiques and shopping, you'll love Abbeville. As with most towns, modern businesses have migrated to the suburbs. The historic downtown is crammed with antiques and crafts shops, art galleries, and trendy boutiques. The **Uptown Exchange on the Square,** 102 Trinity Street (864–459–2224), contains several antiques and specialty shops.

Take SC 81 north to I–85 and return to Atlanta.

There's More

Abbeville, South Carolina

Outdoor activities. Calhoun Falls State Park and Marina, SC 81 (864–447–8267), on Richard B. Russell Lake, has swimming, fishing, camping, tennis, and boat ramps. The lake has 500 miles of shoreline and is perfect for all water sports. An overlook at the dam gives an excellent view of the lake.

Aiken, South Carolina

Canoeing. Aiken State Natural Area, 1145 State Park Road, Windsor (803–649–2857).

Hunting. Eleven hunting clubs and preserves provide hunting for deer, quail, turkey, and dove. Contact Thoroughbred Country or the Aiken Chamber of Commerce for more details (see page 171).

Riding to the hounds. If you are a qualified rider, contact the Aiken Chamber of Commerce to put you in touch with one of the hunts (see page 171).

Wineries. Montmorenci Vineyards, 2989 Charleston Highway, Montmorenci (803–649–4870), grows its own grapes, hand-picks them, and gently presses and ferments them in small lots to create award-winning wines. Visit for a tasting Wednesday through Saturday from 10:00 A.M. to 6:00 P.M.

Aiken Winery, 137 West Laurens Street Southwest (803–642–WINE; www.aikenwinery.com), uses California grapes aged in imported French oak barrels to produce Chardonnay, Pinot Noir, and Cabernet Sauvignon. Located behind the Carriage House Inn, the winery is open for tours and tastings Monday through Saturday.

Crawfordville, Georgia

Auction. Every Friday and/or Saturday night there's an auction across from the fire station on Askin Street. Items include everything from antiques to tools to farm equipment. (706) 756–3333.

Special Events

Abbeville, South Carolina

May. Abbeville Spring Festival, centered on the square, features live entertainment, a beauty pageant, an antiques and car show, home tours, a Civil War encampment, food, and crafts. (864) 459–2157.

December. Historic Christmas in Abbeville includes holiday shopping in decorated shops and home tours. (864) 459–2157.

Aiken, South Carolina

February. Confederate and Union encampments and Battle of Aiken reenactment. (803) 649–9475.

March. The Triple Crown Events: flat racing, steeplechase, polo. Contact the Aiken Chamber of Commerce at (803) 641–1111.

May. The Lobster Race, held at the festival area on Newberry Street downtown. Real lobster races at the World's First Official Thoroughbred Lobster Racing Track. Gourmet seafood, beach bands, kiddie rides, and entertainment. (803) 641–1111.

November. Blessing of the Hounds is an annual event that marks the beginning of the Aiken Hounds hunt season. Horses, riders, and hounds meet on Thanksgiving morning near the Memorial Gate in Hitchcock Woods to be blessed. Contact the Aiken Chamber of Commerce at (803) 641–1111.

Steeplechase–Hunt Meet. The last steeplechase event in a yearlong season, sanctioned by the National Steeplechase and Hunt Association. Ford Conger Field. Contact the Aiken Steeplechase Association at (803) 648–9641.

December. During Christmas in Hopelands Garden, the illuminated gardens are open for concerts and choral performances nightly the two weeks before Christmas. Contact the Aiken Chamber of Commerce at (803) 641–1111.

Crawfordville, Georgia

September. Annual Labor Day Fair is an old-time country fair with parades, children's activities, games, an arts-and-crafts show, Civil War living-history demonstrations, a reenactment, and period crafts. (706) 456–2229.

December. During Victorian Christmas at Liberty Hall, the house is alive with music, decorations, and refreshments. (706) 456–2602.

Other Recommended Restaurants and Lodgings

Abbeville, South Carolina

Village Grill, 110 Trinity Street (864–459–2500), specializes in rotisserie chicken and ribs. Lunch and dinner Monday through Saturday.

Yoder's Dutch Kitchen, SC 72 (864–459–5556), one of the "Top 10 Pennsylvania Dutch Restaurants in the Country," serves Mennonite country cooking for lunch Wednesday through Saturday and dinner Thursday through Saturday.

The Vintage Inn Bed and Breakfast, 1205 North Main Street (864–459–4784).

Aiken, South Carolina

Annie's Inn, US 78, Montmorenci (803–649–6836), is a bed-and-breakfast in an antebellum farmhouse. Six cottages are perfect for longer stays.

Carriage House Inn, 139 Laurens Street Northwest (803–644–5888), offers comfortable elegance in historic downtown.

The Guesthouse at Houndslake Country Club, 897 Houndslake Drive (803–648–9535 or 800–735–4589), is located on the grounds of a private country club. Guests have use of the twenty-seven-hole golf course, eight tennis courts, Olympic-size pool, and three restaurants.

Malia's Restaurant, 120 Laurens Street Southwest (803–643–3086), is open daily for lunch and dinner. Features a changing blackboard international menu. Located in a historic storefront.

No. 10 Downing Street, 241 Laurens Street (803–642–9062), located in an 1837 house, features four cozy dining rooms with fireplaces. Lunch and dinner Tuesday through Saturday. Bakery, gift shop, attractive gardens. Reservations are recommended on weekends and holidays. International gourmet cuisine.

Olive Oil's Restaurant, 233 Chesterfield Street (803–649–3726), serves Italian cuisine and offers an extensive Italian wine list. Casual dining room, porch, and patio dining seven nights a week. Located in a Victorian cottage.

Up Your Alley, 222 The Alley (803–649–2603), has the feel of a neighborhood pub. Exposed brick, oak antiques, and stained glass create a warm, friendly ambience. Open for dinner only. Closed Sunday.

The West Side Bowery, 151 Bee Lane (803–648–2900), is a historic pub and restaurant with patio dining on the Alley. Extensive lunch and dinner menus—mostly American and Italian. Bar open until 1:00 A.M.

For More Information

Aiken Chamber of Commerce, 121 Richland Avenue, Aiken, SC 29802. (803) 641–1111.

Greater Abbeville Chamber of Commerce, 107 Court Square, Abbeville, SC 29620. (864) 366–4600 or (800) 333–6262.

Taliaferro County Commissioners, 113 Monument Street, Crawfordville, GA 30631. (706) 456–2494.

Thoroughbred Country, P.O. Box 850, Aiken, SC 29802. (803) 649–7981 or (888) 834–1654.

EASTBOUND ESCAPE SIX

Savannah/Tybee Island, Georgia

Queen City of the South / 2 Nights

Savannah, a gracious city with the romantic allure and refinement of the Old South, was hewn from the wilderness in 1733, when English general James Oglethorpe founded the first city in the Georgia colony. Its important location on Yamacraw Bluff overlooking the Savannah River created a buffer between rich Carolina tobacco fields and Spanish invaders in Florida. Early colonists experimented with making silk, but it never became a strong component in the economy. When cotton became king, Savannah prospered as a port city. It served as the temporary state capital of the colony, then the state, from 1733 to 1782. Savannah was the site of Georgia's first Declaration Celebration on August 10, 1776. Although Button Gwinnett, Lyman Hall, and George Walton—Georgia's three signatories of the Declaration of Independence—had affixed their signatures on July 4, the copy of the document didn't reach Savannah until August 10. It was taken to Liberty Pole to be read aloud, after which there was a great torchlight procession.

- ☐ River Street
- ☐ Historic homes
- ☐ Museums
- ☐ Gardens
- ☐ Beaches

The meticulous blueprint that Oglethorpe drew for the city remains one of Savannah's most abiding and beguiling attributes. The city was laid out on a grid with twenty-four parklike squares; over the last 250 years, these have become bounteous with mature, moss-draped live oaks that create a green canopy over shiny magnolias, brilliant azaleas, and prominent monuments or fountains.

Around the squares, stately homes, churches, and businesses blossomed. During the 1950s some of these gems were razed in the name of "progress." In 1966, however, a 2.2-square-mile area was designated as a National Historic Landmark District, one of the largest in the country. Almost 1,500 structures have been preserved and restored. Today the stately structures serve not only as private homes and businesses, just as

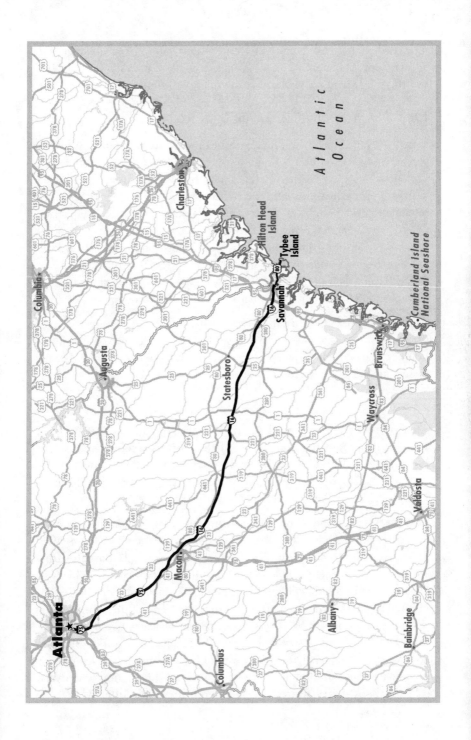

they used to, but also as museums and intimate inns. In recent years the notoriety of John Berendt's book *Midnight in the Garden of Good and Evil* and the subsequent movie have greatly increased tourism.

Day 1 / Morning/Afternoon

Take I–75 south to Macon, then go east on I–16 to **Savannah.** Whether you arrive before or after dark, go to the tourist heart of Savannah, which stretches along the Savannah River. Anchored by River Street and Factor's Walk, a 9-block area of warehouses was renewed to house shops, galleries, restaurants, and nightspots. **Riverwalk Plaza,** a brick-paved esplanade dotted with benches, plantings, and fountains, is *the* meeting or people-watching spot. From here you can catch a sightseeing cruise aboard the paddle wheeler *Savannah River Queen,* River Street Riverboat Company, 9 East River Street (912–232–6404 or 800–786–6404). The company also does brunch and dinner cruises between April and October.

DINNER: River House Restaurant, 125 West River Street (912–234–1900), serves seafood and steak in an old former cotton ware-house enhanced by Savannah gray brick walls and old pine beams. Reservations are suggested but not required.

Evening

After you dine, visit some of the district's nightspots, such as **Wet Willie's,** 101 East River Street (912– 233–5650); the **Cotton Exchange,** 201 East River Street (912–232–7088); **Spanky's,** 317 East River Street (912–236–3009); **Olympia Cafe,** 5 East River Street (912–233–3131); or **Huey's,** 115 East River Street (912–234–7385).

LODGING: Savannah offers a treasure chest of wonderful bed-and-breakfasts and small inns (more than thirty-eight of them), all so wonder-ful that it's hard to choose just one to recommend. The **Ballastone Inn,** 14 East Oglethorpe Avenue (912–236–1484 or 800–822–4553; www .ballastone.com), is the Tiffany's of Savannah's small intimate hostelries. Housed in an 1853 mansion, it has been named one of the most roman-tic inns in the country by *Bride's Magazine* and *Glamour.* Guest rooms are furnished with rice poster and canopy beds and other antiques. Some have working fireplaces and/or whirlpool baths. Complimentary port or brandy, midday refreshments, afternoon tea, pre-dinner hors d'oeuvres, robes, turndown service, fresh flowers, and fruit are also offered.

Savannah town houses

Day 2 / Morning

BREAKFAST: Enjoy a sumptuous breakfast served on a tray in your room or in the tearoom, parlor, lounge, or out in the courtyard.

Begin a tour of Savannah by visiting the **Central of Georgia Railroad Station,** 301 Martin Luther King Boulevard (912–944–0460; www.chsgeorgia.org), an 1860 depot that houses the Savannah Visitors Center. After watching the orientation presentation, pick up some brochures and get advice from the friendly staff. Most tour companies pick up passengers from the visitor center.

Among the dozen-plus tour companies in Savannah, a few options include **Gray Line Trolley Tours,** 1115 Louisville Road (912–234–8687); **Old Town Trolley,** 234 Martin Luther King Jr. Boulevard (912–233–0083); and **Carriage Tours of Savannah,** 10 Warner Street (912–236–6756). Among the alternatives, **Haunting Tours,** 229 East Point Drive (912–234–3571), offers ghost walks.

Before you leave to explore the rest of the city, however, there are two nearby attractions you should see. Adjacent to the visitor center is the

Savannah History Museum, 303 Martin Luther King Boulevard (912–238–1779), which chronicles 250 years of the city's past. The building, which was the passenger station for the Central of Georgia Railroad, houses a variety of exhibits, including an 1890 steam locomotive, a cotton gin, and artifacts from Savannah's wars.

Next door is the **Roundhouse Railroad Museum,** 601 West Harris Street (912–651–6823; www.chsgeorgia.org). Built prior to the Civil War, it is the oldest and most complete antebellum locomotive repair shop and roundhouse still in use in this country. Thirteen original structures still standing include the massive roundhouse and turntable and the magnificent 125-foot-tall smokestack. Exhibits include two of the oldest surviving steam engines, a 1914 steam locomotive, antique machinery, and rolling stock.

LUNCH: If you're visiting Savannah on a weekday, the lower level of a modest town house, 107 Jones Street (912–232–5997), houses **Mrs. Wilkes' Dining Room,** a world-famous, all-you-can-eat, family-style restaurant. What other restaurant do you know about that until recently kept its phone number a secret, doesn't advertise, doesn't take reservations, makes you wait in line, seats you with strangers, doesn't provide menus, and makes you take your dirty dishes to the kitchen? Well, you'll just have to try Mrs. Wilkes' Dining Room to understand its appeal. Visitors come from all over the world to eat here. It's open for lunch Monday through Friday 11:00 A.M. to 3:00 P.M.

Afternoon

In order to appreciate Savannah's outstanding architecture, visit the **Massie Heritage Interpretation Center,** 207 East Gordon Street (www.massie school.com), housed in the only remaining building of Georgia's oldest chartered school system. Exhibits include "The Elements of Greek, Roman, and Gothic Architecture: Their Influence on Savannah's Architectural Heritage," "Savannah's Victorian Era: Loss and Regeneration," and "Savannah's City Plan: A Unique Environment for a Diverse Citizenry." Open Monday through Friday.

Once you understand Savannah's architectural styles and know what to look for, go and inspect some of the city's historic house museums—all of them superbly furnished with appropriate antiques.

Isaiah Davenport House Museum, 324 East State Street (912–236–8097; www.davenportsavga.com), built between 1815 and 1820 by master builder Isaiah Davenport, features delicate plasterwork, an elliptical cantilevered staircase, and Ionic Tuscan columns.

The **Juliette Gordon Low Birthplace,** 10 East Oglethorpe Avenue (912–233–4501; www.girlscouts.org/birthplace), childhood home of the founder of the Girl Scouts, has been restored to the period of her childhood, 1860–86. The Regency town house, built around 1820, features Egyptian Revival and classical interior details and is furnished with many original family pieces.

The **Andrew Low House,** 329 Abercorn Street (912–233–6854; www.andrewlow.com), was the home of Juliette Gordon Low's father-in-law, Andrew Low, a cotton merchant. Built in 1848, the classical design shows West Indian plantation influence. William Makepeace Thackeray and Gen. Robert E. Lee were both guests here. It was from this house that Juliette Gordon Low organized the first Girl Scout troop in America, in 1912.

Designed by William Jay for cotton merchant and banker Richard Richardson, the **Owens-Thomas House Museum,** 124 Abercorn Street (912–233–9743), is an outstanding example of Regency architecture.

Telfair Museum of Art, 121 Barnard Street (912–232–1177; www.telfair.org), is the oldest public art museum in the South. Opulent period rooms are authentically restored to their 1819 appearance and serve as display space for fine and decorative arts, including American, French, and German Impressionist paintings.

Ships of the Sea Maritime Museum, 41 Martin Luther King Boulevard (912–232–1511; www.shipsofthesea.org), exhibits ship models, paintings, and maritime antiques primarily from the eighteenth and nineteenth centuries. The collection is housed in the elegant William Scarborough House. Scarborough was an owner of Steamship Savannah and was president of the Savannah Steamship Company. The museum garden is a delightful oasis.

Flannery O'Connor's childhood home is at 207 East Charlton Street on LaFayette Square (912–233–6014). Ask about special literary programs presented in the fall and spring.

DINNER: The restaurant at the **17 Hundred 90 Inn,** 307 East President Street (912–236–7122 or 800–487–1790; www.17hundred90.com), serves continental cuisine and has earned numerous awards, including "the Most Elegant Restaurant in Savannah" from *Gourmet* magazine. Also offers B&B accommodations.

LODGING: The Ballastone Inn.

Day 3 / Morning

BREAKFAST: At the inn.

Take a drive out toward the beach. Wilmington and Tybee Islands are reached from Savannah via US 80 and Skidaway Island by State Loop 26. You won't even realize you're on an island as you cross heavily built-up **Wilmington Island.** Separated from the mainland by the Intracoastal Waterway, it is between the waterway and Tybee Island.

Robert E. Lee's first assignment after his graduation from West Point was at **Fort Pulaski,** US 80 East (912–786–5787; www.nps.gov/fopu/), now a national monument. Designed by Napoléon's military engineer and built between 1829 and 1847, it was a masterpiece among brick-and-masonry forts. When the Confederates captured the fort in 1861, they thought they had an invincible obstruction of the Savannah River; however, bombardment by the Union's new rifled artillery in 1862 forced the Confederates to surrender in less than thirty hours. Later the fort was used as a Union military prison.

Continue on US 80 to **Tybee Island,** a popular family beach resort. Tybee (pronounced TIE-bee) comes from the Euchee Indian word for "salt." Rather than salt, the island offers 5 miles of silvery sand beach. Tybee Island, the site of the 1996 Olympic beach volleyball events, retains a 1950s ambience with one-story and low-rise motels; a variety of cottages; small, casual mom-and-pop restaurants; and surf and charter boat fishing.

The **Tybee Island Light Station,** 30 Meddin Drive (912–786–5801; www.tybeelighthouse.org), has been guiding mariners safely into the Savannah River for more than 270 years. The Tybee Island Light Station is one of America's most intact, having all of its historic support buildings. Rebuilt several times, the current 154-foot lighthouse, which was built in 1887 on the base of a previous one, wears its 1916 daymark (color scheme). The lighthouse has 178 stairs and is one of only seven lighthouses to have its First Order Fresnel lens. The Head Keeper's Cottage has been beautifully restored and furnished to represent an earlier era. An adjacent museum contains lighthouse artifacts.

The **Tybee Island Marine Science Center** on Tybee Island, 1510 Strand at Fourteenth Street (912–786–5917; www.tybeemsc.org), is an interpretive center with aquariums and exhibits. Open only in the summer.

LUNCH: Cafe Loco, 1 Old Tybee Road (912–786–7810), is a funky hangout on an inland waterway. Great for boiled or fried seafood.

Return to Atlanta via I–16 and I–75.

There's More

Air Force history. The Mighty Eighth Air Force Heritage Museum, 175 Bourne Avenue, Pooler (912–748–8888 or 800–421–9428; www.mighty 8thmuseum.com), is dedicated to the Mighty Eighth, which was created in Savannah in 1942 and grew to be the greatest air armada ever committed to battle. This museum honors the sacrifice, bravery, resolve, and teamwork of the more than one million men and women who have served in the unit. Great for aircraft enthusiasts, the museum houses extensive Air Force memorabilia. Dynamic state-of-the-art displays of historic battles and missions tell the story of the Mighty Eighth's role from the World War II air war over Europe up through Desert Storm.

Black history. Savannah has a significant Black history. That heritage can be explored at the King-Tisdell Cottage of Black History Museum, 502 East Huntingdon Street (912–234–8000), an outstanding historic project of the Georgia Trust for Historic Preservation, and at the Beach Institute, 502 East Harris Street (912–234–8000). The newest museum to explore African-American history and culture is the Ralph Mark Gilbert Civil Rights Museum, 460 Martin Luther King Jr. Boulevard (912–231–8900; www.savannahcivilrightsmuseum.com). Pick up the brochure *Negro Heritage Trail,* which presents three separate walking or driving tours, from any of the museums.

Jogging. 5K, 8K, and 10K routes have been devised by the Savannah Striders Club. Request a map from the Convention and Visitors Bureau (912–644–6400 or 877–728–2662).

Outdoor adventures. Wilderness Southeast, 711 Sandtown Road (912–897–5108), a unique outdoor school, offers overnight wilderness discovery adventures, including sailing, canoeing, and hiking.

Skidaway Island State Park, 52 Diamond Causeway (912–598–2300), reached by State Loop 26, offers tent and trailer sites, a swimming pool, fishing, and hiking trails.

Aquarium. The Skidaway Marine Science Complex and Aquarium, 30 Ocean Science Circle (912–598–2496), is an oceanographic center that conducts studies on area sea life and its potential uses. The 12,000-gallon aquarium exhibits Georgia marine life. Other displays include archaeological finds and economic patterns from aboriginal times to the present.

Special Events

Savannah

Celebrations in Savannah, the "Hostess City of the South," rival those of New Orleans, well known as a party city. Both St. Patrick's Day and Christmas are popular holidays in Savannah.

All year. First Saturday Festivals, with changing themes, occur at Riverfront Plaza. Call the Savannah Riverfront Association at (912) 234–0295.

March. The second-largest St. Patrick's Day celebration in the country takes place in Savannah, which hosts 300,000 people every year for the wearin' of the green. Savannah's festival and parade are so popular that you need to make hotel reservations at least a year in advance. Many lodgings, in fact, require a prepaid, three-nights-minimum stay. This is one time that guaranteeing your room by credit card probably won't do. Innkeepers want cash, up front. If you have trouble getting reservations, try the surrounding towns for accommodations. Call the St. Patrick's Day Parade Committee, 5 West Liberty Street, at (912) 233–4804.

The profusion of blooms in late spring is the signal for the Tour of Homes and Gardens. The four-day event includes daylight, twilight, and candlelight walking tours; receptions, luncheons, and seminars; and a sunset dinner cruise. Call the Historic Savannah Foundation, 321 East York Street, at (912) 234–8054.

April. Known locally as NOGS because of the location "North of Gaston Street," Hidden Gardens of Historic Savannah tours include two homes, eight gardens, and light refreshments at the Green-Meldrim Mansion. (912) 644–6400 or (877) SAVANNAH.

December. Christmas in Savannah includes a festival of trees, open house in several shops and artists' studios, a tour of inns, a holiday doors contest, and a tour of homes. Call the Convention and Visitors Bureau at (877) 728–2662.

Tybee Island

August. Annual Seafood and Music Fest offers live concerts on the north beach parking lot and other family-oriented activities. (912) 786–5444.

December. Annual Tybee Island Christmas Boat Parade, a fantasy of whimsically decorated boats. Call Lazaretto Creek Marina at (912) 786–5848 or Frank's Outboard and Jetsports at (912) 786–4032.

Wilmington Island

June. At Thunderbolt, a quaint shrimping village on Wilmington Island, you can see the annual June Blessing of the Fleet.

Other Recommended Restaurants and Lodgings

Savannah

Savannah boasts a potpourri of delightful, intimate inns and bed-and-breakfasts. Many offer extras such as afternoon tea or a cocktail hour. To help you choose the best inn for you, check the Web sites: www.romantic innsofsavannah.com and www.historicinns-savannah.com.

Two historic inns right on the river are the Olde Harbor Inn, 508 East Factor's Walk (912–234–4100 or 800–553–6533), and the River Street Inn, 115 East River Street (912–234–6400 or 800–253–4229). Just across East Bay Street are the East Bay Inn, 225 East Bay Street (912–238–1225 or 800–500–1225), and the Mulberry Inn, 601 East Bay Street (912–238–1200).

The Senator's Gate Bed and Breakfast, 226 East Hall Street (912–233–6398; www.thesenatorsgate.com), offers gracious accommodations in a beautifully restored Italianate Victorian mansion built in 1885 for R. E. Lester, who among his many careers was a state senator. Elegant rooms, a gourmet breakfast, and tender loving care from friendly hosts guarantee a delightful stay.

Several other outstanding B&Bs in Savannah include Gaston Gallery Bed and Breakfast, 211 East Gaston Street (912–238–3924 or 800–671–0716); the Gastonian, 220 East Gaston Street (912–232–2869 or 800–322–6603); and the Hamilton-Turner House, 330 Abercorn Street (912–233–1833 or 888–448–8849).

Breathing new life into the revitalization of Broughton Street, the Marshall House, 123 East Broughton Street (912–644–7896 or 800–589–6304), began life as one of Savannah's premier hotels. Once abandoned, the hotel had a multimillion dollar face-lift and reopened as an intimate sixty-eight-room inn. Two on-site restaurants are 45 Bistro, which features modern interpretations of southern classics, and Chadwick's, for afternoon tea and evening cocktails and jazz.

You'll never run out of outstanding places to eat in Savannah:

Elizabeth on 37th, 105 East Thirty-seventh Street (912–236–5547), is a past winner of the James Beard Award.

Garibaldi, 315 West Congress Street (912–232–7118), serves local seafood specialties.

You can order contemporary and colonial Georgian cuisine at the Olde Pink House, 23 Abercorn Street (912–232–4286), one of Savannah's oldest mansions.

Pirates House, 20 East Broad (912–233–5757), which specializes in seafood, is located in an authentic 1733 tavern.

Among some other outstanding Savannah restaurants are Bistro Savannah, 309 West Congress Street (912–233–6266); The Cafe at City Market, 219 West Bryan Street (912–236–7133); Crystal Beer Parlor, 301 West Jones Street (912–232–1153); Il Pasticcio, 2 East Broughton Street (912–231–8888); and the Sapphire Grill, 110 West Congress Street (912–443–9962).

Tybee Island

The Breakfast Club, 1500 Butler Avenue (912–786–5984), with an observation kitchen, serves breakfast and lunch. A fixture on Tybee since 1976, the restaurant has been voted Savannah's Best Place to Eat Breakfast for more than a decade.

An old fish camp is what the Crab Shack at Chimney Creek, 40-A Estill Hammock Road (912–786–7009), reminds us of. You can eat in the ramshackle building, but we enjoyed a meal on the huge deck at picnic tables with a hole in the middle and a garbage can underneath in which to pitch the shells from shrimp, crabs, and other shellfish.

Hunter House Bed and Breakfast, 1701 Butler Avenue (912–786–7515), offers accommodations and has a well-known restaurant. Open for dinner.

Tybee Island Inn, 24 Van Horn Street (912–786–9255 or 866–892–4667), is located in the old recreation building of the long-gone fort hospital near the Tybee Island lighthouse and the museum at Fort Screven.

Locals recommend the North Beach Grill, 41-A Meddin Drive (912–786–9003), for its Caribbean and southern cuisine; George's, 1105 US 80 East (912–786–9736); and Tango, 1106 US 80 East (912–786–8264).

Tybee Cottages, Inc., P.O. Box 1226, Tybee Island 31328 (912–786–6746 or 877–524–9819), offers a variety of small to large cottages on the island—many waterfront.

Wilmington Island

Chow down on some fresh seafood—especially Low Country Boil—at Williams Seafood, 8010 East US 80 (912–897–2219).

For More Information

Savannah Area Convention and Visitors Bureau Chamber of Commerce, 101 East Bay Street, Savannah, GA 31401. Mailing address: P.O. Box 1628, Savannah, GA 31402. (912) 644–6400 or (877) SAVANNAH; www.savannah-visit.com or www.savannahchamber.com.

Savannah Waterfront Association, 130 East Factor's Walk, Savannah, GA 31402. (912) 234–0295; www.savriverstreet.com.

Tybee Island Visitors Center, US Highway 80 at Campbell Avenue, Tybee Island, GA 31328. (912) 786–5444 or (800) 868–BEACH; www.tybee online.com or www.tybeeisland.com.

WESTBOUND
ESCAPES

WESTBOUND ESCAPE ONE

Tuskegee to Selma, Alabama

Center Stage in the South / 2 Nights

Montgomery presents a legacy of American history. Conquistadores, other conquerors, Confederates, and kings played a part in its evolution. De Soto staked the first Spanish flag on the Alabama River in 1540. The French created Fort Toulouse in 1717. That fort became Fort Jackson under the British in 1814. The actual birth of Montgomery occurred in 1819 when the towns of East Alabama and New Philadelphia merged to form a town named after the Revolutionary War hero Gen. Richard Montgomery. The city became the capital of Alabama in 1846 and served briefly as the capital of the Confederacy.

Montgomery became the catalyst of the 1960s civil rights movement. Rosa Parks's refusal to give up her seat to a white man sparked a yearlong, eventually victorious bus boycott. A momentous march from Selma ended on the capitol steps.

☐ Alabama State Capitol

☐ Civil rights sites

☐ Alabama Shakespeare Festival

A cultural giant, Montgomery has a rich musical history. Some of the city's musical luminaries include Hank Williams Sr., Nat King Cole, Clarence Carter, Toni Tenille, Metropolitan Opera singer Nell Rankin, and blues singer Willie Mae "Big Mama" Thornton. On the literary/artistic front, F. Scott and Zelda Sayre Fitzgerald (who was from Montgomery) met and married here. Montgomery boasts the Wynton M. Blount Cultural Park, home to the Alabama Shakespeare Festival and the Montgomery Museum of Fine Arts, as well as a symphony, ballet, and dance theater.

The area around Montgomery shares the capital city's significant African-American history. Tuskegee is the site of one of the first universities established to educate Blacks. Selma was the scene of many civil rights meetings, protests, and marches before the fateful march from Selma to

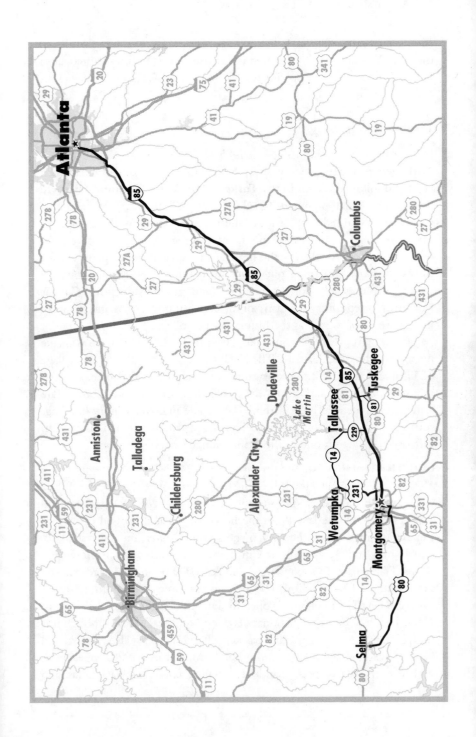

Montgomery. In addition, Selma was the site of one of the last battles of the Civil War and was thus spared destruction of its beautiful antebellum homes. Tallassee deserves a visit just for lunch, and Wetumpka boasts several attractions.

Day 1 / Morning

Leave Atlanta in midmorning via I–85 to AL 81 and go south toward **Tuskegee.** At the intersection of AL 81 and Old Montgomery Road, turn right and follow the signs to the **Tuskegee Institute National Historic Site,** 1212 Old Montgomery Road (334–727–3200), established as a university in 1881 to educate African Americans. Booker T. Washington, born a slave, became the university's president. George Washington Carver, also born into slavery, worked as the head of the Agriculture Department for forty-seven years, carrying out many agricultural experiments. Tour the **Oaks,** Washington's home, and the **George Washington Carver Museum,** a repository for many of his personal possessions, the results of his experiments, as well as the history of the college.

Retrace AL 81 to I–85 and take it west to AL 229, which you will take north to **Tallassee,** Alabama. The small town began as the Indian village of Talisi. A huge, 1852 five-story mill was once one of Alabama's largest industrial complexes. During the Civil War the town's Confederate armory produced Tallassee Carbine Rifles. The mill and armory buildings survive and await restoration. The horizontally arched Benjamin Fitzpatrick Bridge is one of the world's longest curved bridges.

LUNCH: Hotel Talisi, 14 Sistrunk Street (334–283–2769). Beginning in 1928 as the Woodall Hotel, the inn had seventy-two rooms, the Palace Cafe, and several stores. Although it survived the Great Depression and World War II, by the late 1950s the hotel had virtually ceased operation. Purchasing it in 1962, the new owners concentrated on the restaurant, which grew and grew and grew. Current owners/partners Bob Brown and Roger Gaither tell us the restaurant cooks 6,000 pounds of fried chicken per month and feeds 450 to 600 persons on Sunday, 1,000 to 1,100 on Mother's Day. The restaurant is open for lunch through dinner daily except Labor Day, July Fourth, Christmas Day, and New Year's Day. Although it is undoubtedly the restaurant that has kept the Hotel Talisi alive, Brown and Gaither are gradually restoring the hotel proper to its 1920s appearance, with flowery red carpets, chandeliers, ceiling fans, camelback sofas, and velvety crimson draperies. The hotel doesn't need to hire a band—it is one: The lobby contains three baby grand pianos, three uprights, and a player spinet, as well as two electric organs. An organist entertains during lunch. Upstairs, 10-foot-wide hallways are crammed with a variety of antiques, including a century-old Steinway piano. Eighteen rooms, including five suites, with private baths are eclectically furnished as they may have been in the 1920s. Guests may encounter one or more of the three lady ghosts.

Afternoon

Take AL 14 to **Wetumpka,** then go north on AL 9. **Morrione Winery,** 3865 Central Plank Road (334–567–9957), a family endeavor, uses old-world procedures and new-world technology to transform Muscadines into light, fruity wines—Majestic White, Magnolia, Welder, Regal Red, and Blush. Tours, tastings, sales.

Go south on AL 9, then continue south on US 231 and watch for signs to **Fort Toulouse/Jackson Park,** 2521 West Fort Toulouse Road off US 231 (334–567–3002). Located on 165 acres at the junction of the Coosa and Tallapoosa Rivers, the fort/park offers archaeological excavations, a museum, historic buildings, an Indian mound, nature trails, the William Bartram Arboretum, and a campground. French living-history programs are presented spring through fall.

Take US 231 south to **Montgomery.**

DINNER: Dawson's at Rose Hill, 11250 Highway 80 East (334–215–7620), offers a romantic ambience enhanced by candlelight and fine linens in a historic home in the country. The cuisine is primarily Northern Italian. Reservations are strongly suggested.

Evening

Take in a performance at the **Alabama Shakespeare Festival,** Carolyn Blount Theatre, 1 Festival Drive, in the Wynton M. Blount Cultural Park (334–271–5353 or 800–841–4ASF), which operates year-round. The only American theater invited to fly the flag of England's Royal Shakespeare Company, the Alabama Shakespeare Festival is the fifth-largest Shakespeare festival in the world and offers world-class classical and contemporary theatrical productions. Performances of two different plays are given simultaneously in the large and small theaters.

LODGING: From the porch or the gazebo of **Red Bluff Cottage,** 551 Clay Street (334–264–0056), a bed-and-breakfast, you'll have great views of the capitol and the Alabama River. Poised high above the Alabama River in the historic Cottage Hill District of pre– and post–Civil War homes, Red Bluff Cottage has an unusual raised style.

Day 2 / Morning

BREAKFAST: At the B&B.

Begin with a visit to the **Montgomery Visitor Center,** located in historic Union Station, 300 Water Street (334–262–0013), where you can watch a video about Montgomery and get information on all the attractions and events the city offers. Admire the gargantuan, Romanesque Revival **Union Station** built between 1893 and 1896. At that time Montgomery was a thriving railroad center, with six rail lines and forty-four passenger trains a day. Today the station is divided into offices.

Take the underground tunnel that was once used to transport cotton to and from steamboats to **Riverfront Park,** a two-acre esplanade on the Alabama River that features a playground, picnic areas, an amphitheater, and the *Betsy Anne,* an authentic stern-wheeler.

A good place to get a feel for old Montgomery is **Old Alabama Town,** 301 Columbus Street (334–240–4500 or 888–240–1850; www.oldalabamatown.com), near the heart of downtown in the Old North Hull Street District. Thirty restored and, in some cases, relocated buildings permit you to examine urban and rural life between 1800 and 1900. Begin at Lucas Tavern, where pioneers stopped when they entered the Alabama Territory in 1817. You can explore an 1820 cabin, an 1890 schoolhouse, a fully stocked turn-of-the-twentieth-century grocery store, a church, Campbell's Cottage, an 1850 town house, a pole barn, the Ordeman-Shaw Italianate town house, and an authentically restored turn-of-the-twentieth-century cotton gin. Dependencies include a kitchen, laundry room, and well. Participate with working craftspeople at the Rose-Morris Craft House. Other attractions include the depression-era Alabama Pharmaceutical Association Drugstore Museum.

LUNCH: Have a delicious southern-cooked lunch at the **Blue Sky Restaurant** located in the 1850 Young House, 231 North Hull Street (334–262–4465), in Old Alabama Town. You can purchase a ticket that includes the tour and lunch.

Afternoon

Just 4 blocks from Old Alabama Town is the 1850 Greek Revival **Alabama State Capitol,** Bainbridge Street and Dexter Avenue (334–242–3184), one of the few state capitols designated as a National Historic Landmark. For nearly 150 years the capitol has overlooked downtown from its majestic hilltop setting. It is the state's top tourist attraction, with more than one million visitors annually. A small brass star imbedded in the floor of the Dexter Avenue portico marks the spot where Jefferson Davis was inaugurated as president of the Confederate States of America.

A magnificent pair of three-story spiral stairways dominates the original entrance hall. They are believed to have been the handiwork of Horace King, a freed slave who went on to become a noted engineer and bridge builder. The rotunda features a stained-glass skylight and eight large, vibrantly painted murals. The Senate Chamber, the most historic room in the capitol, is where delegates from the seceding southern states organized the Confederate government in February 1861. The chamber has been restored to its Civil War–era appearance with a reproduction of the oil-burning chandelier that hung there and desks and chairs replicating several originals that survive. The House of Representatives, old Supreme Court Chamber, and original Governor's Office have been returned to their Victorian-period elegance.

Across Washington Avenue is the **First White House of the Confederacy,** 644 Washington Avenue (334–242–1861). The 1835 Italianate house was home to the Davises during the brief period that Montgomery was the capital of the Confederacy. It is furnished with many of the Davises' personal belongings, some of their furniture, and other Civil War artifacts. All articles in the President's Bedroom belonged to Davis and were presented by Mrs. Davis and placed according to a diagram she drew before her death in 1906. Memorabilia include his slippers, collar box, suspenders, spittoon, valise, umbrella, and walking stick. The 1889 photograph is the last that was taken of Davis.

The nation's first **Archives and History Museum,** established in 1901, makes its home in Montgomery. The Alabama Department of Archives and History, 624 Washington Avenue (334–242–4435), next door to the First White House of the Confederacy, exhibits Native American projectile points, grinding stones, cooking vessels, burial urns, quilts, toys, medical paraphernalia, and a Hank Williams display. The children's gallery is called Grandma's Attic.

About a block away, the Reverend Martin Luther King Jr. accepted his first pulpit in 1954 at what is now the **Dexter Avenue King Memorial Baptist Church,** 454 Dexter Avenue (334–263–3970). Plans for the bus boycott and civil rights marches were organized at the church. Now listed as a National Historic Landmark, the church boasts a powerful mural that traces King's odyssey from Montgomery to his assassination in Memphis and includes individuals who were instrumental, positively and negatively, in the events of the period, among them Rev. Vernon Johns, Stokely Carmichael (who coined the phrase "Black Power"), Dick Gregory, Andrew Young, Ralph Abernathy, Jesse Jackson, Coretta Scott King, and the King children.

Rosa Parks Library and Museum, 252 Montgomery Street (334–241–8615), pays tribute to the unassuming seamstress who sparked the 1955 Montgomery bus boycott and became the mother of the civil rights movement. The state-of-the-art interactive museum was built on the site where she waited for the bus. A re-created street scene and a replica of the bus let visitors put themselves in her place. Exhibits include video footage, artifacts, historical documents, and a life-size statue of Ms. Parks.

Still in the same area and within easy walking distance is the **Civil Rights Memorial,** Washington Avenue and Hull Street at the Southern Poverty Law Center. The major events of the movement, as well as the names of forty people who gave their lives in the struggle between 1954 and 1968, are carved around the edge of the round granite tabletop. Cooling, healing water pours down the wall and bubbles up and runs across the tabletop, then spills into a shallow pool.

DINNER: Jimmy's Uptown Grille, 540 Clay Street (334–265–8187), offers casual fine dining and overlooks downtown and the Alabama River. The local newspaper's readers voted the restaurant the Most Romantic Restaurant in Montgomery. The Lounge is open until 2:00 A.M.

Evening

See another performance at the Alabama Shakespeare Festival.

LODGING: Red Bluff Cottage.

Day 3 / Morning

BREAKFAST: Enjoy another morning repast at the bed-and-breakfast.

If you're an early riser, there are several outdoor sights you can see before most attractions start to open at noon or 1:00 P.M.

Country-music fans will want to visit the **Hank Williams Sr. Memorial and Statue.** Williams and his family moved to Montgomery when he was thirteen, and he soon won a professional singing contest that led to a career that culminated at the Grand Ole Opry. A promising future was cut short when he died in a car accident at age twenty-nine. The unveiling of his tombstone in the Oakwood Cemetery Annex at 1304 Upper Wetumpka Road was attended by 60,000 people. The memorial features the opening notes from "I Saw the Light," a bronze plaque of Hank playing the guitar, a stone replica of his cowboy hat, and replicas of pages of sheet music. A bronze statue honoring Williams, located in Lister Hill Plaza on Perry Street, was commissioned by Hank Williams Jr. It shows the singer holding a guitar and wearing his trademark suit, cowboy boots, and hat. The **Hank Williams Museum,** 118 Commerce Street (334–262–3600), contains the actual 1952 Cadillac in which the singer died.

At 11:00 A.M. you can take a backstage tour of the Carolyn Blount Theatre at the Alabama Shakespeare Festival. You'll visit both theaters, as well as the scenery, costume, and prop shops, and see some of the state-of-the-art equipment. You must make advance reservations with the box office (see Evening, Day 1).

Take a leisurely tour through the **Montgomery Museum of Fine Arts,** 1 Museum Drive, in the Wynton M. Blount Cultural Park (334–244–5700; www.mmfa.org). Rich in southern works, it is the repository of the Blount Collection of American Art—forty-one paintings and watercolors that span the period from the 1700s to the present. Works by John Singer Sargent, Edward Hopper, and many others illustrate the evolution of American art. The museum's permanent collection of more than 2,500 pieces includes American and European works such as drawings, etchings, engravings, and graphics by Dürer, Matisse, Rembrandt, Whistler, and others. ARTWORKS, by far, is the most outstanding interactive art gallery and hands-on art studio for children we've ever seen. High-tech activities include the use of computers, an exploration of optics, art-related discovery boxes, books, puzzles, games, and quiet activities for the whole family.

LUNCH: Enjoy a light lunch of salads, soups, or sandwiches while overlooking the lake-studded parkland at the Terrace Cafe at the Montgomery Museum of Fine Arts.

Afternoon

From Montgomery take US 80 west to **Selma.** This charming small city was laid out by William Rufus King, a vice president of the United States. He is buried at **Old Live Oak Cemetery** (off US 22; 334–875–7241), as are Confederate soldiers and prominent Selma citizens such as Elodie B. Todd, half sister of Mary Todd Lincoln, and congressman Benjamin Sterling Turner, an ex-slave who became the first Selmian elected to the U.S. House of Representatives.

Selma boasts several historic districts. The **Historic Water Avenue District** encompasses Water Avenue, a restored nineteenth-century commercial district that runs along the river. It has been updated with brick streets and sidewalks and several pocket parks. Two museums anchor this district, which is filled with antiques shops, restaurants, and a historic hotel. The oldest residential area is the **Old Town Historic District.** The **Martin Luther King Jr. Street Historic District** runs from Selma Avenue to Jeff Davis Avenue and contains several churches and memorials. Pick up a *Windshield Tour* brochure and audiotape describing 116 historic sites from the **Selma–Dallas County Chamber of Commerce,** 912 Selma Avenue (334–875–7241 or 800–45–SELMA).

Selma's pride and joy is **Sturdivant Hall,** 713 Mabry Street (334–872–5626), built in 1853. An extraordinary representation of neoclassical architecture, the mansion is filled with period furniture and surrounded by formal gardens. The adjacent original kitchen building contains a museum gift shop.

Among the city's museums, the **Old Depot Museum,** 4 Martin Luther King Jr. Street (334–874–2197), located in a beautiful Victorian railroad depot, contains extensive collections of memorabilia that relate to local history as well as a Black heritage exhibit.

Selma became known to the nation during the civil rights struggles of the 1960s—especially the attempted and successful marches from Selma to Montgomery. The **Edmund Pettus Bridge** earned its bad reputation as the place where protestors were attacked by state troopers on Bloody Sunday, March 7, 1965.

A bust of Dr. King stands in front of the **Brown Memorial A.M.E. Church,** 410 Martin Luther King Jr. Street (334–874–7897). A 1907 Byzantine-style church, it served as a local headquarters for the civil rights movement and as the staging place for many marches. On the same street, the **First Baptist Church** was the site of mass meetings and demonstrations. Built in 1894, it was designed by a local Black architect and is a superb example of nineteenth-century Black churches. Twenty memorials along the avenue tell stories of the movement through searing pictures and the words of those who came together in a common cause.

Overlooking the Edmund Pettus Bridge, the **National Voting Rights Museum and Institute,** 1012 Water Avenue (334–418–0800), houses history in the form of firsthand accounts of participants in the pivotal events.

Return to Montgomery and take I–85 back to Atlanta.

There's More

Montgomery

Historic church. Confederate president Jefferson Davis rented a pew at the 1855 St. John's Episcopal Church, 113 Madison Avenue (334–262–1937). It was built without a slave gallery and instead features an organ and choir loft.

Museum. Scott and Zelda Fitzgerald Museum, 919 Felder Avenue (334–264–4222), was the one-time home of author Francis Scott Key Fitzgerald, distantly related to the composer of "The Star Spangled Banner," and his wife, Zelda Sayre, a Montgomery native whom he met while he was stationed at nearby Camp Sheridan after World War I. They were married in 1920 and had one daughter. Enormously talented in her own right, Zelda wrote short stories, plays, and novels and was an accomplished ballerina and a gifted painter. One of her paintings is displayed at the Montgomery Museum of Fine Arts. Unfortunately, after several mental breakdowns she was diagnosed with schizophrenia and spent most of the rest of her life in institutions. She died in a sanitarium fire in Asheville, North Carolina. The museum collection contains personal artifacts from the couple's personal and private lives.

Spectator sports. Sports fans will enjoy the Montgomery Motor Speedway, 480 Booth Road (334–262–6101), as well as VictoryLand Greyhound Racing Park, exit 22 off I–85 (334–269–6087). The latter offers wagering on thirteen greyhound races nightly and matinees four days a week; a grandstand; a glass-enclosed, climate-controlled clubhouse; and restaurants and cocktail lounges.

Zoo. Completely renovated in 1991 and enlarged to forty acres, the Montgomery Zoo and Mann Wildlife Learning Museum, 2301 Coliseum

Parkway off North Boulevard (334–240–4900), features barrier-free exhibits of animals from five continents; a walk-through, free-flight aviary; and a reptile building. A narrated train ride travels past most of the exhibits. Indoor/outdoor dining at the Overlook Cafe.

Special Events

Montgomery

March–April. Southeastern Livestock Exposition Rodeo and Livestock Week is a Wild West rodeo. Call the Alabama Cattleman's Association at (334) 265–1867.

December. Christmas on the Coosa in nearby Wetumpka includes caroling, pageants, historic tours, and a boat parade. (334) 567–5147.

Old Alabama Town Christmas celebrates a nineteenth-century holiday. (334) 240–4500.

Other Recommended Restaurants and Lodgings

Montgomery

Outside town, just off I–85, is Colonel's Rest Bed and Breakfast/East Folk Farm, 11091 Atlanta Highway (334–215–0380). All units, some attached to the main house or in separate cottages, have kitchen facilities.

Farmer's Market Cafe, two locations: 315 North McDonough (334–262–1970) and 1659 Federal Drive (334–271–1885). Serves country cooking and barbecue.

Selma

Faunsdale Bar and Grill, US 80, Faunsdale (334–628–3240), is a casual cafe in a historic building where steak and seafood lead the menu. Live entertainment is offered on the weekend.

Major Grumbles, 1 Grumbles Alley (334–872–2006), located in a historic building, has indoor dining and a patio overlooking the river.

St. James Hotel, 1200 Water Street (334–872–3234), located in a restored 1837 riverfront property, is Selma's only full-service hotel with a restaurant and the original bar. The three-story building, originally the Brantley

Hotel, sports iron balconies overlooking the river. Forty-two intimate rooms feature antiques and reproductions.

Tally Ho, 509 Magnum Avenue (334–872–1390), located in what began as a log cabin that has been enlarged several times, serves fish and steak entrees.

For More Information

Alabama Bureau of Tourism and Travel, 401 Adams Avenue, Montgomery, AL 36103-4309. (334) 242–4169 or (800) ALABAMA.

Montgomery Chamber of Commerce Convention and Visitors Division, 300 Water Street, Montgomery, AL 36101. (334) 262–1100 or (800) 240–9452; www.visitingmontgomery.com.

Selma–Dallas County Chamber of Commerce, 912 Selma Avenue, Selma, AL 36702. (334) 875–7241 or (800) 45–SELMA.

Cave Spring, Georgia, and Huntsville, Alabama

Huntsville's a Blast / 2 Nights

In the early 1800s John Hunt heard Native American tales that on the west side of the Great Smoky Mountains was a Big Spring from which flowed endless fresh, clear water. In 1805 he came through the foothills to find it and built a log cabin near the spring and limestone bluffs. Other settlers followed, and a county was formed in 1808. In 1810 the town of Twickenham was established, named after the English home of Alexander Pope. Nonetheless, because of anti-English sentiment and the War of 1812, the town's name was changed to Huntsville to honor the first settler.

□ Spaceships

□ Historic homes

□ Railroad museum

The Alabama Constitution was written there in 1819, and the city became the state's temporary capital. River-borne transportation for cotton barges provided by the Tennessee River, stagecoach lines, and a railroad made the city a transportation hub by the 1850s. It was the railroad that led to the capture of Huntsville by Union troops in 1862; however, because Huntsville was occupied throughout the Civil War, most structures were spared in order to be used as headquarters, residences, and offices.

Textiles led to recovery after the Civil War. Around the turn of the twentieth century, tourists were attracted to Monte Sano, the "Mountain of Health," but it was World War II that brought Redstone Arsenal and started Huntsville down the technology path. In 1950 Dr. Wernher von Braun and 118 German scientists arrived. Their research and development of space flight turned Huntsville into the nation's first technological center. The city's current high-tech workforce is the third largest in the nation. You're just as likely to hear foreign accents and Yankee brogue as you are to hear soft southern drawls.

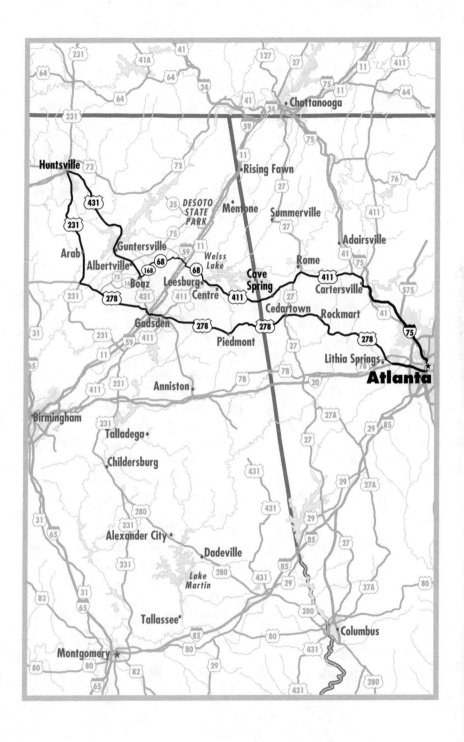

Day 1 / Morning

Take I–75 north from Atlanta to US 411 and travel west, bypassing Rome. Continuing west on US 411, you'll come to **Cave Spring,** renowned for the number and variety of its antiques shops. The town, established in 1832, was named for the mineral spring that flows from a large limestone cave in what is now **Rolater Park,** just off the town square at the intersection of State 100 and US 411/GA 53 (706–777–3962). Legend says that Native American tribal meetings and games were held near the cave and springs. At the turn of the twentieth century, visitors came to Cave Spring for the purity of the water and its medicinal qualities: chlorine, manganous oxide, silica, sulphur trioxide, sodium oxide, lime, magnesia, alumina, and ferric oxide.

During the summer you can tour the huge, 300,000-year-old cave and admire the many impressive stalagmites, among which is the legendary **Devil's Stool** formation. Excess water from the spring flows into a pond and then into a one-and-a-half-acre, Georgia-shaped pool—the second largest in Georgia. Another popular activity is fishing for trout in the stream that flows through the park.

Two significant buildings anchor the twenty-nine-acre park, once the site of the Cave Spring Manual Labor School, which later became Hearn Academy. The **Hearn Academy Classroom Building** is undergoing restoration by the Cave Spring Historical Society (706–777–8865), and the 1839 building that served as the school's dormitory has been completely restored and functions as the **Hearn Inn** (see "Other Recommended Restaurants and Lodgings"), a bed-and-breakfast operated by the historical society. On the park grounds you can see a quaint old brick church erected in 1851 and noted for its stained-glass windows and slave balcony. You can peek into an old log cabin, built in the mid-1800s, that was moved to the park.

The Cave Spring Presbyterian Church, Alabama Street, another project of the historical society, is the home of the **Cave Spring Art Gallery.** Among the ninety Gothic-, Victorian-, and plantation-style buildings listed on the National Register of Historic Places, many have been adapted to other uses. More than forty antiques shops beckon shoppers and browsers.

Continue west on US 411 across the state line into Alabama. Take AL 68 north toward Leesburg, and take AL 168 to US 431 to **Huntsville.**

LUNCH: **Papou's**, 110 Southside Square (256–534–5553), serves Greek and Mediterranean cuisine.

Afternoon

In 1819 forty-four delegates to a Constitutional Convention met in a vacant cabinetmaker's shop in Huntsville to write Alabama's constitution, allowing Alabama to become the twenty-second state in the Union. **Constitution Village,** 109 Gates Avenue (256–564–8100 or 800–678–1819; www.earlyworks.com or www.stepintohistory.com), re-created on the site, is a living-history museum that depicts life in early-nineteenth-century northeast Alabama.

Reconstructed on the original sites are the Neal House, cabinet-maker's shop, print shop, Confectionery Shop, library, and post office from the 1805–19 period. Enter and exit through the Confectionery Shop on Gates Avenue, which also serves as a gift shop. Costumed guides will take you around, beginning with the cabinetmakers, who will demonstrate methods of fine woodworking with nineteenth-century tools and techniques and even let you turn the great wheel lathe. The Neal Residence, home of Madison County's first sheriff, features a main house, detached kitchen, dairy, well house, stables, carriage house, and barn. Guides demonstrate cooking over an open fire, harvesting the garden, pressing cider, carding cotton, spinning, weaving, making soap and starch, washing clothes, quilting, needleworking, basket weaving, and candle dipping.

In the Boardman Complex you'll see a Ramage Press like the one used to print the Constitution of the State of Alabama as well as the *Alabama Republican* newspaper. Sample sheets are printed daily. The library was the first one incorporated in Alabama. Subscribers, limited to men, were allowed to check out books only one hour a day, two days a week. Also in this complex are slaves' and servants' quarters. In the Federal-style, two-story Clay Building are Mr. Clay's law office, federal land surveyor's office, and post office. Did you know that in those days, the recipient, not the sender, paid for mail? But the recipient could refuse to accept it. Wouldn't that be nice?

As you leave through the Confectionery Shop, browse through the gift items, such as pottery, hand-blown glass, hand-forged iron items, and Shaker-style furniture. Just a few of the period children's toys include whimmy diddles, buzz saws, marbles, fifes, and tin whistles. Take some fudge, fresh-baked cookies, jams, jellies, and relishes with you.

Just around the block is the **Harrison Brothers Hardware Store,** 124 Southside Square (256–536–3631; www.harrisonbrothershardware .com), Alabama's oldest hardware store. Originally founded as a tobacco wholesale store in 1879, the emporium moved to this location in 1897 and evolved into a hardware store. Better than a museum, the store also offers items for sale. Still boasting a coal-fired potbellied stove, creaky wooden floors, and a hand-operated rope elevator, the store is stocked from floor to ceiling with tiny numbered drawers, reached by tall rolling ladders. Every available surface is covered with old-fashioned tools. An ancient desk is loaded with an untidy mound of old ledgers, invoices, catalogs, and calendars. A massive hand-operated cash register still rings up sales. One side of the shop is devoted to modern gadgets, gift items, candy, cast-iron cookware, oak rocking chairs, garden gadgets, and bird feeders for sale.

DINNER: Cafe Berlin, 4800 Whitesburg Drive South (256–880–9920), specializes in German food.

LODGING: Spend the night outside of town at the **Church House Inn,** 2017 Gimwood Road, Toney (256–828–5192), which resembles a church and even sports an authentic church steeple. Located on ten acres, the B&B offers three guest rooms and serves a full breakfast.

Evening

See if there are any performances of the **Huntsville Opera Theater,** the only all-volunteer opera company in the United States. Performances are held at the Von Braun Center. Call the Arts Council at (256) 881–4796 or log on to www.huntsvilleopera.org/about.asp.

Day 2 / Morning

BREAKFAST: Dine at the B&B, or try **Eunice's Country Kitchen,** 1006 Andrew Jackson Way Northeast (256–534–9550). This simple restaurant, which serves a hearty country breakfast, including ham and molasses, is *the* place to see and be seen. Political candidates know to breakfast here to press the flesh. The day we were there, the mayor was refilling coffee cups. When we said that Aunt Eunice, as she is known, could tell a lot of stories, she said, with a laugh, "People pay me *not* to tell stories." There's a large communal table called the Liar's Table, and Aunt Eunice will be happy to give you a Liar's License.

Two neighborhoods on the National Register of Historic Places, **Twickenham** and **Old Town,** offer a 4-mile living museum of eighteen decades of architecture. With more than sixty-five pre–Civil War structures, Twickenham is one of the largest concentrations of antebellum homes in the South, while Old Town comprises Victorian homes built between 1870 and 1930. In some places original brick sidewalks and car-riage blocks survive. A brochure for a walking tour is available from the **Huntsville Convention and Visitors Bureau,** 500 Church Street (256–551–2230 or 800–772–2348; www.huntsville.org). It describes the architectural gems and provides fascinating information about them. You can contact the Twickenham Historic District at (256) 533–5723.

The only Twickenham home open to the public, the **Weeden House Museum,** 300 Gates Avenue (256–536–7718), was the birthplace and life-long home of noted artist and poet Maria Howard Weeden. The 1819 Federal-style High House features fanlight windows with original glass, elaborate hand-carved woodwork, and an architecturally perfect can-tilevered spiral staircase. During the Civil War the family was reduced to poverty, and Weeden began to paint watercolor portraits and party favors to earn money. After the Civil War she continued to support her impov-erished family by teaching, writing poetry, and painting. She began to paint character portraits of ex-slaves and was able to capture their humor and philosophy of life in the poems she wrote in their dialect. Her books were published by major publishers of the day. Many of Weeden's works are displayed in the museum. Open Monday through Friday.

Some private homes of note that you can drive by include: the **Morgan-Neal House,** 558 Franklin Street; the **Carlos Smith House,** 704 Adams Street; the **Banister House,** 702 Adams Street; **Westlawn,** 413 McClung Drive; and the **Cox House,** 311 Lincoln Street.

The **Episcopal Church of the Nativity,** 208 Eustis at Green (256–533–2455), a product of the "Ecclesiological Movement," whereby buildings were patterned after English parish churches of the Middle Ages, is considered one of the finest examples of Gothic Revival architecture in the United States. Built in 1859, the edifice features a 151-foot-tall spire and exquisite stained-glass windows. It was the only church not comman-deered by the Union during the Civil War; an officer was going to use it to stable horses but reconsidered after reading the words REVERENCE MY SANCTUARY engraved over the entrance.

Dogwoods and magnolias shade the final resting place of five Alabama governors; Confederate Secretary of War Leroy Pope Walker; architect George Steele, who was responsible for many of Huntsville's most glori-ous mansions; Studebaker president Russel Erskine; the mother of actress Tallulah Bankhead; and many others at **Maple Hill Cemetery,** 202 Maple Hill Street Southeast (256–539–5537), a treasure trove of ornate gravemarkers and mausoleums.

LUNCH: Clementine's, 4701 Meridian Street North (256–512–0697), serves lunch and home-baked goods.

Afternoon

The 1860 **Huntsville Depot and Museum,** 320 Church Street (256–564–8100 or 800–678–1819; www.earlyworks.com), Alabama's oldest surviving railroad depot and the only one from the antebellum period, is an example of the architectural magnificence of railroad stations of the era. During the Civil War the depot was a temporary prison for Confederate soldiers. Graffiti left by these soldiers still punctuates the walls. A multimedia presentation relates Huntsville's history. Exhibits include rolling stock, a one-eighth-scale narrow-gauge steam locomotive, and an HO-scale model railroad that re-creates Huntsville as it was in the 1860s. Children are particularly fascinated by Andy Barker, the robotic ticket agent who operates a 1912 telegraph office. From the depot you can take a thirty-minute streetcar tour through historic downtown. You can disembark from the trolley at any attraction and reboard later.

The **Huntsville Museum of Art,** 300 Church Street (256–535–4350 or 800–786–9095), is noted for its permanent collection of nineteenth- and twentieth-century American paintings and graphics.

Visit the thirty-acre **Huntsville/Madison County Botanical Garden,** 4747 Bob Wallace Avenue (256–830–4447 or 877–930–4447; www.hsvbg.org), a 112-acre oasis of rose, daylily, and iris collections as well as woodland paths and meadows. A butterfly house is open in summer.

Located high atop Round Top Mountain at the tip of Monte Sano is **Burritt Museum and Park,** 3101 Burritt Drive (256–536–2882; www.burrittmuseum.com), from which you can get a striking panorama of Huntsville. The fourteen-room mansion was built by a prominent physician who had the foresight to stuff the walls with hay for insulation in order to protect residents from the cool mountain breezes. Browse through two rooms of original furniture and the exhibits of Native American artifacts, rocks and minerals, 150 years of medical and pharmaceutical instruments, nineteenth-century decorative arts, and photographs and memorabilia from the 1887 Monte Sano Hotel and Health Resort— all of which depict regional history. Explore the collection of nineteenth-century rural structures, including log cabins, blacksmith shop, smokehouse, and wood-frame church. You can picnic or hike one of the nearby wildflower trails past mountain springs, cascading waterfalls, and a nineteenth-century coal mine. Walk along the 1840 Big Cove Turnpike,

U.S. Space and Rocket Center

site of a Confederate surrender in 1865. The park boasts an award-winning Handicap Nature Trail. Living-history programs take place during the summer.

DINNER: For fine dining and an excellent wine list, try **801 Franklin**, 801 Franklin Street (256–519–8019).

LODGING: Church House Inn.

Day 3 / Morning

BREAKFAST: A full breakfast is served at the Church House Inn.

It's best to allow a whole day to explore the **U.S. Space and Rocket Center,** 1 Tranquillity Base (256–837–3400 or 800–637–7223; www.ussrc .com). You'll spend forty-five minutes in the Spacedome Theater viewing an IMAX movie, two to four hours in the Space Museum, and forty-five minutes on the bus tour of the Marshall Space Flight Center, where actual research occurs and where you can see the original rocket-testing grounds. You'll also want to leave time to stroll through the gigantic rockets on display outside in Rocket Park, as well as to eat and to browse through the gift shops. At the Space and Rocket Center, you'll find sixty hands-on activities as well as exhibits, demonstrations, films, and simulations. Highlights include a model of the Hubble Telescope and a life-size Space Shuttle. The *Pathfinder*, with its distinctive black-and-white nose and 57-foot tip, weighs ninety-eight tons. The 363-foot *Saturn V* replica in front of the museum is the only "standing" moon rocket in the world. Also on the grounds are the Space Camp, which hosts 19,000 children annually, and the Space Academy, which offers similar experiences for "big kids."

Take US 231 to US 278 through Gadsden. Pass through Piedmont, Alabama, and Cedartown and Rockmart, Georgia, on your way back to Atlanta.

There's More

Outdoor activities. Nearby Monte Sano State Park, 5105 Nolen Avenue (256–534–3757), towers 1,000 feet above the edge of Huntsville and offers rustic cabins, camping, and hiking trails.

A nature trail on Green Mountain, South Shawdee Road (256–883–9501), includes a sixteen-acre lake, wooded paths, chapel, covered bridge, wildlife area, and braille trail.

Huntsville Cross Country Running Park, Airport Park, follows a 2- to 3-mile loop between the old airport and the Municipal Golf Course.

Water sports. Madison County Lake, 2501 Country Lake Road (256–776–4905), covers 105 acres and offers boat rentals and a bait and tackle shop. Open weekends only in December and January.

Ditto Landing Marina, 293 Ditto Landing Road (256–882–1057), is the area's major access to the Tennessee River. The 253-acre park features boat docks and a bicycle motorcross course.

Special Events

Cave Spring, Georgia

June. The Cave Spring Arts Festival offers quality handcrafted art objects, such as sculpture, wheel-thrown and hand-built pottery, wood carvings, toys, basketry, metalwork, fine needlework, and unusual crafts, music, dance, food, and several fun runs. Proceeds go to the Cave Spring Historical Society for restoration and preservation of historic structures. Contact Shirley Voyles at (706) 777–3043.

Huntsville, Alabama

May. Huntsville Pilgrimage permits visitors to tour four homes and four churches. (256) 551–2230, (256) 553–5723, or (800) 772–2348.

September. The Big Spring Jam music festival attracts tens of thousands of music lovers to Big Spring Park in front of the Von Braun Center.

December. Special holiday meals are prepared at Constitution Village. (256) 564–8100.

Other Recommended Restaurants and Lodgings

Cave Spring, Georgia

Hearn Inn, 13 Cedartown Street in the park (706–777–8865), is simply furnished, as befits its origins as a dormitory.

Huntsville, Alabama

Bibb House Bed and Breakfast, 11 Allen Street (256–772–0586; www.bibbhouse.com), offers two rooms in an 1867 house on two acres. A country breakfast is included.

Dogwood Manor, 707 Chase Road (256–859–3946; www.bridge net11.com/dogwood), offers four rooms in a two-story Federal-style home. A gourmet breakfast is included.

For More Information

City of Cave Spring, P.O. Box 365, Cave Spring, GA 30124. (706) 777–3382.

Huntsville Convention and Visitors Bureau, 500 Church Street, Suite One, Huntsville, AL 35801. (256) 551–2230 or (800) 772–2348; www .huntsville.org.

WESTBOUND ESCAPE THREE

Tuscaloosa to Marion, Alabama

Heart of Alabama / 2 Nights

Established in 1816, Tuscaloosa served as the second capital of Alabama.

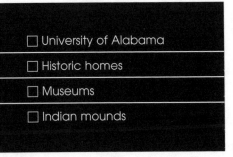

- ☐ University of Alabama
- ☐ Historic homes
- ☐ Museums
- ☐ Indian mounds

Not long after, the University of Alabama was founded. The city suffered severe destruction during the Civil War, but parts of it have managed to preserve an Old South atmosphere. Although the university is the heart of the city, there are many other attractions: Magnificent antebellum mansions, historic sites, wildlife, natural attractions, antiques shops, and several quaint small towns draw today's visitors to the region.

Day 1 / Morning

Take I–20 west from Atlanta toward Birmingham. On the way you'll pass close by Anniston and Talladega, which are described in the "There's Still Magic in the Magic City" escape (see p. 218). If you're not stopping in Birmingham, take the I–459 Bypass around the city and rejoin I–20/59 to **Tuscaloosa,** which was named for a Native American chief who opposed Spanish explorer Hernando de Soto. Just be forewarned: Try to avoid Tuscaloosa on football weekends.

LUNCH: Owned by former pro football player Bob Baumhower and popular with the college crowd, **Bob Baumhower's "Wings" Sports Grille,** 500 Harper Lee Drive (205–556–5658; www.wingsportsgrille .com), is famous for its buffalo wings.

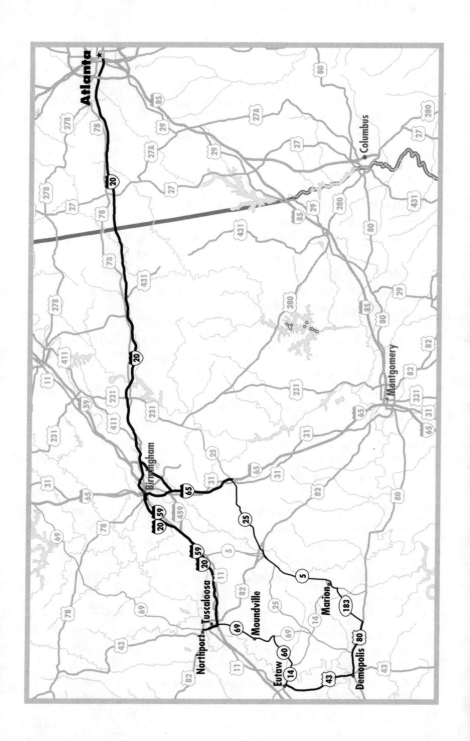

Afternoon

The centerpiece of Tuscaloosa is the University of Alabama. "Roll Tide!" is the slogan of the university's Crimson Tide football team, and you'll see evidence of the town's obsession with football everywhere. Tuscaloosa, however, had a history long before there was a university and a football team. Its humble beginnings go back to the late eighteenth century. Although nothing remains from that period, several structures survive from the early 1800s.

The city served briefly as the capital of Alabama (1825–46), and **Capitol Park,** University and Twenty-eighth Avenues (205–758–2238; www.historictuscaloosa.com), contains several reminders of that period. In the park, the **McGuire-Strickland House,** 2828 Sixth Street, a wood-frame raised cottage built circa 1820, is considered to be the oldest wooden structure in Tuscaloosa. Its square nails, wooden pegs, and hand-hewn timbers typify early Alabama workmanship. Currently being used as a school, it is not open to the public. Some fragments of columns and other architectural elements are all that remain of the **Old Capitol.** Relocated to the park is the **Old Tavern,** 2800 Twenty-eighth Avenue (205–758–2238), a former stagecoach stop built in 1827. Memorabilia from the capital era are displayed inside. Open Tuesday through Friday.

Tuscaloosa suffered significant damage during the Civil War, but the **Battle-Friedman House and Gardens,** 1010 Greensboro Avenue (205–758–6138), the 1835 Greek Revival town house of wealthy planter and businessman Alfred Battle, survives. Later it was owned by Bernard Friedman, a Hungarian immigrant. Beautifully restored and furnished with high-quality period pieces, the mansion now serves as a house museum and cultural center. Closed Monday. Drive by the **Dearing-Swain Home,** 2111 Fourteenth Street, a private home that is considered to be the most perfect example of Greek-temple architecture in the state.

You wouldn't want to go to Tuscaloosa without spending some time on the university campus, so tour the **Gorgas House,** Capstone Drive (205–348–5906; www.museums.ua.edu/gorgas). Built in 1829, it is the oldest structure on campus, the oldest structure built by the state of Alabama, and one of the first buildings in the state constructed specifically for higher education. A raised cottage, it was originally designed as a "hotel" or "steward's hall"—a dormitory and dining hall for cadets. The family of the seventh college president and Confederate general Josiah Gorgas and his wife, Amelia Gayle Gorgas, lived in the house from 1879 to 1953. Even during that time the house continued to be used as a university post office and hospital. Numerous family treasures are displayed. Open Tuesday through Saturday.

See exhibits of natural history, geology, and mineralogy at the **Alabama Museum of Natural History,** Smith Hall, Sixth Avenue, University of Alabama campus (205–348–7550; www.museums .ua.edu/history). Smith Hall, the first university building constructed in the twentieth century, is considered to be the finest example of Beaux Arts architecture in the region. The Grand Exhibition Hall contains displays from the age of dinosaurs, the Ice Age, and the Coal Age. See the Hodges meteorite, the only meteorite known to have struck a human being. Take a photographic journey to "The Land that Time Forgot: Michael Leahy's Explorations of Highland New Guinea, 1930–35." Comprised of pictures and artifacts, the exhibit describes Australian explorer Michael Leahy's series of gold-prospecting trips to New Guinea. Closed Sunday and Monday.

Football season never ends at the **Paul W. Bryant Museum,** 300 Paul W. Bryant Drive (205–348–4668; www.museums.ua.edu/bryant). The museum is not only a monument to the Crimson Tide but also to the university's most beloved coach, the late "Bear" Bryant. Displays include a re-creation of Bryant's office; his famous houndstooth hat (and a replica of it in Waterford crystal); state-of-the-art videos with highlights of great Bama coaches, players, and unforgettable plays; football art; and other memorabilia.

Visit the **Westervelt Warner Museum of American Art,** North River Yacht Club, 8316 Mountbatten Road (205–343–4540; www.warner museum.org), to see one of the most extensive collections of American fine art anywhere. Gulf States Paper Corporation CEO Jack Warner amassed this personal collection of sculptures, porcelains, paintings, and primitive artifacts. Closed Monday.

DINNER: Cypress Inn, 501 Rice Mine Road North (205–345–6963; www.cypressinn.restaurant.com), overlooks the Black Warrior River. Enjoy a drink on the outdoor patio, then move inside to savor a meal of traditional beef, chicken, and seafood selections.

LODGING: Expect casual elegance and Southern hospitality at the **Crimson Inn Bed and Breakfast,** 1509 University Boulevard (205–758–3483 or 877–424–6622; www.bbonline.com/al/crimsoninn/), a Dutch colonial home not far from the campus. If you're a real Bama fan, you might enjoy staying in Mikal's Bama Room, which is decorated with Crimson Tide memorabilia. You can walk to the stadium from the bed-

and-breakfast. Gather in the parlor with your hosts and fellow guests to savor some dessert and conversation before you turn in.

Day 2 / Morning

BREAKFAST: Morning begins with the savory aroma of coffee outside your door, followed by a southern gourmet breakfast.

Art aficionados should drive across the river to **Northport** to visit the **Kentuck Art Center and Museum,** 501 Main Avenue (205–758–1257; www.kentuck.org), where you can watch potters, photographers, woodworkers, jewelers, glassblowers, a metalsmith, and other artisans at work. Although they do many pieces on commission, most of the works displayed are for sale.

Return to Tuscaloosa and take AL 69 south to **Moundville,** site of a large collection of ancient Indian mounds. The **Moundville Archaeological Park,** AL 69 (205–371–2234; www.museums.usa.edu /moundville), occupies part of what was once the largest and most powerful community of Native Americans during the Mississippian period (A.D. 1000–1500). These early Americans built huge earthwork mounds along the Black Warrior River, on which they constructed temples, council houses, and homes for the nobility. Two dozen of these mounds, of varying heights and sizes, remain.

Operated by the Alabama Museum of Natural History at the University of Alabama in Tuscaloosa, the park, in addition to the mounds, has the **Jones Archaeological Museum** (205–371–2572), filled with artifacts from archaeological excavations of the site. A re-created temple and huts give visitors a glimpse of what life must have been like. In addition, the park has a boardwalk nature trail.

Take AL 60/69 south to AL 14 and go west to **Eutaw,** a town cotton made.

LUNCH: Cotton Patch, Union Road (205–372–4235), is a casual, down-home restaurant.

Afternoon

Eutaw was spared during the Civil War, and fifty-three mansions survive from that period. Drive around to see and photograph these architectural masterpieces. The most beautiful of all is **Kirkwood Mansion,** 111 Kirkwood Drive (205–372–2694), the most photographed home in Alabama, which you can tour. The gorgeous Greek Revival home is surrounded by soaring Corinthian columns and crowned by an enormous belvedere. Kirkwood is furnished with an unparalleled collection of antebellum pieces. Open Monday through Saturday 9:00 A.M. to 5:00 P.M. and Sunday 1:00 to 5:00 P.M. Pick up a brochure for a walking/driving tour of the town from the **Greene County Visitor Center,** in the Vaughn-Morrow House, 110 Main Street (205–372–9002).

From Eutaw go south on US 43 to **Demopolis,** originally settled in 1817 by exiles from Napoléon's army. Although they were aristocrats who knew little or nothing about farming, their plan was to start a colony. It's little surprise that it failed, but a community was established. Two important historic homes there should be on your itinerary:

Bluff Hall, 405 North Commissioners Avenue (334–289–9644), built in 1832, is named for its location on a high chalk cliff. It was originally a simple Federal-style town house, but in 1850 the addition of a columned portico turned it into a Greek Revival home. Confederate president Jefferson Davis, general Leonidas Polk, and others were guests there. Now a museum house, Bluff Hall is furnished with antiques. The *pièce de résistance* is the impressive collection of antique clothing. A gift shop is on-site. Closed Monday.

A Demopolis masterpiece is **Gaineswood Antebellum House Museum,** 805 South Cedar Avenue (334–289–4846), formerly the home of Nathan Whitfield, who took seventeen years to build the twenty-room mansion. It has been described by the *Smithsonian Guide to Historic America: The Deep South* as "one of the three or four most interesting houses in America." Rooms filled with original furnishings feature ceiling domes, plaster friezes, and cast-iron ornamentation.

After leaving Demopolis, go east on US 80 to AL 183 and north to **Marion.**

DINNER: For a substantial meal the most popular place in town is the **Gateway Inn Dinner Club,** 1615 AL 5 South (334–683–9166). Well known for its rib-eye steak, the restaurant also serves fried, baked, or broiled catfish; boiled or fried shrimp; pastas; and a large variety of vegetables.

LODGING: Myrtle Hill, 303–5 West Lafayette Street (334–683–9095), was the 1840 Greek Revival home of Confederate general George D. Johnson. Today it operates as a bed-and-breakfast. Furnished with eighteenth- and nineteenth-century antiques, Myrtle Hill offers luxurious guest rooms.

Day 3 / Morning

BREAKFAST: Enjoy a sumptuous plantation breakfast at the bed-and-breakfast.

Spared during the Civil War, Marion is what you might envision when you imagine the serenity, elegance, and beauty of the Old South. More than one hundred and fifty antebellum homes, churches, and other structures survive. The gracious town has an illustrious past as a cultural and educational center; at one time Marion boasted five institutions of higher learning. Two of these survive: Judson College and the Marion Military Institute.

Judson College, founded in 1838, is one of the oldest women's colleges in the nation and the only one in Alabama. Visit the campus to see the **Alabama Women's Hall of Fame,** A. Howard Bean Hall (334–683–5184; www.awhf.org), which honors such Alabama luminaries as Helen Keller, Tallulah Bankhead, Lurleen Wallace, Julia Strudwick Tutwiler, Amelia Gayle Gorgas, and Mildred Westervelt Warner. Bronze plaques, portraits, letters, and other memorabilia describe their contributions to the state.

Marion Military Institute, 1101 South Washington Street (334–683–2343), founded in 1842, is a military preparatory school and junior college. Eighty-five percent of its graduates go on to one of the U.S. military academies. Among the sites of general interest on the campus are the lovely **chapel** and the **Alabama Military Hall of Honor Museum.** The 1857 chapel served as a hospital during the Civil War, and names and initials of former students and patients are carved into the handmade brick exterior walls. Early in the twentieth century the chapel was the recipient of several stunning stained-glass windows. Portrait plaques and artifacts of inductees are displayed in the Hall of Honor, which is located in an 1832 building moved to the campus.

Visit the **monument to Harry the Slave** in the Marion Cemetery, Lafayette Street. Harry lost his life during an 1854 fire while waking all the students at Howard College. As a result of his efforts, only one student died. Harry was honored with a well-attended funeral followed by burial in the main part of the cemetery rather than in the slave section. His bravery is immortalized on a large monument erected by students and the Alabama Baptist Convention.

Antiques hunters find fertile feeding grounds in Marion. Several shops are located in historic homes or turn-of-the-twentieth-century commercial buildings. For more information call the Perry County Chamber of Commerce at (334) 683–9622.

LUNCH: Kalico Kitchen, Highway 5 (334–683–6739), is a casual eatery with a wide variety of menu choices.

Afternoon

To return to Atlanta from Marion, take AL 5 to AL 25 east to I–65. Go north toward Birmingham, take the I–459 Bypass around the city, then I–20 back to Georgia.

There's More

Greyhound racing. Greenetrack, the Greene County Greyhound Park, Inc., I–59 at exit 45, Eutaw (205–372–9318), offers racing you can watch from the comfort of a climate-controlled clubhouse.

River cruise. The **Bama Belle** (205–339–1108), Tuscaloosa's newest attraction, is a modern-day replica of an early 1900s paddle wheeler that makes sightseeing, birding, and dinner cruises on the Black Warrior River.

Water sports. Demopolis is considered the gateway to the 234-mile Tennessee-Tombigbee water system. The Demopolis Yacht Basin, Highway 43, Demopolis (334–289–4374), offers full-service facilities for pleasure boats. Lake Lurleen State Park, 13226 Lake Lurleen Road, Coker (205–339–1558), near Tuscaloosa, offers fishing, swimming, and boating as well as more than 1,600 acres to hike and explore.

Special Events

Demopolis

December. A spectacular weeklong Christmas festival on and around the river includes Santa's arrival by boat, a lighted boat parade, musical show, living Christmas-tree choir, candlelight tours of Gaineswood, children's street parade, arts-and-crafts festival, Civil War reenactors camp out, barbecue cook-off, and fireworks. (334) 289–0270.

Moundville

October. The annual Moundville Native American Festival includes a recreation of an 1800 Creek hunting camp, performances of traditional songs and dances, storytelling, tool and craft making, games of Indian stick-ball, and a Lantern Tour of the Living History Camp. (205) 371–2234.

Northport

October. The Kentuck Arts Festival attracts 30,000 art lovers who come to see nearly 200 artisans as well as enjoy storytelling, music, demonstrations of pioneer skills, and good food. (205) 758–1257.

Other Recommended Restaurants and Lodgings

Marion

The cafeteria at Judson College, Jewett Hall, 302 Bibb Street (334–683–5100), is open to the public, and meals are very reasonably priced.

Northport

The Globe, 430 Main Street (205–391–0949), re-creates the Globe Theater in England, has a publike bar, and has a restaurant with a varied, multiethnic menu.

Tuscaloosa

Dreamland Barbecue, 5535 Fifteenth Avenue East (205–758–8135), is the place to go for ribs. This location is the original.

Four Points Hotel, 320 Paul Bryant Drive (205–752–3200), located on the campus, is a modern hotel with a restaurant, lounge, live entertainment, and a swimming pool.

Kozy's Fine Dining, 3510 Pelham Loop Road (205–556–0665), is the place to splurge for a romantic special occasion. The ambience is pure 1940s, and the menu ranges from pasta to duck.

The Waysider, 1512 Greensboro Avenue (205–345–8239), located in a historic home, serves great breakfasts and lunches and is known for its biscuits.

For More Information

Demopolis Area Chamber of Commerce, 102 East Washington Street, Demopolis, AL 36732. (334) 289–0270.

Eutaw Chamber of Commerce, 110 Main Street, Eutaw, AL 35462. (205) 372–9002.

Perry County Chamber of Commerce, 1200 Washington Street, Marion, AL 36756. (334) 683–9622.

Tuscaloosa Convention and Visitors Bureau, 1305 Greensboro Avenue, Tuscaloosa, AL 35401. (205) 391–9200 or (800) 538–8696.

WESTBOUND ESCAPE FOUR

Anniston/Talladega/ Birmingham, Alabama

There's Still Magic in the Magic City / 2 Nights

Birmingham, often called the Magic City because it appeared to grow like magic out of the wilderness, was founded in 1871 at the crossing of two railroad lines. It progressed rapidly from yellow-pine shacks and boxcars to cotton plantations and tobacco farms, then to an industrial steel center, and finally, in the late twentieth century, to a medical and technological center.

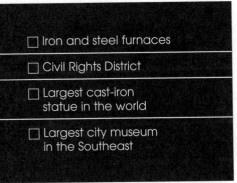

- ☐ Iron and steel furnaces
- ☐ Civil Rights District
- ☐ Largest cast-iron statue in the world
- ☐ Largest city museum in the Southeast

Riding the foothills of the Appalachians in a series of ridges, Birmingham—"the Pittsburgh of the South"—was named for the great industrial steel center in England. All that remains of the city's steel industry are the statue *Vulcan,* the Roman God of the Forge, and the Sloss Furnaces, the world's only industrial plant of its size that is being preserved.

Anniston, the "Model City of the South," was founded in 1872 by industrialist Samuel Noble as an iron foundry. Today it is the home of one of the South's premier natural-history museums.

During the Creek War of 1813, the Battle of Talladega, a decisive victory for Andrew Jackson and his Tennessee Volunteers, was the forerunner of engagements that eventually broke the power of the Native Americans in the Southeast. Settlers streamed into the area in the 1830s when the Creeks were forced off their lands. Today Talladega is known for the roar of auto racing and, as the home of the Alabama School for the Deaf, has the largest population of hearing-impaired citizens in the country.

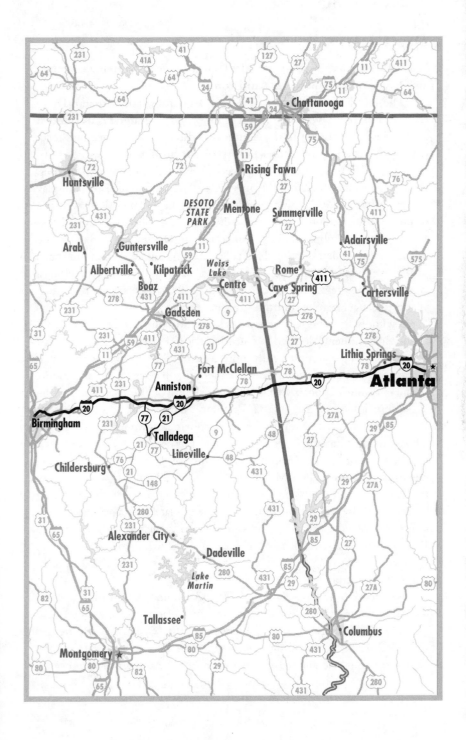

Day 1 / Morning

Leave Atlanta after breakfast and take I–20 west toward Birmingham, then take US 431/AL 21 north to **Anniston.**

The **Anniston Museum of Natural History,** 800 Museum Drive (256–237–6766; www.annistonmuseum.org), the largest city-funded natural-history museum in the Southeast, boasts one of the nation's most extensive collections of natural-history specimens. The best aspect of this museum is that most displays have been taken out from behind glass cases, thereby increasing their impact on visitors. The "Dynamic Earth" display features a meteorite, dazzling gemstones, and a hurricane ball, as well as a re-created Pteranodon flying over a 20-foot-long Albertosauros and fossilized plants and animals millions of years old. "Designs for Living" is one of the nation's oldest diorama bird collections. Assembled around the turn of the twentieth century, the displays boast hand-painted habitat settings. Because of the age of the collection, you'll be able to see extinct birds such as the passenger pigeon and the Carolina parakeet, as well as the endangered whooping crane and the red-cockaded woodpecker. In "Adaptations to the Environment," located in Lagarde African Hall, you can take a safari and have a close encounter with more than one hundred African animals in a re-created natural savanna environment that includes a life-size model of an enormous baobab tree. On the grounds of the museum are the Wildlife Garden, the Eugenia G. Brannon Nature Trail, and the Bird of Prey Trail. Closed Monday except during summer, and closed Thanksgiving, Christmas Eve and Day, and New Year's Day.

Next door to the Anniston Museum of Natural History is the **Berman Museum,** 840 Museum Drive (256–237–6261; www.berman museum.org), the repository of more than 6,000 objects collected over seventy years by Col. Farley L. Berman and his late wife, Geraldine. Their collection includes priceless works of fine artists such as Remington and Russell, as well as rare, ornate, or unusual items from around the world, such as weapons, a 2,000-year-old Greek helmet, a World War I bunker, and suits of armor.

Retrace US 431/AL 21 past I–20 and continue south on AL 21 to **Talladega,** known worldwide for its fast and furious motor racing.

The **Talladega Superspeedway,** 3366 Speedway Boulevard (256–362–7223; www.talladega.com/superspeedway), draws fans to the heart-pounding excitement of two annual NASCAR Nextel Cup events.

Bus tours of the track are conducted on nonrace days. Other major events at the speedway include the ARCA (Automobile Racing Club of America) Food World 500K, the International Race of Champions, and the Fram Filters 500K NASCAR Busch Race.

More than one hundred racing vehicles and memorabilia from 1902 to the present are exhibited, along with paintings and awards that honor the inductees, at the **International Motorsports Hall of Fame and Museum,** 3198 Speedway Boulevard (256–362–5002; www.motor sportshalloffame.com), across from the speedway. The complex features five other halls of fame: the Alabama Sports Writers Hall of Fame, the ARCA Hall of National Champions, the Western Auto Mechanics Hall of Fame, the Quarter Midgets of America Hall of Fame, and the World Karting Hall of Fame. Enormous showrooms display a galaxy of mint-condition and not-so-mint-condition racing vehicles, in every color of the rainbow, poised as if waiting for the checkered flag. The entire collection is valued at more than $18 million.

Return to town. In downtown Talledega between Talladega City Hall and Short Street and bordered by Spring and Court Streets, the **Talladega-Texaco Walk of Fame and Davey Allison Memorial** honors Alabama notables in racing history. The **Silk Stocking District,** a 113-acre area south of the courthouse square, was the enclave of leading merchants, lawyers, doctors, and local officials around the turn of the twentieth century. The wives of these wealthy citizens were the only ladies in town who could afford to wear silk stockings—hence the name. Get an audiotape and a brochure that describe the seventy-five houses included in *A Tour of Talladega's Silk Stocking District* from the **Greater Talladega Chamber of Commerce,** located in the 1906 Louisville and Nashville Railroad Depot, 210 East Street South (256–362–9075). The station was an active passenger depot until the 1950s and continued to be used as a freight terminal until the 1970s, when it was bought by the city.

Other historic districts you might want to explore include the Talladega College Campus District, the Courthouse Square District, and the Boxwood Historic Complex.

From Talladega take AL 77 north to I–20, and take I–20 west to **Birmingham.** Even though you've packed a plethora of activities into your morning, remember: You gained an hour as soon as you crossed into Alabama and the central time zone. So if you aren't fainting from hunger, save your appetite for a soul food lunch in Birmingham's Civil Rights District before touring the sights.

LUNCH: La Vase, 328 Sixteenth Street North (205–328–9327), serves down-home family cookin' and soul food.

Afternoon

The centerpiece of the **Civil Rights District** is **Kelly Ingram Park,** Sixth Avenue North at Sixteenth Street, dedicated as "a place of revolution and reconciliation." During the civil rights movement, it was the focal point of grassroots resistance rallies. The Freedom Walk through the park features chilling sculptures of snarling dogs and water cannons pummeling demonstrators. In contrast to the violent scenes, however, all paths lead to the center of the park, where a statue of Martin Luther King Jr. and a long black marble pool create a peaceful meditative oasis.

In 1963 the **Sixteenth Street Baptist Church,** 1530 Sixth Avenue North (205–251–9402), tragically burst into international prominence when a bomb killed four little girls attending Sunday school. The fatal explosion became a rallying cry for unity among Blacks and concerned whites around the country, and the church served as a headquarters for mass meetings and demonstrations. A large stained-glass window, a gift from the people of Wales, memorializes the young victims.

Across the street is the **Birmingham Civil Rights Institute,** 520 Sixteenth Street North (205–328–9696; www.bcri.bham.al.us), where you can explore the history of the civil rights movement from post–World War I to the present day. An awe-inspiring journey on the road to equality, the trip begins with a film on Birmingham's history and segregation. A series of galleries include the Barriers Gallery, Confrontation Gallery, Movement Gallery, and Processional Gallery. Inclined walkways depict the uphill struggle for civil rights. Lifelike figures, sound effects, and detailed exhibits depict slices of everyday life as well as pivotal incidents. Dramatic moments are retold on film in four minitheaters. The journey ends with an exhibit gallery that chronicles contemporary human rights violations and triumphs throughout the world.

Housed in the nearby historic Carver Theater for the Performing Arts, the **Alabama Jazz Hall of Fame,** 1631 Fourth Avenue North (205–254–2731; www.jazzhall.com), honors great jazz artists with ties to Alabama, such as Nat King Cole, Duke Ellington, Lionel Hampton, and Erskine Hawkins. Visitors travel from the beginnings of boogie-woogie to the jazz space journeys of Sun Ra and his Intergalactic Space Arkestra. Interactive TV allows visitors to learn about specific performers, instruments, bands, and other facets of jazz.

Birmingham Civil Rights Institute

DINNER: The **Grille at the Tutwiler,** 2021 Park Place North (205–322–2100), features continental cuisine served in an upscale atmosphere.

Evening

Check to see if there are performances at the **Alabama Theatre,** 1817 Third Avenue North (205–252–2262; www.alabamatheatre.com), the largest theater in the state. Built in 1927, it is designed to resemble a Spanish palace with Moorish details such as spiraling terra-cotta columns, a two-story Hall of Mirrors, marble columns, gold-leaf ornamentation, elaborate chandeliers, and stained-glass arches. Lavish lounges are decorated in different styles, such as a Chinese tearoom and an English hunting lodge. The interior is crowned with an elliptical dome. A massive Mighty Wurlitzer pipe organ is the star each year during Horror Week, an October Fright Fest of horror films, when the organist is delivered to the stage in a candelabra-topped coffin. Throughout the year film series and rock concerts are interspersed with live theater performances.

LODGING: The **Tutwiler,** Park Place North (205–322–2021;

http://tutwiler-birmingham.wyndham-hotels.com), is a hotel created from the renovated 1913 Ridgely Apartment Building. Chosen as one of Alabama's three representatives in the National Trust for Historic Preservation's Historic Hotels of America, the hotel features Italianate architectural details, elegant turn-of-the-twentieth-century antiques and reproductions, and an art collection, some of its pieces lent by the Birmingham Museum of Art. Pub for casual dining and cocktails.

Day 2 / Morning

BREAKFAST: At the hotel.

The impressive sculptural setting of massive furnaces, webs of pipes, and tall smokestacks at the **Sloss Furnaces National Historic Landmark,** 203 South Second Street (205–324–1911; www.slossfurnaces.com), is now not only a museum of the industry but also a community center that serves as a venue for festivals and performances. The interpretive center recounts the legend of Birmingham's spectacular ascension to eminence as the South's premier industrial city.

Adventures in learning are on tap at the **McWane Center,** 200 Nineteenth Street (205–714–8300; www.mcwane.org), a downtown science museum in a renovated department store where you can indulge in a hands-on examination of the world around us. Everyone is encouraged to touch and play with the exhibits, which range from watery habitats to space exploits. In addition, the museum features an IMAX theater.

LUNCH: John's, 112 Twenty-first Street North (205–322–6014), a downtown landmark, specializes in seafood served family-style.

Afternoon

Eight decades of aviation history are displayed at the **Southern Museum of Flight and Alabama Aviation Hall of Fame,** 4343 Seventy-third Street North (205–833–8226; www.bham.net/flight/museum/html), just 2 blocks east of the airport. Exhibits include mementos from the World War I encounter between the notorious Red Baron and Canadian Roy Brown, a World War II Link trainer used to train pilots to fly "blind," mementos from the Flying Tigers, fifteen restored aircraft spanning the period from 1912 to 1990, and hundreds of civilian and military models. Airplanes are refurbished or rebuilt in the fully equipped shop on the premises. An imposing McDonnell Douglas F-4 Phantom commands the lawn.

DINNER: Cafe Bemone, at the Redmont, 2101 Fifth Avenue North (205–324–2101), is a Cajun bistro with a sidewalk cafe.

Evening

Check to see what cultural or sports events are on tap. Making up the **Birmingham-Jefferson Convention Complex,** 1 Civic Center Plaza (205–458–8400), are the 3,000-seat Concert Hall, the 1,000-seat theater, and the 19,000-seat Coliseum, home of the Birmingham Bulls of the East Coast Hockey League. It is also used for performances by top-name artists, Southeastern Conference basketball tournaments, and traveling shows such as ice shows and circuses.

LODGING: The Tutwiler.

Day 3 / Morning

BREAKFAST: Niki's West, 233 Finley Avenue West (205–252–5751), serves a buffet and is such a longtime favorite, you may have to wait. Breakfast is served from 6:00 to 10:00 A.M.

Originally built as Birmingham's contribution to the 1904 St. Louis World's Fair, and recently extensively renovated, *Vulcan,* Twentieth Street South and Valley Avenue (205–933–1409; www.vulcanpark.org), the second largest statue in the United States after the Statue of Liberty and the largest cast-iron statue ever made, has stood watch over the city from his own park since 1939. A glass-walled elevator to the top of the statue affords a panorama of the formal gardens and a wide vista of the city.

A living museum encompassing sixty-eight acres, the **Birmingham Botanical Gardens,** 2612 Lane Park Road (205–414–3900 or 205–414–3961; www.bbgardens.org), has thousands of flowers, trees, and shrubs and more than 230 species of native birds. Special collections include roses, wildflowers, camellias, irises, lilies, and vegetables, as well as a fine collection of sculpture and one of the largest glass conservatories in the Southeast.

From the **Temple of Sibyl,** Shades Mountain on US 31 at the entrance to the city of Vestavia Hills, a replica of a Greek temple, you can get tremendous views of Shades Valley and the Samford University campus.

LUNCH: Cafe Bottega, 2240 Highland Avenue (205–933–2001), a casual trattoria, boasts pizza from a wood-burning oven.

Afternoon

One of the finest museums in the South, the **Birmingham Museum of Art,** 2000 Eighth Avenue North (205–254–2565; www.artsbma.org), contains among its 15,000-work permanent collection the Hitt Collection of French eighteenth-century decorative arts; the Kress Collection; Asian art; the most extensive collection of Wedgwood outside of England; art of the Old West, including notable Native American art; 1,200 objects of African art; the Education Gallery, a children's hands-on discovery museum; an impressive collection of Alabama art; and a multilevel, outdoor sculpture garden.

Located amid six acres of well-tended gardens, the 1842 Greek Revival **Arlington Antebellum Home and Garden,** 331 Cotton Avenue (205– 780–5656; www.informationonbirmingham.com/arlington), was built by Judge William S. Mudd, one of the ten founders of Birmingham. It is filled with authentic period furnishings and decorative arts. Closed Monday.

Take I–20 back to Atlanta.

There's More

Birmingham

Horse and greyhound racing. Visitors are eager to get to the starting gate at the Birmingham Race Course, 1000 John Rogers Drive (205–838–7500 or 800–998–UBET; www.birminghamracecourse.com), for live greyhound and simulcast thoroughbred and greyhound racing.

Outdoor activities. Oak Mountain State Park, just off I–65 about 15 miles south of Birmingham (205–620–2520), is the state's largest, at 10,000 acres. Its valleys and ridges offer improved and primitive campsites, cottages, golf, hiking, tennis, a bicycle motorcross racetrack, three lakes, and a nature center.

Admire an unusual view of Birmingham's skyline from the Ruffner Mountain Nature Center, 1214 South Eighty-first Street (205–833–8264; www.bham.net/ruffner). The urban forest features native plants, animals, unusual geologic formations, and free-flowing springs. Seven miles of trails crisscross the mountain. Exhibits explain the mountain's natural and mining history.

Shopping. Five Points South is a historic neighborhood around Twentieth

Street South that contains a rich collection of architecture of various periods, from Spanish Baroque to art deco, as well as restaurants, bars, shops, fountains, the exquisite Pickwick Hotel, and a legitimate theater.

Special Events

Anniston

February. Black Heritage Festival explores the lifestyles and rich heritage of African Americans through song, dance, and storytelling. (256) 237–6766.

Birmingham

April. The internationally recognized Birmingham International Festival is the city's oldest and largest cultural festival. It is consistently listed in the Top Twenty Events in the Southeast. A different county is highlighted each year. (205) 252–7652.

Other Recommended Restaurants and Lodgings

Anniston

The Victoria, 1600 Quintard Avenue (256–236–0503 or 800–260–8781), an elegant Queen Anne Victorian mansion built in 1888, offers bed-and-breakfast accommodations and has an elegant, full-service restaurant and lounge. Perched on a wooded hillside—the highest spot in town—the house features a three-story turret, brilliant stained-glass windows, a conservatory, and colonnaded verandas. Inside features include high ceilings and original hardware, mantels, flooring, and woodwork. The first floor has four individual dining rooms, a piano lounge, and a glass-enclosed veranda. Upstairs are three opulent, antiques-filled guest rooms. A three-story addition to the mansion wraps around the courtyard and pool. Each of the units is furnished with antiques and reproductions. The historic Guest House has been converted to a one-bedroom suite featuring a whirlpool bath, a wet bar, and doors that open to a private patio and pool.

Birmingham

Cobb Lane Restaurant, 1 Cobb Lane (205–933–0462), has been famous since 1948 for its Chocolate Roulage and its She-Crab Soup.

Higlands Bar and Grill, 2011 Eleventh Avenue South (205–939–1400), which offers fine dining at is best, has been among the city's premier restaurants for years.

The Pickwick, 1023 Twentieth Street South (205–933–9555 or 800–255–7304; www.pickwickhotel.com), is an intimate art deco gem in the trendy Five Points South district.

Crowne Plaza Redmont Birmingham Downtown, 2101 Fifth Avenue North (205–324–2101), is a historic downtown hotel.

For More Information

Calhoun County Convention and Visitors Bureau, 1330 Quintard Avenue, Anniston, AL 36202. (256) 237–3536 or (800) 489–1087.

Greater Birmingham Convention and Visitors Bureau, 2200 Ninth Avenue North, Birmingham, AL 35203. (205) 458–8000 or (800) 458–8085; www.bcvb.org.

Greater Talladega Area Chamber of Commerce, 210 East Street South, Talladega, AL 35160. (256) 362–9075.

Nashville, Tennessee

Country Music Meets Ancient Greece / 3 Nights

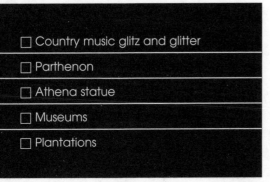

- ☐ Country music glitz and glitter
- ☐ Parthenon
- ☐ Athena statue
- ☐ Museums
- ☐ Plantations

MYTH: You have to be a country-music fan to appreciate Nashville.
FACT: The infectious, exuberant mood of the city captivates everyone. While a good 50 percent of the points of interest revolve around the musical entertainment world, not all of the music is country. Jazz, in particular, plays a large role in the Music City's identity. In addition, Nashville displays other faces. Impressive museums and elegant antebellum plantations vie with parks, gardens, and a huge lake for the visitor's attention.

We readily admit that country music isn't our favorite, so we felt some trepidation about our first visit. Our fears were groundless. Not only did we thoroughly enjoy the varied entertainment options, but we were entranced by the historical and cultural attractions found there. We've returned again and again and still haven't seen all there is.

Nashville has so much to offer that we've created a four-day escape with two days devoted to the country-music sights and two days spent on the city's alter ego and still haven't included everything. You could easily break this itinerary into two or more shorter trips.

Day 1 / Afternoon

Leave Atlanta via I–75 to Chattanooga, then take I–24 west to Nashville.

The Music City's foremost attraction is **Gaylord Opryland Resort,** 2800 Opryland Drive (615–871–6800 or 888–777–OPRY; www.opry.com or www.gaylordhotels.com). This massive complex includes the Grand Ole

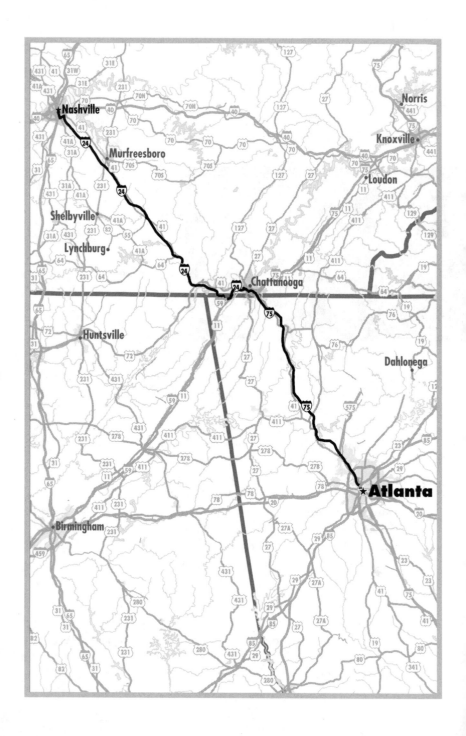

Opry, the Nashville Network, the Roy Acuff Museum, the *General Jackson* showboat, and one of America's largest hotels.

A good place to start is the **Grand Ole Opry Museum,** 2802 Opryland Drive (615–889–3060), which pays tribute to Hall of Fame members, current stars, and to the Opry itself with audio and video electronic effects and interactive devices. Among the stars honored are Patsy Cline, Marty Robbins, Tex Ritter, Roy Acuff, Minnie Pearl, Little Jimmy Dickens, George Jones, Jim Reeves, Garth Brooks, and Reba McEntire.

DINNER AND LODGING: Normally, we don't recommend gargantuan properties, but the massive **Gaylord Opryland Hotel,** 2800 Opryland Drive (615–889–1000), is a destination in itself. One of the nation's largest hotels, the eight-building complex covers several acres and contains almost 2,900 sleeping rooms, three gigantic atriums, lounges, shops, swimming pools, important art collections, including murals depicting Nashville in the 1880s and 1890s, and more. Restaurants include the informal Cascades in the water garden, Old Hickory Restaurant for super continental cuisine, simple fare and country charm at Rachel's Kitchen, Beauregard's, Ristorante Volare for Italian cuisine, and casual fare at the Springhouse Golf Club. A huge addition is under construction.

The exotic plantings, waterfalls, and pools in the atriums would rival those of any botanical garden. The Conservatory area covers two acres, and the two-acre Cascades features two waterfalls splashing off a fabricated mountain into a 12,500-square-foot lake. You can actually ride a flat-bottom boat down the river through the four-acre Delta, which also boasts an 85-foot-tall fountain.

The hotel is adjacent to all the other Opryland attractions. You can walk, drive your own car, or take a hotel shuttle bus within the complex.

Evening

The **Grand Ole Opry,** 2804 Opryland Drive (877–777–6779; www.opry.com), once housed in downtown's historic Ryman Auditorium, now occupies a modern structure at the park. Performances include a matinee and two evening shows. A wide variety of long-established and beginning entertainers keeps audiences spellbound. Some of the performances are live radio broadcasts, and some are taped for TV. You'll be in for a treat of foot-stomping, hand-clapping fun. Shows are held on Tuesday and Friday, and there are two performances on Saturday.

Day 2 / Morning

BREAKFAST: At the hotel.

Start your day in town, at the **Country Music Hall of Fame,** 222 Fifth Avenue South (615–416–2096 or 800–852–6437; www.country musichalloffame.com). The museum provides a delightful stroll through the development of Nashville as Music City USA. Pictures and memorabilia trace the history of the Grand Ole Opry as well as country music itself. We particularly enjoyed the flamboyant sequined costumes and musical instruments performers have donated, as well as Elvis's solid gold Cadillac. Closed Tuesday January through March as well as Thanksgiving, Christmas, and New Year's Day.

Visit the place where it all began: **Ryman Auditorium,** 116 Fifth Avenue North (615–889–3600 for reservations; www.ryman.com), the most famous home of the Grand Ole Opry. Completely restored, it is open daily for tours. The auditorium was a religious tabernacle before it served as the home of the Grand Ole Opry between 1943 and 1974. Hence the shrine is nicknamed the Mother Church of Country Music.

Ever have a hankering to make your own recording or music video? Well, you can do that at the **Music Machine Recording,** 185 Second Avenue North (615–742–0888), in one of several sound booths or a videotape studio. Background music and song sheets are provided. You supply the voice and the talent. Get copies made for your family and friends.

LUNCH: Return to Opryland for a luncheon cruise aboard the *General Jackson,* 2802 Opryland Drive (615–889–6611), a modern, diesel-driven paddle wheeler. Of course, you may buy a ticket for the cruise only. If you get hungry after all, a sweetshop and a snack bar will solve your problem. Continuous entertainment and views of the river and the passing land-scape vie for the passenger's attention. An authentic showboat review with singing, dancing, jokes, and skits accompanies the buffet. Some participants are recruited from the audience to join the fun. Jugglers, Dixieland bands, folksingers, and comedians perform throughout the boat.

Afternoon

You could stay on the Opryland property or the immediate vicinity for the entire weekend and never run out of things to see. Directly across the street from the Grand Ole Opry Museum is the **Nashville Car**

Museum, 2611 McGavock Pike (615–885–7400), which exhibits antique cars, street rods, and cars of the stars.

Music Valley Wax Museum, 2515 McGavock Pike (615–883–3612), features likenesses of fifty stars and the Sidewalk of Stars, where more than 200 stars have placed their footprints, handprints, and signatures.

The **Willie Nelson and Friends Showcase Museum,** 2613A McGavock Pike (615–885–1515), presents tributes to Patsy Cline, Audie Murphy, Roy Orbison, Elvis, and many Grand Ole Opry stars. Nelson's memorabilia include gold and platinum albums, guitars, and other personal items.

DINNER: Jack's Barbecue, 334 West Trinity Lane (615–228–9888), specializes in Texas barbecue.

Evening

You never know what might be going on at the **Wildhorse Saloon,** 120 Second Avenue (615–902–8200; www.wildhorsesaloon.com). First of all, the decor is a showstopper with whimsical horses and cows "saddled up" to the bars; then there might be line-dance lessons, a live performance, or a special being taped. And, oh yeah—lunch and dinner are served daily. Open until 3:00 A.M.

Across the street from the Opryland complex, you can find more musical entertainment at the **Nashville Palace,** 2400 Music Valley Drive (615–885–1540), where you'll see Nashville headliners. The **Ernest Tubb Midnight Jamboree,** 2414 Music Valley Drive (615–889–2474), features top Opry stars and new talent each week.

LODGING: Opryland Hotel.

Day 3 / Morning

BREAKFAST: Nashville Nightlife Breakfast and Dinner Theater, Music Valley Drive (615–885–5201 or 800–308–5779; www.nashville nightlife.com), offers a full country breakfast buffet accompanied by a live variety show featuring Grand Ole Opry stars Del Reeves and Jeannie Seely.

Head for Riverfront Park for a tongue-in-cheek introduction to some of Tennessee's most famous citizens at the **Tennessee Fox Trot Carousel.** It doesn't matter whether you're a tiny tot or a senior citizen, everyone will love this fantasy ride/work of art—whether you're there to look or to ride. Seeing's believing. Instead of horses or circus animals, Nashville native and internationally renowned artist Red Grooms carved and then brightly painted thirty-six caricatures of Nashvillians and Tennesseans, such as Andrew Jackson and Davy Crockett. The carousel is named for the ballroom dance that was popular in the 1940s and for the slow mixed gait of a horse as it trots with its forelegs and paces with its hind legs.

While you're at Riverfront Park, visit **Fort Nashborough,** 170 First Avenue North (615–862–8400), on the riverfront, which celebrates the founding of the city on Christmas Eve 1779. Costumed guides present an interpretive program about the fort—a replica of the original. One of the first settlers was Rachel Donelson, who became the wife of Andrew Jackson. Before you leave Fort Nashborough, get a brochure for **City Walk,** a walking tour of downtown beginning at Fort Nashborough and ending at **Hatch Show Print.** Explore **"the District,"** actually several historic districts, including Second Avenue, Broadway, and Printers Alley.

LUNCH: B. B. King's Blues Club and Restaurant, 152 Second Avenue North (615–256–2727; www.bbkingbluesclub.com), open for lunch and dinner, has live entertainment nightly.

Afternoon

Next head for the **Bicentennial Mall State Park,** 600 James Robertson Parkway (615–741–5280 or 888–TNPARKS). The nineteen-acre outdoor history museum north of the State Capitol gives you a tour of Tennessee's history by way of a 200-foot granite map of the state with thirty-one fountains representing the state's major rivers. Marble columns divide the timeline into decades. Other points of interest in the park include the Wall of History, Court of Three Stars, Walk of Counties, World War II memorial, Centennial memorial, McNairy Springs Fountain, an amphitheater, and a gift shop. The many fountains entice young and old alike to get wet on a hot day.

Completed in 1859, the Greek Revival–style **Tennessee State Capitol,** Charlotte Avenue between Sixth and Seventh, dominates downtown, standing 170 feet above the highest hill. Many areas have been restored to their nineteenth-century appearance. Tennessee's three native sons who became President of the United States are commemorated on the grounds. President and Mrs. James K. Polk are buried there, and there are statues of Andrew Jackson and Andrew Johnson. Guided tours are given Monday through Friday on the hour (except noon).

Enjoy the exhibits of the **Tennessee State Museum,** 505 Deaderick Street (615–741–2692; www.tnmuseum.org), which chronicle the history of Tennessee beginning 12,000 years ago and continuing through the early 1900s. Gigantic mastodon bones greet you. On the upper level, which you see first, you begin with prehistoric times and progress through frontier days. Downstairs you'll continue through the turn of the twentieth century. Closed Monday, Easter, Thanksgiving, Christmas, and New Year's Day.

Nashville is a graceful city, boasting seventy-two public parks, the largest of which is **Centennial Park,** 2600 West End Avenue at Natchez Trace (615–862–8431; www.parthenon.org), crowned by a complete **replica of the Greek Parthenon**—the only full-scale replica in existence. Originally built as a temporary structure to house an art exhibit during the 1897 Centennial Exposition, it has, due to popular demand, been restored several times to become a permanent edifice.

Downstairs are galleries for permanent and traveling art shows. Upstairs two halls re-create the Naos and the Treasury of the original Parthenon. On display are copies of the Elgin Casts—copies made from the original pediment fragments of the Parthenon—from which sculptors re-created the friezes for the outside of the building. Two sets of gargantuan bronze doors, seven and a half tons each, are the largest sets of matching bronze doors in existence.

The most outstanding exhibit, however, is a colossal, 42-foot statue of the goddess Athena. The original statue, created by Phidias in the fifth century B.C., was formed of gold and ivory plates covering a wooden frame. This copy, by Nashville sculptor Alan LeQuire, is the largest indoor sculpture in the Western world. She holds a human-size figure of Nike, the winged goddess of victory, in her right hand, while her left hand supports a shield and spear. A serpent rests at her feet. Open Tuesday through Saturday September through May and Tuesday through Sunday June through August.

Cheekwood-Tennessee Botanical Gardens and Museum of Art, 1200 Forrest Park Drive (615–356–8000; www.cheekwood.org), was once an elegant private estate. The majestic, three-story, Georgian-style mansion built in 1932 and surrounded by fifty-five acres of gardens is now a museum of art that contains a permanent collection of nineteenth- and twentieth-century American art, silver, sculpture, photography, snuff bottles, and a world-class Worcester porcelain collection. Additionally, the new

The Parthenon, Nashville

Frist Learning Center, which occupies the garage and stables, has interactive exhibits and contemporary art galleries. The grounds include a water garden, color garden, seasonal gardens, a serene Japanese garden, herb garden, dogwood garden, wildflower garden, boxwood gardens, orchid and camellia greenhouses, and the Woodland Sculpture Trail. Cheekwood contains the Botanical Garden Library in Botanic Hall, Pineapple Room restaurant, and a gift shop. The grounds are also the site of many summer concerts. A shuttle bus makes a continuous loop around the property. Closed Monday except Memorial Day and Labor Day.

DINNER: A hot spot to see and be seen as well as to enjoy a delicious meal and an extensive wine list is the **Sunset Grill,** 2001-A Belcourt Avenue (615–386–3663), in the trendy Hillsboro Village neighborhood. Music-business people and sports personalities often hang out there. For a more casual meal in good weather, eat on the patio; in winter it's enclosed. The main dining room is more formal. Try the Voodoo Pasta, a melange of chicken, shrimp, andouille sausage, marinara sauce, and Black Magic seasonings over Cajun fettuccine. Other menu choices range from lamb to duck. But save room for the to-die-for desserts.

LODGING: Gaylord Opryland Hotel.

Day 4 / Morning

BREAKFAST: At the hotel.

Belle Meade Plantation, 5025 Harding Pike (615–356–0501; www.bellemeadeplantation.com), is known as the Queen of Tennessee Plantations, although it began life in the late 1700s as a simple log cabin, which remains on the property. In 1816 Belle Meade acquired a reputation as a stud farm, and this aspect made the property prosperous—so affluent, in fact, that in 1853 a magnificent Greek Revival mansion was built. One of the showplaces of the South, it hosted all of Nashville's society as well as several U.S. presidents. Belle Meade—a National Historic Landmark—has been restored to the extravagant elegance of the nineteenth century. Spared during the Civil War, although the front is riddled with bullet holes, the estate went on to even greater prominence in the thoroughbred field. It was once the home of Iroquois, until 1954 the only American-bred winner of the English Derby. The exquisitely restored mansion is elegantly furnished with nineteenth-century antiques and art. The colossal 1890 Carriage House and Stable houses one of the largest antique carriage collections in the South.

Other surviving outbuildings include a 1790 log cabin—one of the oldest log structures in Tennessee—the garden house, smokehouse, and mausoleum. Costumed guides lead tours that offer a look at the lifestyles of the rich and famous of early Nashville. A visitor center, located in a building that blends perfectly with the stables, houses an impressive gift shop and Martha's Cafe at the Plantation (615–353–2828), where lunch is served. Closed Thanksgiving, Christmas, and New Year's Day.

One of Nashville's hidden treasures is **Belmont Mansion,** 1900 Belmont Boulevard (615–460–5459; www.belmontmansion.com). Tucked away on the grounds of Belmont University, the home was built in the 1850s by Adelicia Acklen. One of the wealthiest women in America, she was what we would now call a Steel Magnolia. Although constructed as a "summer home," the immense mansion is in the style of an opulent Italian villa set in elaborate gardens. In fact, it is the only Italian villa–style mansion ever built in Tennessee. Eventually the house contained thirty-six rooms and 11,000 square feet of living space—not counting the 8,400 square feet of service area. Fifteen of the rooms are open to tour. They are furnished in period antiques, similar to what might have been in the mansion; however, an outstanding collection of marble statues, gaslight chandeliers, and ornate gilded mirrors are original.

The estate included a water tower to provide irrigation to the gardens, as well as to supply water to the fountains, a greenhouse, and a conservatory. Today the water tower remains as a Carillon Bell Tower. Most of the formal garden survives, accented by statuary and several ornate ironwork gazebos—composing the largest collection of nineteenth-century garden ornaments in the country. Other features of the estate included an art gallery, bowling alley, bear house, and zoo. Because no public park existed in Nashville at the time, Mrs. Acklen opened the estate grounds for the enjoyment of the populace. Closed major holidays.

Nashville's oldest plantation home open to the public, **Travellers Rest Historic House,** 636 Farrell Parkway (615–832–2962; www.travellersrest plantation.com), was a haven for weary travelers from the time it was built in 1799 by Judge John Overton, whose descendants continued to live in the house until 1948. Confederate general John Bell Hood used the house as his headquarters just before the 1864 Battle of Nashville. Set well back from the road, the house is hidden behind ancient magnolias. The Federal-style house began humbly as a two-story, four-room house, but additions throughout the 1800s increased it to the size you see today. Restored to reflect the era of the original owner and furnished with simple early-nineteenth-century Tennessee furniture, Travellers Rest gives you a glimpse into how wealthy Nashvillians lived in the early 1800s. You'll also want to stroll through the boxwood garden and visit the outbuildings and gift shop. Closed Thanksgiving, Christmas, and New Year's Day.

LUNCH: South Street Original Crab Shack and Authentic Dive Bar, 907 Twentieth Avenue South (615–320–5555), specializes in low-country seafood recipes and ribs.

Afternoon

Visit the **Hermitage/Andrew Jackson Home,** 4580 Rachel's Lane (615–889–2941; www.thehermitage.com), home of Andrew Jackson, and see the mansion much as he left it in 1845. On the grounds are several log cabins where the family lived while the mansion was being built and later while it was being restored and enlarged, as well as a smokehouse and springhouse. Beside the mansion is Rachel's formal garden, first laid out in 1819. Both husband and wife are buried here under a Greek Revival columned dome. The tour begins with a movie in the modern visitor center, which also houses a museum that contains some of the Jacksons' clothing, personal possessions, and carriages. Next an audiocassette presentation guides you through the house. The furnishings are original purchases made about 1835. The interior reflects elegant simplicity—no fancy moldings or ornate draperies. Closed Thanksgiving, Christmas, and the third week in January.

Also included on the tour are Tulip Grove, the nearby home of Jackson's nephew, and the Old Hermitage Presbyterian Church.

Return via I–24 and I–75 to Atlanta.

There's More

Horseback riding. Ramblin' Breeze Ranch, 3665 Knight Road, Whites Creek (615–876–1029), features 120 acres of scenic trails.

Other sightseeing attractions. Some other things to see and do around Nashville include the Adventure Science Museum (615–862–5160); Farris Agricultural Museum (615–837–5197); Hartzler–Towner Multicultural Museum at Scarrett-Bennett Center (615–340–7481); Hatch Show Print (615–256–2805); Nashville Zoo (615–833–1534); Historic RCA's Studio B (615–256–5167), where Elvis recorded; the Upper Room Chapel and Museum (615–340–7207); and Carl Van Vechton Gallery, Fisk University (615–329–8720). Several tour companies offer tours past the homes of the music stars.

Special Events

May. The Iroquois Steeplechase, Nashville. (615) 322–4814.

June. International Country Music Fan Fair, Nashville. (615) 889–7503.

November–December. Belle Meade Plantation Victorian Christmas, Nashville. (615) 356–0501.

Other Recommended Restaurants and Lodgings

The Arcade, located between Fourth and Fifth and Church and Union in Nashville, houses a collection of small, fun places to eat. You'll find something for every taste.

Belle Meade Brasserie, 106 Harding Place (615–356–5450), bills itself as a "New American Bistro." Closed Sunday.

Chaffin's Barn Dinner Theater, 8204 TN 100 (615–646–9977 or 800–282–BARN), offers an all-you-can-eat Southern Buffet and a performance of *Broadway Comes to Nashville*. Thursday through Saturday.

Historic Nashville hotels include the Hermitage Hotel, 231 Sixth Avenue North (615–244–3121), and the Union Station Hotel, 1001 Broadway (615–726–1001), originally Nashville's railway station, now restored and converted into a hotel.

The Nashville area contains a dozen bed-and-breakfasts. Go to www.bbonline.com/tn/nashville.html or contact the Natchez Trace Bed and Breakfast Reservation Service (800–377–2770).

For More Information

Music Valley Information and Ticket Center, 2416 Music Valley Drive, Nashville, TN 37214. (615) 871–4005.

Nashville Convention and Visitors Bureau, 211 Commerce Street, Nashville, TN 37201. (615) 259–4700 or (800) 657–6910; www.nashville cvb.com.

WESTBOUND ESCAPE SIX

Lynchburg/Murfreesboro/Franklin, Tennessee

*War, Whiskey, Walking Horses,
and What Nots / 2 Nights*

☐ Civil War history

☐ Sippin' whiskey

☐ Tennessee Walking Horses

☐ Presidential home

☐ Plantations

☐ Antiques

Middle Tennessee was one of the richest areas of the state when cotton was king; however, the Civil War touched almost every site in this area, although many historic structures survived. An area of gently rolling hills and wide open spaces, middle Tennessee today has only one large city: Nashville (see the "Country Music Meets Ancient Greece" escape, p. 229). The remainder of the region is characterized by sleepy small towns that retain their nineteenth-century charm. Visitors come, not only to visit antebellum and Civil War sites, but to tour the whiskey distilleries, to see Tennessee Walking Horse competitions, to shop for antiques and crafts, and to enjoy the out-of-doors.

Many of the attractions in this itinerary are found on the **Tennessee Antebellum Trail**—a loop through middle Tennessee that includes fifty-five sites. It might make sense to purchase an Antebellum Trail ticket, which includes admission to nine historic sites, rather than purchasing tickets to each site separately. For information call (800) 381–1865. Three of the attractions on the Antebellum Trail (Belmont Mansion, Belle Meade Plantation, and Travellers Rest) are described in the Nashville chapter, which can be combined with this itinerary for a longer getaway.

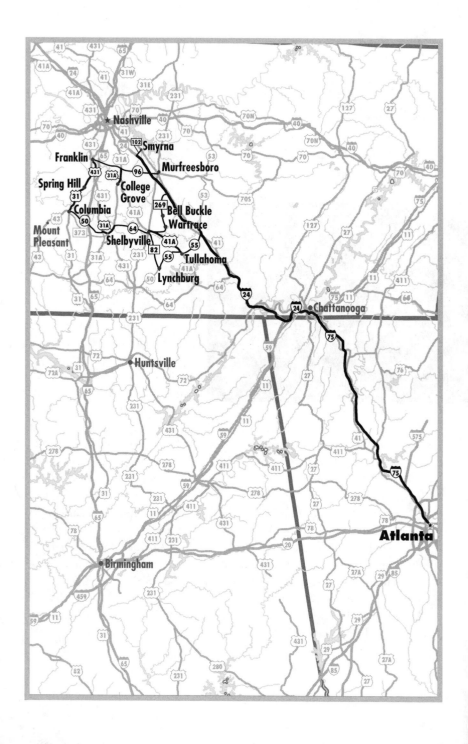

Day 1 / Morning

Take I–75 north from Atlanta to Chattanooga, then go west on I–24 to Manchester. Go southwest on TN 55 to **Lynchburg** to visit **Jack Daniel's Old Time Distillery,** 280 Lynchburg Highway (931–759–4221; www.jackdaniels.com), the oldest registered distillery in the country. Observe every step of sour-mash whiskey making, including the charcoal mellowing process (which is what makes it sippin' whiskey instead of bourbon) that has been used for more than 125 years. Highlights include Daniel's original office; a life-size statue of Mr. Jack; and Cave Spring, which provides the iron-free, pure limestone water. The gift shop, the only liquor store operating in a dry county, offers Jack Daniel's gifts and, thanks to a recent referendum, for the first time since 1866, is able to sell its products to visitors, but only in commemorative decanters. Closed Thanksgiving, Christmas Eve and Day, New Year's Eve and Day. White Rabbit Bottle Shop closed Sunday.

LUNCH: Miss Mary Bobo's Boarding House, 295 Main Street (931–759–7394), located in a stately 1866 mansion, serves southern cuisine family-style in a traditional boardinghouse atmosphere. The menu varies daily. Some specialty recipes use Jack Daniel's whiskey. Reservations required.

Afternoon

Retrace TN 55 to TN 82 and turn north to **Shelbyville.** Although Shelbyville was the site of a Civil War encampment and has a perfectly proportioned, often-copied town square, it is really famous for its Tennessee Walking Horses. You'll drive by farm after farm that breed and train the high-steppers.

To learn more about this American-bred horse, stop at the **Tennessee Walking Horse Museum and the Celebration,** Calsonic Arena, 721 Whitthome Street (931–684–5915; www.twhnc.com). The small museum showcases the history of the Tennessee Walking Horse with artifacts and a movie. View the wall of grand champions, beginning with the very first—Strolling Jim, in 1939. The World Grand Championships—known as the Celebration—where the high-stepping horses compete for more than a half million dollars in prizes, is a ten-day event in late August, which also includes trade fairs, dog shows, a petting zoo, good food, and elaborately decorated barns. Make lodging reservations way in advance. The arena also hosts thirty-five other horse shows annually.

Take TN 64 to Wartrace, then TN 269 north to **Bell Buckle.** Tourists come to Bell Buckle, which is a mecca for artisans, craftspeople, antiques, good food, and fun. As small as the town is, it boasts a half dozen B&Bs. The downtown crossroads center, TN 82, has numerous crafts and antiques stores.

DINNER: Bell Buckle Cafe and Music Parlor (913–389–9693; www.bellbucklecafe.com) serves prizewinning hickory-smoked barbecue and down-home specials every day. Live entertainment Thursday through Sunday, including a live radio show Saturday at 1:00 P.M.

Continue north on TN 269, then take US 231 north to **Murfreesboro,** a lovely turn-of-the-twentieth-century town. In 1834 it was determined that the exact geographic center of Tennessee is located on Old Lascassas Pike, 1 mile from the Middle Tennessee State University campus in Murfreesboro.

LODGING: Byrn-Roberts Inn, 346 East Main Street (615–867–0308 or 888–877–4919; www.byrn-roberts-inn.com), is a redbrick, 12,000-square-foot, Queen Anne Victorian mansion, which was built in 1903 by Charles and Allie Byrn. Current owners Julie and David Becker have added six bathrooms, some with whirlpool tubs. Faux finishes, beautiful antiques and reproductions, and accessories make for a sophisticated look.

Day 2 / Morning

BREAKFAST: Breakfast is served in the dining room of the Byrn-Roberts Inn. Expect specialties such as buttermilk pancakes with strawberry sauce and whipped cream or stuffed French toast. Julie will, however, cater to any dietary restrictions with prior notice.

Get an idea what life in the early nineteenth century must have been like by visiting the **Cannonburgh Pioneer Village,** 312 South Front Street (615–890–0355), a living-history museum that depicts early Southern experiences. Tour a log cabin, blacksmith shop, general store, gristmill, one-room schoolhouse, church, and museum. The grounds are open year-round, but the buildings are only open April through December 1. Closed Monday.

Murfreesboro was named for Col. Hardy Murfree, who once owned the land on which **Oaklands Historic House Museum,** 900 North Maney Avenue (615–893–0022; www.oaklandmuseum.org), now stands. One of the area's most elegant homes, the antebellum plantation house was built in four stages between 1815 and 1860. During the Civil War it was alternately occupied by Confederate and Union troops. It was also the site of a successful raid by Confederate general Nathan Bedford Forrest, after which he received the surrender of the city there, and a visit by Jefferson Davis in 1862. Furnished with original and period pieces, the house has been restored to its 1860 appearance.

LUNCH: The **Bunganut Pig Olde English Pub and Eatery,** 1662 West Northfield Boulevard (615–893–7860; www.bunganutpig.com), serves English-style fare in a rustic atmosphere. Live music nightly. Closed Sunday.

Afternoon

The 570-acre **Stones River National Battlefield,** 3501 Old Nashville Highway (615–893–9501; www.nps.gov/stri), was the site of a Civil War battle that took place between December 31, 1862, and January 2, 1863. Although both sides claimed victory, when the Confederate troops withdrew, the Union army controlled middle Tennessee. Stop at the visitor center to see an audiovisual presentation about the battle and pick up a copy of the self-guided tour map or a recorded guide. Markers along the route identify the stages of the battle. Exhibits along the 0.5-mile trail through Fortress Rosecrans describe the role of the largest earthen fort constructed during the Civil War. During the summer, living-history artillery and infantry demonstrations are scheduled. The site includes a national cemetery and the oldest intact Civil War memorial, which marks "Hell's Half-Acre," where Union soldiers held their ground against Confederate attacks.

From Murfreesboro take I–24 north to TN 102 to **Smyrna,** home of Sam Davis, who was known as the Boy Hero of the Confederacy. He enlisted in the Confederate army at nineteen and served as a courier. He was captured, tried as a spy, and sentenced to be hanged. The trial officer, however, offered him his freedom if he would reveal the source of his information. Davis replied, "If I had a thousand lives, I would give them all gladly rather than betray a friend." He was hanged in Pulaski, Tennessee, on November 27, 1863. The farmhouse where Davis grew up is now the **Sam Davis Home Historic Site,** 1399 Sam Davis Road (615–459–2341; www.samdavishome.org). The Greek Revival home was built around 1820 and enlarged around 1850. The tour includes the main house, original kitchen, smokehouse, and overseer's office. Special events are held at the site year-round.

Retrace TN 102, go west on TN 96 to Triune and then go south on US 31A to **College Grove,** where you will spend the night.

DINNER AND LODGING: The focal point of the **Peacock Hill Country Inn,** 6994 Giles Hill Road (615–368–7727 or 800–327–6663; www.bbonline.com/tn/peacock), which sits on a 700-acre working cattle ranch, is a one-story 1850s farmhouse to which owners Anita and Walter Ogilvie have added several spacious guest rooms. High ceilings; exposed, hand-hewn red-cedar beams; brick fireplaces; clapboard walls, a checker-board floor; and a brick-floored sun porch all combine to create an upscale country home. Guest rooms vary in style and theme from country to Victorian to spring garden to Americana, but they all sport the modern amenities today's sophisticated travelers expect. The Grainery and an old smokehouse boast suites. Located just a short distance down the road, McCall House is another antebellum farmhouse, which has been completely restored and renovated to house three luxurious suites. If it's not too late when you arrive, sit on the porch or in the trellised garden or stroll the grounds. When you make your reservations (be sure to ask for detailed directions when you call), make arrangements to have dinner there as well. With advance notice and $20 per person, the Ogilvies will prepare a romantic, several-course dinner for you.

Day 3 / Morning

BREAKFAST: At Peacock Hill Country Inn.

Retrace US 31A to Triune and go west on TN 96 to **Franklin,** best known for the fierce Battle of Franklin, which occurred on November 30, 1864. Today Franklin is one of the prettiest towns in Tennessee, with a beautifully restored nineteenth-century town square and main street. The entire 15-block historic downtown, which features specialty shops, restaurants, and antiques stores in historic buildings, is listed on the National Register of Historic Places.

Begin by stopping at Franklin's visitor information center, which is housed in the **McPhail Office,** 209 East Main Street (615–591–8514). Built in 1817, it was Dr. Daniel McPhail's office and was used as a headquarters by Union generals the morning of the Battle of Franklin.

The most famous house in Franklin is the 1830s **Carter House,** 1140 Columbia Avenue (615–791–1861), which was caught in the center of the battle. The 1830 redbrick neoclassical house was commandeered by Union forces as a command post while the Carter family and their friends and neighbors hid in the cellar. Captain Tod Carter, one of three Carter sons who served the Confederacy, was wounded just 175 yards from the house. After the battle, Carter was carried inside and ministered to by family, but he died forty-eight hours later. All the surviving buildings are bullet riddled, but the farm office and smokehouse are believed to be the most battle-damaged buildings still standing from the Civil War. The fascinating tour includes the visitor center/museum, video presentation, and the house and grounds.

Just outside town is the historic **Carnton Plantation,** 1345 Carnton Lane (615–794–0903; www.carnton.org), an antebellum neoclassical plantation house built in 1826 by former Nashville mayor Randal McGavock. The home was a social and political center where President and Mrs. Andrew Jackson were frequent visitors and Sam Houston and James K. Polk visited as well. The house served as a hospital during the Battle of Franklin. After the war John McGavock donated two acres of land adjacent to the family cemetery for the purpose of the reinternment of 1,481 Confederate soldiers killed at Franklin. The shady plot is the largest privately owned Confederate cemetery and is maintained by the United Daughters of the Confederacy.

LUNCH: Sandy's Downtown Grill, 108 Fourth Avenue South (615–794–3639), is an upscale eatery where lunch choices range from sandwiches to salmon, steak, or liver.

Afternoon

Continue your tour by taking US 431 south to US 31 south to **Spring Hill.** The area's claim to fame is that it is the home of the **Saturn Corporation automobile plant.** A restored horse barn houses the visitor center. Call (800) 326–3321 in advance to make arrangements for a plant tour.

Spring Hill may be better known for several incidents in Civil War history and for its lovely collection of antebellum and late-nineteenth-century homes. **Rippavilla Plantation,** 5700 Main Street (615–486–9037; www.rippavilla.org), has been graciously restored to its 1860 appearance and is furnished with appropriate pieces, many of them family heirlooms. Family photos, jewelry, dolls, furniture, and other memorabilia tell the stories of the families that made their mark on this home—not only the wealthy owners, but their slaves as well. Several rooms upstairs compose a museum about the plantation and the Civil War Armies of the

Tennessee. Rippavilla also serves as the headquarters of the Tennessee Antebellum Trail.

Go south on US 31 to **Columbia.** Columbia's reputation as a mule-trading center is still celebrated today with an annual Mule Day festival. Columbia's Main Street, historic downtown square, and historic district permit visitors to take a walk back in time. Stop by the **Middle Tennessee Convention and Visitors Bureau,** 8 Public Square (931–381–7176 or 888–852–1860), to pick up a brochure for a self-guided tour past fourteen historic sites in addition to Rippavilla. Although these are private homes and not open to the public, you'll enjoy seeing them from the exterior. Ferguson Hall, the home of Martin Cheairs—brother of Rippavilla's Nathaniel Cheairs—is identical to it. The McKissack House combines Georgian, Federal, and Classic Revival elements. Oaklawn, which looks quite similar to Rippavilla and Ferguson Hall, was the headquarters of Gen. John Bell Hood.

Even more important than mules and historic buildings is the fact that the eleventh president of the United States, James Polk, began his legal and political career from the 1816 home he shared with his parents, now the **James K. Polk Ancestral Home,** 301 West Seventh Street (931–388–2354; www.jameskpolk.com). This house, Polk's only surviving residence besides the White House, is furnished with many of his personal belongings, including portraits, china, silver, and furniture used by the Polks in the White House, as well as Mexican War memorabilia and one of Mrs. Polk's ball gowns.

The **Athenaeum Rectory,** 808 Athenaeum Street (931–381–4822; www.athenaeumrectory.com), is all that remains of the Columbia Athenaeum, an unusual girls' boarding school from the nineteenth century. The building, with Moorish Gothic architecture, was built in 1835. The first occupant was the Reverend Franklin Gillette Smith, who came to Columbia to be the rector of the Columbia Female Institute. In 1852 Smith built his own school, the Columbia Athenaeum, which operated until 1904, teaching physics, calculus, chemistry, and biology in addition to literature, French, history, archery, croquet, riding, and dancing. The restored house contains many original features, among which are the colorful flashed glass around the front door, the fountain on the front lawn, and the wood-carpeting floors.

The Athenaeum Rectory is open for tours Tuesday through Saturday, except that it is closed the last week in December through January. The

Athenaeum is also the headquarters for the Majestic Middle Tennessee Christmas Tour the first full weekend in December.

To return to Atlanta from Columbia, go southeast on TN 50, then take US 431 south to Lewisburg. Go east on TN 64 to Shelbyville, then south on US 41A to Tullahoma. Go northeast on TN 55 to I–24, then retrace it to Chattanooga and take I–75 south to Atlanta.

There's More

Natchez Trace. Running through this area of middle Tennessee is the scenic Natchez Trace (800–305–7417; www.nps.gov/natr), which stretches 450 miles from Nashville to Natchez, Mississippi. In the days of the flatboat, traders would float their merchandise downriver to New Orleans and then walk back. With the invention of the steamboat, the return walk became unnecessary, but the route remains. Today it is operated by the National Park Service, and the northern terminus is west of Franklin. There are several waterfalls and scenic overlooks along the route.

Outdoor activities. See wetlands and abundant waterfowl at the Tennessee Wildlife Observation–Monsanto Ponds, Monsanto Road/TN 50 West, Columbia (931–381–7176). Recreation World, 7115 South Springs Avenue, Franklin (615–771–7780), is a family fun center with go-karts, miniature golf, batting cages, bumper cars, and an in-line skating rink. Percy Priest Lake, near Smyrna and Murfreesboro, attracts thousands of visitors each year.

Special Events

Bell Buckle

June. The highlights of the RC and Moon Pie Festival are Tennessee's largest Moon Pie and the Moon Pie Toss, but the festival also features a 10-mile run, fun run, country fair, carnival, weight lifting and other contests, beauty pageant, parade, and more. (931) 389–9663.

Maury County

For the following Maury County Pilgrimages call the Middle Tennessee Visitors Bureau at (931) 388–2155 or (888) 852–1860.

May. Spring Pilgrimage, usually the last weekend in April, features plantation and antebellum city homes and gardens.

December. Plantation Christmas, usually held the first weekend in December, features private plantation homes in period holiday finery.

Other Recommended Restaurants and Lodgings

Franklin

Namaste Acres Farm Bed and Breakfast, 5436 Leipers Creek Road (615–791–0333), offers theme rooms on a working horse farm.

Lynchburg

Lynchburg Bed and Breakfast, 107 Mechanic Street (931–759–7158), built in 1877, is within walking distance of downtown, the Jack Daniel's Old Time Distillery, and Miss Mary Bobo's Boarding House restaurant.

Mulberry

Dream Fields Country Bed and Breakfast Inn, 9 Backstreet (931–438–8875), is a wonderful old farmhouse in a peaceful rural setting outside Lynchburg.

Murfreesboro

Carriage Lane Inn, 411 North Maney Avenue (615–890–3630 or 800–357–2827; www.carriagelaneinn.com), is a quaint turn-of-the-twentieth-century cottage with cozy but elegant guest rooms.

For More Information

Bell Buckle Chamber of Commerce, P.O. Box 222, Bell Buckle, TN 30720. (931) 389–9633; www.bellbucklechamber.com.

Lynchburg Chamber of Commerce, P.O. Box 421, Lynchburg, TN 37352. (931) 759–4111.

Middle Tennessee Convention and Visitors Bureau, P.O. Box 1076, Columbia, TN 38402-1076. (931) 381–7176, (931) 388–2155, or (888) 852–1860.

Rutherford County Chamber of Commerce, 501 Memorial Boulevard, Murfreesboro, TN 37129. (615) 893–6565 or (800) 716–7560; www.rutherfordchamber.org.

Shelbyville/Bedford County Chamber of Commerce, 100 North Cannon Boulevard, Shelbyville, TN 37160. (931) 684–3482 or (888) 662–2525.

Tennessee Antebellum Trail, 1345 Carnton Lane, Franklin, TN 37064. (800) 381–1865.

Williamson County/Franklin Chamber of Commerce, P.O. Box 156, Franklin, TN 37065-0156. (615) 794–1225 or (800) 356–3445; www.williamson-franklinchamber.com.

FARTHER AFIELD
ESCAPES

Charleston, South Carolina

Changing but Changeless Charleston / 2 Nights

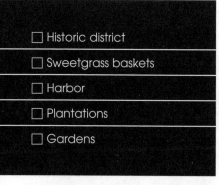

☐ Historic district

☐ Sweetgrass baskets

☐ Harbor

☐ Plantations

☐ Gardens

In September 1989 Hurricane Hugo pounded historic Charleston with a fury rarely experienced in the twentieth century. Although damage was extensive, most of the proud old buildings withstood the onslaught. Massive repairs were begun immediately, and the city scarcely missed a beat in its tourism industry. In fact, Charleston has endured many wars, earthquakes, fires, and massive storms, but the exquisite city always bounces back—better than ever.

Barely changed since it was founded in 1670, the port city of Charleston has done an outstanding job of preserving its past. The genteel town boasts 73 prerevolutionary structures, 136 from the late eighteenth century, and more than 600 others built prior to 1840.

There's a delightful story told about a wealthy matron that exemplifies why Charleston is such a magnet for tourists. When asked why she never used her money to travel, she answered, "But my dear, why should I travel when I'm already here?" Charleston has much to offer the visitor depending on the amount of time that can be spent there. If you have only a weekend, you will probably want to stay in the historic district, where delightful hotels and bed-and-breakfasts put you within easy walking distance of sights, restaurants, and entertainment. If you have longer, you'll want to explore the nearby plantations and beaches, the forts, naval ships, or the new aquarium.

Day 1 / Morning/Afternoon

Take I–20 east to Columbia, South Carolina, then I–26 east to **Charleston.** If it's still light when you arrive, spend a little while at **Waterfront Park,** located just off East Bay Street on Concord, at the intersection of Vendue Range. The area, once a seedy neighborhood of

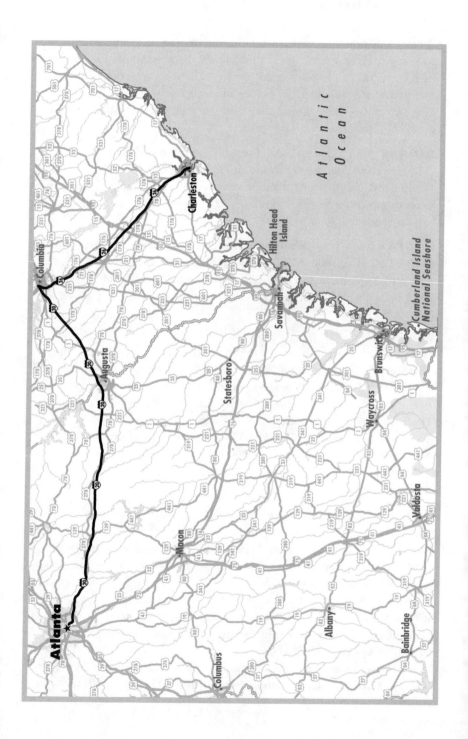

derelict warehouses, is now a magnificent new park on the harbor. Blocks of grassy areas and sidewalks are punctuated by numerous park benches, trees, fountains, and flower-filled planters. The long wharf that leads out into the harbor provides old-fashioned swings in covered arbors. If you arrive after dark, have dinner, then visit the park. It's particularly striking at night—lit up like a birthday cake.

DINNER: 82 Queen, 82 Queen Street (843–723–7591; www .82queen.com), located in a National Historic Landmark building with a lovely courtyard, is famed for its Charleston She-Crab Soup, other low-country specialties, raw bar, wine bar, and lounge. Lunch and dinner reservations suggested.

LODGING: The **Planters Inn,** 112 North Market Street (843–722–2345 or 800–845–7082; www.plantersinn.com), dating from the 1840s, is ideally located in the heart of the historic district and next to the outdoor market. Afternoon refreshments; turndown service. Expensive.

Evening

Check ahead to see if there are performances at the historic **Dock Street Theater,** 135 Church Street (843–720–3968), where the Charleston Stage Company (133 Church Street; 843–577–5967; www.charlestonstage.com) performs. Also check the **North Charleston Coliseum and Performing Arts Center,** 5001 Coliseum Drive (843–529–5050; www.coliseumpac.com); **Gaillard Municipal Auditorium,** 77 Calhoun Street (843–577–7400); or any of the other entertainment venues.

Day 2 / Morning

BREAKFAST: Silver-service continental breakfast in your room at the inn.

Begin at the **Charleston Area Convention and Visitors Bureau and Visitor Reception and Transportation Center,** located in a renovated freight depot, 375 Meeting Street (843–853–8000 or 800–774–0006; www.charlestoncvb.com), for an excellent film, *Forever Charleston;* it explains the city's history and orients you to what you'll be seeing. Staff members have information on hundreds of shops, restaurants, accommodations, tours, and services.

Another outstanding film is *Charleston, Secrets of a Southern City,* shown at the **Historic Charleston Foundation Museum Shop and**

Bookstore, 108 Meeting Street (843–724–8484; www.historic charleston.org). Much of the narration in the prizewinning presentation is by descendants of Civil War–era planters and slaves. Many quality Charleston reproductions and gifts are for sale.

After a filmed orientation we recommend taking one of Charleston's excellent variety of guided tours. Using any one of the more than fifty sightseeing companies, you can tour by van, trolley, or horse-drawn carriage. Walking tours offer an intimate glimpse into many prominent buildings and hidden courtyard gardens. We recommend **Charleston Strolls**'s Walk with History, P.O. Box 1651, Charleston 29402 (843–766–2080; www.charlestonstrolls.com), and **Charleston Tea Party Walking Tour,** 198 King Street (843–722–1779). Another option is to tour on your own by using the DASH city transit system (843–724–7420), which allows you to park at the visitor center and buy an all-day pass to ride the trolley. You can tour the harbor by boat and, in fact, can reach Fort Sumter only by boat. Although there are several sightseeing and dinner-cruise boats that tour the harbor, our favorite is the schooner *PRIDE* (843–559–9686), onboard which one of our daughters had a small romantic wedding.

While you're touring, look for Charleston's unique architectural features. One example is the seemingly ordinary front door. When you look at a historic house head-on, you'll see an unadorned housefront broken by simple windows and a doorway to one side. You assume that the door opens directly into the house. When viewing the house from the side, however, you'll see that the door actually opens onto the first-floor porch or piazza that runs front-to-back along the side of the house. Each house usually has a piazza for each floor, so what looks like a plain, unassuming house from the front is magnificent and stately when viewed from the side. Also look for circles, crosses, or stars on the facades of houses. Not just decorative, these are actually the end plates of metal earthquake rods that run completely through the building.

LUNCH: Magnolia's—Uptown/Down South, 185 East Bay Street (843–577–7771), serves low-country cuisine, or **Blossom's,** next door (843–722–9200), operated by the same company. (For more information about either, log on to www.magnolias-blossom-cypress.com.)

Afternoon

Spend the afternoon exploring some of Charleston's elegant house museums. The early 1800s **Edmondston-Alston House,** 21 East Battery overlooking the harbor (843–722–7171 or 843–782–3608; www.middleton place.org/eahouse), is a three-story Greek Revival house still lived in by an Alston descendant. Memorabilia on display include documents, portraits, engravings, an outstanding library, furniture, silver, china, and other family heirlooms. Notice the unusual ball-and-rope woodwork.

It was at the Edmondston-Alston House that we were introduced to the traditional Charleston Joggling Board. This long, supple, bench-height board is supported by two upright end pieces. If you sit on one end of the board and jiggle up and down, you'll gradually drift to the middle. As a courting device, a young woman sat at one end, her beau at the other. Before you knew it, they were cuddling in the middle. It was said that no house with a joggling board had an unmarried daughter. You'll see the contraptions on many piazzas in Charleston, and you can purchase one at the **Old Charleston Joggling Board Company,** 652 King Street (843–723–4331).

The 1808 **Nathaniel Russell House,** 51 Meeting Street (843–724–8481), an outstanding example of Adam-style architecture, features an astonishing flying staircase spiraling from floor to floor and a tier of elliptical rooms. Period antiques and works of art evoke the gracious lifestyle of the city's merchant elite.

Another noteworthy house is the 1817 **Aiken-Rhett House,** 48 Elizabeth Street (843–723–1159), residence of early South Carolina governor William Aiken Jr. It was used as the military headquarters of Confederate general Pierre G. T. Beauregard during the 1864 federal bombardment of the city. The beautiful entrance hall features a double staircase with decorative cast-iron banisters. Most of the wallpaper, paint colors, and furnishings are original. Outdoors, wander through the kitchen, slave quarters, stable, and other outbuildings. Combination tickets are available for the Nathaniel Russell and Aiken-Rhett Houses.

The 1803 **Joseph Manigault House** (pronounced MAN-igo), 350 Meeting Street (843–723–2926), is considered to be one of America's most beautiful examples of Adam-style architecture. The stunning front hall boasts a beautiful curving staircase. A fascinating feature is the secret stairway between the second and third floors. The gardens are adorned by a gate temple.

The 1772 **Heyward-Washington House,** 87 Church Street (843–722–2996), was the home of a signer of the Declaration of Independence. George Washington stayed here during his 1791 southern tour. Examine the original, restored kitchen buildings; the carriage house;

and the magnificent garden. Combination tickets are available for the Joseph Manigault and Heyward-Washington Houses as well as the Charleston Museum (see below).

DINNER: Jackie's Lafayette, 402 Church Street (843–546–5033), serves Cajun/New Orleans cuisine in a bistro atmosphere for lunch and dinner.

LODGING: The Planters Inn.

Evening

Check the entertainment schedule—see "Day 1" and also check with the **Charleston Ballet Theater,** 477 King Street (843–723–7334); the **Charleston Symphony Orchestra,** 77 Calhoun Street (843–723–7528); or the **Footlight Players Theater,** 20 Queen Street (843–722–7521; www.footlightplayers.net).

Day 3 / Morning

BREAKFAST: Another elegant breakfast at the inn.

No trip to Charleston would be complete without wandering through the diverse merchandise in the **Old City Market,** South Market and North Market between Meeting and East Bay Streets (800–868–8118), which stretches out for several blocks behind Market Hall. The one-story, covered, open-air sheds have operated for more than one hundred years. If you want the quintessential gift from Charleston, get a sweetgrass basket. These intricately woven containers preserve an art form brought to America by African slaves.

Visit the **Confederate Museum** housed in Market Hall, 188 Meeting Street (843–723–1541), and built in 1841. Since 1898 the Daughters of the Confederacy have run a museum that features flags, uniforms, swords, and other Confederate memorabilia.

LUNCH: Gaulart and Maliclet French Cafe, 98 Broad Street (843–577–9797), is a casual cafe with counter service; it specializes in French sandwiches, soups, quiches, and omelets.

Afternoon

The **Charleston Museum,** 360 Meeting Street (843–722–2996; www.charlestonmuseum.org), established in 1773, is America's first and oldest museum. The city's natural history is reflected through exhibits of animal and plant life. Other collections focus on Native Americans, settlers, and African Americans, through clothing, furniture, ceramics, glass-ware, pewter, silver, games, vehicles, photographs, and other memorabilia. The Discover Me Room is full of things for children to touch, see, and do. Outside is a full-scale replica of the Confederate submarine *Hunley.* The only thing we don't understand is why a city that lives off its history would ever have approved the nondescript modern building that now houses the museum collection. Combination tickets are available for the museum as well as the Joseph Manigault and Heyward-Washington Houses.

Much more attractive, architecturally, is the **Gibbes Museum of Art,** 135 Meeting Street (843–722–2706; www.gibbesmuseum.org). In addition to changing exhibits, the museum's permanent collection includes views of Charleston, portraits of notable South Carolinians, paintings, prints, and drawings from the eighteenth century to the present.

One of the most priceless exhibits is a collection of miniature rooms. The Elizabeth Wallace Rooms demonstrate the remarkable world of microscopic craftsmanship. The late Elizabeth Wallace of Hilton Head, the donor, was a collector and maker of miniatures. The rooms, which follow the reduction rate of 1 inch to 1 foot, are exact replicas of eight historic American- and two French-style rooms. All the furniture and accessories are rendered proportionally. Also housed in the museum is an outstanding collection of diminutive portraits.

The **Old Exchange Building/Provost Dungeon,** 122 East Bay Street (843–727–2165 or 888–763–0448; www.oldexchange.com), built by the British in 1771, has served as a customs house, city hall, military garrison, and post office. The Constitution was ratified on the front steps. Even pirates were imprisoned on the site.

Return to Atlanta via the same route by which you came.

There's More

Aquarium. South Carolina's watery habitats and their residents are explored at the South Carolina Aquarium, 100 Aquarium Wharf (843–577–FISH or 843–720–1990; www.scaquarium.org). You'll see fish and aquatic animals representing the freshwater streams of the mountain forest and piedmont, as well as the swamps, marshes, and bays of the coastal plain and coast, and the deep waters of the ocean. (Closed Thanksgiving and Christmas Day as well as a half day Christmas Eve.) On the same site you can watch phenomenal movies at the Charleston IMAX Theatre. The aquarium is adjacent to the Fort Sumter Visitor Education Center, which is also the launching point for Fort Sumter Tours. Fountain Walk is filled with restaurants and shops.

Beaches. In warm weather, spend some time at the beach. Public beaches are found at Sullivan's Island, Isle of Palms, Folly Beach, and Beachwalker Park on the west end of Kiawah Island.

Forts. Historic forts include Fort Moultrie, West Middle Street on Sullivan's Island (843–883–3123); Fort Sumter, on a fabricated island in the harbor that can be visited by boat; and the ruins of Colonial Dorchester State Historic Site, on State 642 in nearby Summerville (843–873–1740). Before visiting Fort Sumter, stop in at the new Fort Sumter Visitor Education Center at Liberty Square, 340 Concord Street (843–883–3123 or 843–883–3124; www.nps.gov/fosu), to see exhibits pertaining to national and South Carolina events that led to the Civil War. There is no admission charge, and the center is open daily except Christmas and New Year's Day. To get to Fort Sumter, you need to go via Fort Sumter Tours, which leaves from the Education Center (843–881–7337 or 800–789–3678; www.nps.gov/fosu) three times a day. The aquarium, IMAX theatre, and the shops and restaurants of Fountain Walk are adjacent to the center.

Naval history. Millions of people watched on TV as the Confederate submarine *Hunley* was brought up from its watery grave where it had rested for more than 140 years. The remains of the sailors trapped there all that time were recently laid to rest. On weekends visitors can watch as the submarine is studied and restored at the Warren Lasch Conservation Center, 1250 Supply Street (843–744–2186 or 877–4HUNLEY). Tickets can be purchased by contacting www.etix.com.

Naval buffs can cross the river to Mount Pleasant to the Patriots Point Naval and Maritime Museum, 40 Patriots Point Road (843–884–2727; www.patriotspoint.org), to tour the World War II aircraft carrier U.S.S. *Yorktown*, the submarine *Clagamore*, the destroyer *Laffey*, and the Coast Guard cutter *Ingham*, as well as twenty-five military aircraft, a Vietnam Base Camp, the Congressional Medal of Honor Museum, and the new Cold War Submarine Memorial. Closed Christmas Day.

Plantations/gardens. It takes all day to do justice to Middleton Place National Historic Landmark, 4300 Ashley River Road (843–556–6020 or 800–782–3608; www.middletonplace.org); Magnolia Plantation and Gardens, 3550 Ashley River Road (843–571–1266 or 800–367–3517;

www.magnoliaplantation.com); Audubon Swamp Gardens at Magnolia Plantation (843–571–1266); Drayton Hall Museum, 3380 Ashley River Road (843–766–0188); and Cypress Gardens, 3030 Cypress Gardens Road, Monck's Corner (843–553–0515; www.cypressgardens.org), on the Ashley River. To the east of the Cooper River is Boone Hall Plantation, 1235 Long Point Road, Mount Pleasant (843–884–4371; www.boone hallplantation.com), which could take up another half day.

One of the things we find so delightful about the collections of floriculture at Middleton and Magnolia is their endless variety. The flora isn't glorious only in the spring. Throughout the winter the gardens are splashed with brightly colored winter berries, and camellias abound from fall through spring. At Middleton you can walk down long allées with camellia bushes towering overhead, meeting above the path. Masses of red, pink, white, and variegated blossoms brush your hair and create luxuriant carpets underfoot. In January or early February, you're likely to find azaleas, jonquils, and forsythia already starting to bloom. Magnolia Gardens's peacocks strut across the lawns or perch on the roofs, displaying their finery.

Special Events

February. Southeastern Wildlife Exposition, held Presidents' Day weekend, features conservation exhibits, but the highlight is the display of works by the world's finest wildlife artists. (843) 723–1748; www.sewe.com.

March. Historic Charleston Foundation's Festival of Houses and Gardens is an opportunity to tour private homes and gardens. Plantation picnics at Drayton Hall; historic church tours. (843) 722–3405; www.historic charleston.org.

May–June. The world-famous Spoleto Festival USA entertainment extravaganza features more than one hundred events in opera, chamber music, symphonic concerts, jazz, theater, dance, and art. (843) 579–3100; www.spoletousa.org.

September. Preservation Society of Charleston's Annual Candlelight Tours of Houses and Gardens provides nighttime tours of private homes. Saturday-evening visits include champagne and music at one of the houses. (843) 722–4630; www.preservationsociety.org.

September–October. The Charleston Garden Festival is a much-anticipated event where you can tour many of the city's exquisite private gardens. (843) 722–4630.

December. Christmas in Charleston includes tours of traditionally decorated homes, churches, and public buildings; parades, including the Parade of Boats in the Harbor; and other activities. Many hotels offer special packages. (800) 774–0006; www.charlestoncvb.com.

Other Recommended Restaurants and Lodgings

Restaurants

Anson's, 12 Anson Street (843–577–0551; www.ansonrestaurant.com), features fine low-country dining in a formal atmosphere.

Charleston Chops, 188 East Bay Street (843–937–9300), offers friendly fine dining in an upscale steak house with live piano music. The restaurant is known for the best in certified Angus beef as well as extraordinary seafood and wild-game entrees.

Slightly North of Broad, 192 East Bay Street (843–723–3424; www.slightlynorthofbroad.com), nicknamed SNOB, is billed as a "maverick southern kitchen."

Lodgings

Most visitors to historic Charleston want to stay in a period hostelry. The city brims with such hotels, inns, and bed-and-breakfast establishments. All are elegantly restored properties overflowing with Southern hospitality. Consider some of those listed below, or contact Historic Charleston Bed and Breakfasts, 57 Broad Street (843–722–6606 or 800–743–3583; www.historiccharlestonbedandbreakfasts.com). For beach rentals call Great Beach Vacations (843–768–2300 or 800–686–2120).

Ansonborough Inn, 21 Hasell Street (843–723–1655 or 800–522–2073; www.ansonboroughinn.com), is an all-suite inn located in a former stationer's warehouse convenient to the Market.

For modern accommodations with an old-world attitude, stay at the Charleston Place Hotel, an Orient Express Hotel, 205 Meeting Street (843–722–4900 or 800–611–5545; www.charlestonplace.com). The exterior blends well with the old buildings around it, while the interior replicates the high-ceilinged elegance of older lodgings.

1843 Battery Carriage House Inn, 20 South Battery (843–727–3100 or 800–775–5575; www.batterycarriagehouse.com), offers bed-and-breakfast accommodations at one of the most beautiful mansions on White Point Gardens overlooking the Battery. Guest rooms are in the carriage house in the garden courtyard. Some rooms feature a steam bath or whirlpool bath.

The Francis Marion Hotel, 387 King Street (843–722–0600 or 877–756–2121; www.francismarioncharleston.com), built in 1924, is an upscale hotel with a fine-dining restaurant that features regional Charleston and low-country specialties, as well as two cocktail lounges, a fitness room, and Spa Adagio.

The John Rutledge House Inn, 116 Broad Street (843–723–7999 or 800–476–9741), is an elegant town house noted for its decorative ironwork piazzas.

The Lodge Alley Inn, 195 East Bay Street (843–722–1611 or 800–456–0009), housed in a set of converted warehouses surrounding a courtyard, features rooms and suites furnished in authentic Charleston fashion. Most have a fireplace and minibar; some have kitchens. On-site restaurant and lounge.

The Meeting Street Inn, 173 Meeting Street (843–723–1882 or 800–842–8022), features traditional decor with four-poster beds. Private courtyard with whirlpool. Afternoon wine service.

The Mills House Hotel, 115 Meeting Street (843–577–2400 or 800–874–9600; www.millshouse.com), built in the 1850s, features marble floors, priceless antiques, and impeccable service.

Two Meeting Street, 2 Meeting Street (843–723–7322), is a bed-and-breakfast located in one of the most beautiful houses on the Battery.

The Vendue Inn, 19 Vendue Range (843–577–7970 or 800–845–7900; www.vendueinn.com), overlooking Waterfront Park, features elegantly appointed rooms; suites with fireplace and Jacuzzi; afternoon wine and cheese with chamber music. Fine dining in the Library.

For More Information

Charleston Area Convention and Visitors Bureau, P.O. Box 975, Charleston, SC 29402. (800) 774–0006; www.charlestoncvb.com.

Golden Isles, Georgia

Islas de Oro / *3 Nights*

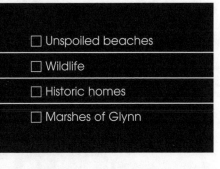

☐ Unspoiled beaches

☐ Wildlife

☐ Historic homes

☐ Marshes of Glynn

The Spanish, who explored them looking for precious metals, called them *Islas de Oro*. Although the explorers didn't find the gold they were searching for, they did find treasures—the coastal barrier islands. We call them Georgia's Golden Isles. If the English hadn't defeated the Spanish in the 1742 Battle of Bloody Marsh on St. Simons Island, we might be speaking Spanish in Georgia today.

The real value of the Golden Isles is their inherent beauty. You don't have to travel to distant, foreign islands to find golden—and often untouched—beaches, luxuriant tropical vegetation, and exotic wildlife. History, recreation, and nature are all available off Georgia's coast.

From north to south Georgia's coastal islands are Tybee, Wilmington, Skidaway, Wassaw, Ossabaw, St. Catherine's, Blackbeard, Sapelo, Wolf, Little St. Simons, St. Simons, Sea, Jekyll, and Cumberland Islands. Tybee Island is described in the "Queen City of the South" escape, page 172. Wassaw, Ossabaw, St. Catherine's, Blackbeard, Sapelo, and Wolf Islands are wildlife refuges; Little St. Simons is a private resort island; and Cumberland Island is a National Seashore—all have limited access. (Although for tourism purposes the state and local organizations classify only St. Simons Island, Sea Island, Little St. Simons Island, and Jekyll Island as the Golden Isles, we think they're all golden treasures, and we discuss several others on this itinerary.)

It would take weeks to explore all these islands. This escape is a mere sampling of St. Simons, Sea, and Jekyll Islands, which are the most accessible and populated. They are often crowded in summer, so why not choose to visit during another time of year? In the fall the air and water temperatures remain ideal. Even winter is popular for everything but

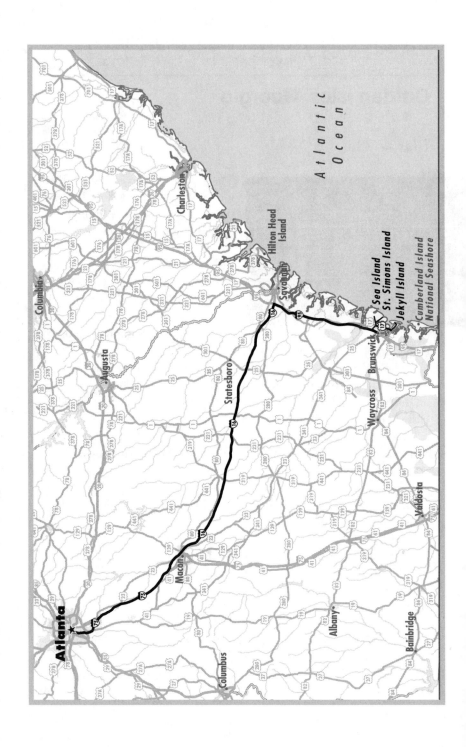

swimming. In the spring the air is delightful, although the water is chilly. At any time of year, reservations are strongly recommended.

Day 1 / Morning/Afternoon

It's a five-and-a-half- to six-hour drive from Atlanta to the Golden Isles, so you'll probably want to drive straight through (pack a lunch) instead of sightseeing along the way. Take I–75 to Macon, then I–16 to Savannah. Turn south on I–95 and go to Brunswick, where you will take the Torras Causeway to St. Simons Island. Between the mainland and the island are endless expanses of waving seagrass—the **Marshes of Glynn,** made famous by the poems of Georgia's beloved nineteenth-century poet Sidney Lanier. In addition to their beauty, the marshes are of critical importance to coastal ecology. They are a buffer between the ocean and the mainland, preventing erosion and providing a rich spawning ground for shrimp and other marine life. Drive across St. Simons Island, which you'll explore tomorrow, and onto **Sea Island.**

DINNER AND LODGING: Treat yourself to a magnificent experience at the world-famous resort the **Cloister,** Sea Island Drive (912–638–3611 or 800–SEA–ISLAND). Since 1928 the resort has entertained presidents, potentates, honeymooners, and families one generation after another. Currently the historic building is being replaced by a new one, but there are numerous other accommodations scattered throughout the property. Even if all meals weren't included in the nightly room rate at the Cloister, you'd want to dine here anyway. You could choose between the resort's Beach Club, Sea Island Club, the Lodge, or St. Simons Island Club, then dance the night away most evenings to a live orchestra.

Evening

Theater is an integral part of island life. Check ahead to see if there are performances by the **Island Players at the Casino Theater,** Neptune Park (912–638–3031), or pursue entertainment options at the hotel.

Day 2 / Morning

BREAKFAST: At the hotel.

The Cloister boasts a complete health spa, manicured golf courses, beach club, shooting school, tennis club, riding stables, fishing, sailing, and special weekends devoted to bridge, cooking, wine, dancing, and other pursuits. Spend the morning at the spa and enjoying the other facilities.

LUNCH: At the hotel.

Afternoon

Explore **St. Simons Island** on your own, or ask at the hotel about guided tours, which are offered by **Island Tours,** 101 Marina Drive (912–638–6882 or 800–250–1764); **Misty Oaks Carriage Company,** 122 Palmetto Street (912–638–6181); or **St. Simons Trolley,** 649 Dellwood Avenue (912–638–8954). Most developed of all the barrier islands, St. Simons offers a look at the past, as well as diverse modern leisure activities. The island was inhabited by Native Americans 4,000 years ago. About 400 years ago Spanish monks came from St. Augustine. Later the English worked their way down the eastern coast from Savannah. Gen. James Oglethorpe built two forts, making St. Simons Island the southernmost English settlement in the New World.

Long a vacation destination, St. Simons Island was popular with mainlanders from the 1880s, when visitors came from the mainland by train and ferry and were transported to and from the village by mule-drawn rail trolleys. Unfortunately, the rambling Victorian hotels of that day are long gone.

Visit **Fort Frederica National Monument,** 6500 Frederica Road (912–638–3639; www.nps.gov/fofr), where you can explore the remains of the 1736 fort, considered to have been the largest and most costly British fortification in North America, as well as the excavated foundations of the town that surrounded it. Both offer glimpses of life in early Georgia. The tabby-powder magazine is particularly interesting. Tabby, a building material peculiar to the Georgia coast, is made from oyster shells, lime, and sand. The visitor center at the fort features a film, a museum, interpretive programs, living history, guided tours, and field exhibitions. Closed Christmas.

The Wesley brothers, founders of Methodism, were among the first settlers of St. Simons Island. **Christ Church,** 6329 Frederica Road (912–638–8683), built in 1820 on a site where they preached, was destroyed during the Civil War. The present church replaced it in 1886. Its superb stained-glass windows display scenes from the island's history. Several ghosts are said to haunt the graveyard.

At the southern tip of the island near the old village, city pier, and Neptune Park is the **St. Simons Island Lighthouse and Museum of**

Coastal History, 101 Twelfth Street (912–638–4666; www.saintsimons lighthouse.org). The original lighthouse was built in 1810 but was destroyed by fleeing Confederate troops at the end of the Civil War. The present light was built in 1867. Still operating although now fully automated, it is one of the oldest continuously functioning lighthouses in the country. Visitors can climb the 129 steps to the top for a splendid panorama. The adjacent Victorian keeper's cottage houses the museum. Also on the property are an 1890 brick oil house and a Victorian gazebo. Closed Thanksgiving, Christmas Eve and Day, and New Year's Day.

A museum and former slave cabins are open to the public at **Epworth-by-the-Sea,** 100 Arthur J. Moore Drive (912–638–8688; www.epworthbythesea.org), a Methodist retreat on what was Hamilton Plantation. The museum is closed Sunday and Monday.

DINNER: For casual dining indoors or out and a view of the sea, **Mullet Bay,** 512 Ocean Boulevard (912–638–0703), offers seafood, sandwiches, po' boys, burgers, and more.

Return to the mainland and take US 17 south. Cross the Sidney Lanier Bridge, then the Jekyll Island Causeway. Stop at the Jekyll Island Welcome Center, 901 Jekyll Causeway (912–635–3636 or 877–453–5955).

LODGING: The imposing, restored **Jekyll Island Club,** 371 Riverview Drive (912–635–2600 or 800–535–9547; www.jekyllclub.com), built at the turn of the twentieth century, is a resort hotel that features four eateries, ranging from the formal Grand Dining Room to the Poolside Bar. The club's guest rooms and suites are custom decorated in a style befitting the elegance expected by the original millionaire owners. Mahogany beds, armoires, and other furniture are enhanced by rich fabrics and plush carpeting. Many rooms feature fireplaces and/or Jacuzzis. Complimentary transportation is provided to the beach and around the island.

Day 3 / Morning

BREAKFAST: At the hotel.

Although Jekyll Island has 10 miles of beaches, four golf courses (including the state's largest), and Summer Waves (an eleven-acre water park), the island is most famous for the **Jekyll Island Club Historic Landmark District.**

From 1886 to 1942 the island was privately owned by one hundred millionaires—including Marshall Field, a Goodyear, Rockefeller, Morgan, Pulitzer, Astor, Gould, and Vanderbilt—for use as a winter hunting retreat. Unlike their summer enclave in Newport, Rhode Island, Jekyll Island was completely closed to the public and provided a secluded haven from the demands of their business and social lives. Nonetheless, a majestic, rambling Victorian clubhouse was built for communal dining and social and sporting activities. Many families built their own "cottages." We'd consider these structures—which were as large as 8,000 square feet—mansions, but many had no kitchens, because everyone ate at the club. Built between 1886 and 1928, the mansions range in style from informal Shingle to formal Italian Renaissance Revival.

The first golf course was laid out in 1898. A wharf was built to handle the residents' yachts. Soon there followed a swimming pool and an indoor tennis center, as well as facilities for bocce ball, croquet, and other recreational activities.

Despite Jekyll Island's isolation, these industrial titans weren't able to stay away from business altogether. The Federal Reserve Act of 1914 was drafted here, and the first transcontinental telephone call was placed from Jekyll Island in 1915.

Unfortunately, World War II, the advent of modern transportation, and the fickleness of the rich and famous when it came to "hot" vacation destinations temporarily spelled the doom of Jekyll Island as a holiday paradise. In 1947 Jekyll Island was bought by the state. One of the most important benefits of state ownership is that building is severely restricted and the island has retained its charm. The prime result, however, has been the massive restoration of the Jekyll Island Club Historic Landmark District, also known as the Millionaires District. The project has become the largest restoration undertaking in the Southeast—240 acres and twenty-five buildings. As each house is restored, it is furnished with period antiques and art and opened to the public.

Begin at the **Jekyll Island History Center,** Stable Road (912–635–4036 or 877–453–5955), located in the old stables, where you can purchase tickets for a tram tour of the district. There are two tours; the shorter one does not include admission to the "cottages." The longer one includes admission to two houses. One of the stops is at **Faith Chapel,** Old Plantation Road (912–635–4036). Built in 1904 of Gothic design, it boasts stained-glass windows by Louis Comfort Tiffany and D. Maitland Armstrong.

Art and traveling exhibitions are on display at **Mistletoe Cottage** and

Goodyear Cottage, which also has a shop that offers fine art and hand-crafted gift items. **DuBignon Cottage** boasts elaborate Victorian interiors. **Indian Mound Cottage** interprets a 1917 lifestyle. A shop in the museum Orientation Center features books and a variety of items that bear the Jekyll Island Club emblem.

An alternative tour is offered by **Victoria's Carriages.** Departing from the History Center, you tour the historic district Monday through Saturday (912–635–9500).

LUNCH: Latitude 31, 1 Pier Road (912–635–3800), specializes in—you guessed it—seafood.

Afternoon

Spend the afternoon on the 10-mile beach, browse through quaint shops, or participate in one of the many sports options. Sixty-three holes of golf are available at the **Jekyll Island Golf Club,** 322 Captain Wylly Road (912–635–2368 or 800–453–5955). Great Dunes is Georgia's oldest course. Joggers and bikers enjoy 20 miles of paths that crisscross the island. From the wharf you can go on fishing trips, dolphin watches, and sunset cruises.

Some special shops in the historic district include the **Cottage on Jekyll,** 32 Pier Road (912–635–2643), for crafts and collectibles; **Nature's Cottage,** 21 Pier Road (912–635–3933), for gifts, books, and art celebrating nature; the **Commissary,** 24 Pier Road (912–635–2878), for specialty food items, gourmet coffees and teas, and fresh-baked goodies; and **Santa's Christmas Shoppe,** 17 Pier Road (912–635–3804), actually a shop for all seasons.

DINNER: The **Grand Dining Room at the Jekyll Island Club** (912–635–2600, ext. 1002 or 800–535–9547) serves continental cuisine. Live entertainment. Reservations recommended.

LODGING: The Jekyll Island Club Hotel.

Day 4 / Morning

BREAKFAST: At the hotel.

Spend the morning on the beach; then retrace I–95, I–16, and I–75 to Atlanta.

There's More

Bicycle rentals. Barry's Beach Service, 420 Arnold Road, St. Simons Island (912–638–8053), and Ocean Motion Surf Shop, 1300 Ocean Boulevard, St. Simons Island (912–638–5225).

Horseback riding. Jekyll Island Experience (888–945–7992) and Victoria's Carriages and Trail Rides, 100 Stable Road, Jekyll Island (912–635–9500).

Nature studies. Wassaw and Wolf Islands are National Wildlife Refuges, and Ossabaw Island is a Heritage Preserve. Blackbeard Island is a Federal Wildlife Refuge accessible for day visits only by boat; book charters from Shellman Bluff or Pine Harbor. Sapelo Island was the home of tobacco millionaire R. J. Reynolds. Today it is a wildlife management area and the home of the Sapelo Island National Estuarine Research Reserve. Tours are available at different times of the year from Meridian (912–485–2251). On St. Simons Island, dolphin, bird-watching, and shelling cruises are offered by Marsh Hen Boat Tours, 310 Magnolia Avenue (912–638–9354). Bird-watching cruises are also offered by Kennedy Charters, 511 Marsh Villa Road (912–638–3214). On Jekyll Island, nature tours are offered by Tidelands Nature Center, 100 South Riverview Drive (912–635–5032; www.tidelands4h.com), Jekyll Island Nature Walks (912–635–9102), and Turtle Walks (912–635–2284).

Outdoor activities. The Lodge on Little St. Simons Island, 1000 Hampton Point Drive (912–638–7472 or 888–733–5774; www.littlestsimonsisland .com), is a 10,000-acre, privately owned island with 6 miles of undeveloped beach. Access is only by private ferry from St. Simons Island. A limited number of guests (thirty) are accepted in the main lodge and four guest houses during certain periods of the year. Wildlife—including more than 200 species of birds—is abundant in the maritime forests, making this island a popular destination for naturalist groups such as the Audubon Society. Little St. Simons Island isn't for everyone. You won't find any golf courses, tennis courts, amusement parks, restaurants, discos, or shopping. Horseback riding is offered early in the morning or late in the afternoon. Canoeing, fishing, long walks, swimming in the ocean or pool, kayak lessons, croquet, and bocce tournaments provide other temptations.

Cumberland Island National Seashore, mainland National Park Service office, 107 St. Marys Street, St. Marys (912–882–4335), is protected in its primitive state. It can be reached only by a ferry run by the National Park

Service from the mainland town of St. Marys. Only 300 visitors—including campers and day-trippers—per day are permitted, and reservations are required. Sixteen miles of pristine deserted beaches are backed by dunes and sea oats. You can occasionally tour thirty-room Plum Orchard, built in 1898, or inspect the ruins of Dungeness. A small Ice House Museum chronicles the island's history. This is a walking experience. No vehicles are permitted.

Tennis. The Jekyll Island Tennis Center, 400 Captain Wylly Road (912–635–3154), has thirteen courts, of which seven are lighted.

Water sports. Barry's Beach Service, King and Prince Resort, St. Simons and Jekyll Islands near the Holiday Inn (912–638–8053); and Island Dive Center, 107 Marina Drive (800–940–3483).

Special Events

Jekyll Island

June. Summer Beach Party Music Festival features well-known entertainers performing country music at the gigantic party on the beach. (912) 635–3636 or (877) 453–5955.

June–July. Jekyll Island Musical Theater Festival. Lively musical theater nightly, except Sunday, at the Jekyll Outdoor Amphitheater on Stable Road. (912) 635–3636 or (877) 453–5955.

Other Recommended Restaurants and Lodgings

Cumberland Island

In addition to campgrounds, one accommodation does exist on Cumberland Island for the more comfort-oriented. Elegant Greyfield Inn (904–261–6408), a 1901 Carnegie mansion on 1,300 acres, has fifteen rooms and suites, and three gourmet meals daily are included in the price. It is accessible only by private ferry from Fernandina Beach, Florida.

Jekyll Island

Best Western, Clarion, Days Inn, Holiday Inn, and Ramada are represented. Rental cottages, villas, and condos are available.

Comfort Inn Island Suites, 711 North Beachview Drive (912–635–2211 or 800–204–0202).

Jekyll Island Campground, 1197 Riverview (912–635–3021 or 877–4JEKYLL), is an eighteen-acre campground with 200 sites.

St. Simons Island

The palatial beachfront King and Prince Resort, 201 Arnold Road (912–638–3631 or 800–342–0212), offers golf, tennis, and sailing, as well as indoor and outdoor pools and a Jacuzzi. Lodging ranges from rooms in the main building to villas.

At Sea Palms Golf and Tennis Resort, 5445 Frederica Road (912–638–3351 or 800–841–6268), you can stay in cottages or villas. In addition to tennis, the resort offers a golf course that is ranked among the top courses in Georgia.

Smaller motels, rental homes, cottages, and condos round out the choice of quarters. There are no campgrounds on St. Simons Island.

For More Information

Brunswick and the Golden Isles of Georgia Visitors Bureau, 4 Glynn Avenue, Brunswick, GA 31520. (912) 265–0620 or (800) 933–COAST; www.bgivb.com.

Cumberland Island National Seashore, P.O. Box 806, St. Marys, GA 31558. (912) 882–4336.

Jekyll Island Convention and Visitors Bureau, 381 Riverview Drive, Jekyll Island, GA 31527. (912) 635–4073 or (877) 453–5955.

FARTHER AFIELD ESCAPE THREE

Alabama Gulf Coast/ Mobile, Alabama

Sun, Sand, Sea, and Southern Belles / 3 Nights

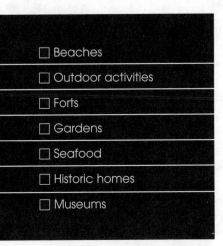

☐ Beaches

☐ Outdoor activities

☐ Forts

☐ Gardens

☐ Seafood

☐ Historic homes

☐ Museums

Only a few of the many Alabama Gulf Coast and Mobile Bay attractions are miles of pristine, powdery white beaches; glamorous, historic Mobile; picturesque small towns and fishing villages; haunting Civil War sites; and a world-famous garden; not to mention excellent fishing and great seafood. Mobile, frequently called New Orleans in Miniature, has more than enough attractions and annual events to be a destination in itself. Mobile claims the first Mardi Gras celebration in the New World and still celebrates it in a big way. Mobile's festivities are much more family-oriented and less crowded than those in the Big Easy.

In few areas of the state are so much history and so many attractions packed into such a small, compact area—most of which is covered by water. Stretched in a huge horseshoe around Mobile Bay, this itinerary can be explored by driving around the bay or taking the auto ferry between Fort Gaines on Dauphin Island and Fort Morgan at Gulf Shores.

Day 1 / Morning

Take I–85 south from Atlanta to Montgomery, Alabama, then head south on I–65 toward Mobile. As you near the city, look for AL 59 and take it south to Gulf Shores. Running east/west along the coast, AL 180 connects **Gulf Shores, Orange Beach,** and **Perdido Key,** collectively known as **Alabama's Gulf Coast.** Located 50 miles southeast of Mobile and 35 miles west of Pensacola, Florida, Alabama's Gulf Coast is a 30,000-acre

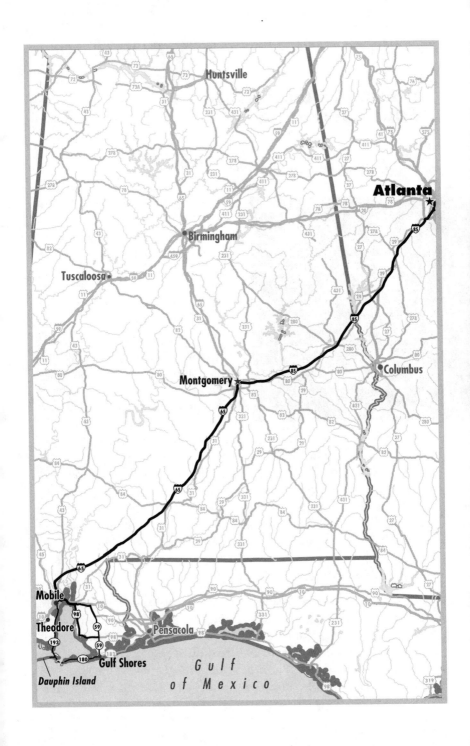

island that offers 32 miles of white-sand beaches. Freshwater lakes, rivers, bayous, and coves add nearly 400,000 acres of protected waterfront.

Alabama's Gulf Coast has a variety of activities. There are four championship golf courses and fourteen public tennis courts in addition to courts at many hotels. Freshwater and saltwater fishing, scuba diving, snorkeling, parasailing, and boat rentals round out the water sports. Other activities include a water park, miniature golf, hot-air ballooning, horseback riding, and a zoo.

Turn right on AL 180 and head straight for your lodgings at the **Beach House,** 9218 Dacus Lane (334–540–7039 or 800–659–6004), so you can drop off your stuff, grab a bite for lunch, and get in some beach time this afternoon. A destination in itself, the Beach House provides almost everything you need for a perfect getaway. The tin-roofed exterior is reminiscent of the grand beach houses built in the early twentieth century. A screened porch wraps around the front of the first floor, and outdoor stairs lead to the hot-tub deck.

The Beach House is filled with modern amenities, but happily, you won't see televisions and telephones. Instead, kites, floats, beach chairs, and even flip-flops are provided.

Perched on high dunes directly on the shores of the Gulf of Mexico, the rambling, three-story Beach House sits on the last lot before the **Bon Secour National Wildlife Refuge** (251–540–7720), which guarantees that the vast stretch of dune-backed beach next door will never be developed. This ideal location provides you with solitude when you want it.

DINNER: The **Beach Club Restaurant** at the Beach Club Condos, 453 Beach Club Trail (251–540–2525), serves seafood, pasta, and salads.

LODGING: All five luxurious guest rooms at the Beach House have their own distinct personality, and all boast fabulous views, king- or queen-size beds, pine floors, and Oriental rugs. Three-night minimum required.

Day 2 / Morning

BREAKFAST: At the Beach House.

Spend the morning at the beach reading, walking, shelling, flying a kite, making sand castles, or whatever your heart desires. Since we all need to be mindful of too much sun exposure, a half day on the beach should be sufficient. Afterward, have lunch and do some exploring.

LUNCH: Go west on AL 180 to the **Round Back Oyster Bar and**

Grill, 8818 AL 180 West (251–540–7800), for a seafood lunch in a casual setting.

Afternoon

West on AL 180 is **Fort Morgan,** 51 AL 180, Mobile Point (251–540–7125). Built between 1819 and 1834, it once guarded the main shipping channel into Mobile Bay. The fort was occupied by Confederate troops for most of the Civil War.

After the Civil War, the fortress was unused until 1898, just before the Spanish-American War. It was then that the fortification was modernized with concrete bastions. During World War I it was used as a training base for artillery troops preparing to go overseas and was one of the first schools for antiaircraft gunners. Abandoned again, the fortification was reactivated during World War II, after which it was donated to the state of Alabama for use as a historical park. Living-history presentations are made daily during the summer, and candlelight tours are given summer Tuesday evenings.

To reach **Fort Gaines** on **Dauphin Island,** on the opposite side of the bay and the beaches beyond, take the scenic thirty-minute ferry ride aboard the auto-passenger **Mobile Bay Ferry,** 351 AL 180 (251–540–7787), which has frequent daily departures from both sides of the bay. Occasionally the ferry has to suspend service because of high seas, in which case you'll have to drive the 100 miles around the bay.

So far, Dauphin Island remains an unrecognized Gulf Coast treasure, maintaining its unhurried atmosphere and pristine beauty. The 15-mile-long island sports white-quartz sand beaches that sometimes boast sand dunes as high as 35 feet. Condominiums and rental homes far outnumber hotels and motels, highways cover only half of the island, and there are no traffic lights—a truly noncommercialized destination.

Dauphin Island was strategically important during the Civil War: Together with Fort Morgan, across Mobile Bay, Dauphin Island's Fort Gaines, 51 Bienville Boulevard (251–861–6992), protected the mouth of the bay and Mobile as well. Established in 1821, the fort was originally a three-story structure, but during the brutal Civil War bombardment the top two stories were blown off.

Artifacts at the Fort Gaines Museum trace various periods of history from the Native American through the English, colonial, American, Civil War, and Spanish/American eras, up to the 1930s. Reenactments, special events, and historical storytellers are also featured.

On Dauphin Island, nature is at its best. The island is a major bird-migration flyway between South America and Canada, making it one of the premier birding spots in the Southeast. Observe more than 340 species of birds at the 160-acre **Audubon Bird Sanctuary,** adjacent to Fort Gaines (251–861–3607). Another harbinger of spring is the first landfall made by monarch butterflies migrating north. Miles of nature walks in the sanctuary, including boardwalks, give access to pine and live-oak forests, magnolia clearings, swampland, and beaches.

Cross the 3-mile Dauphin Island Bridge on AL 193 to the mainland and take Route 59 north to **Theodore,** home of **Bellingrath Gardens and Home,** 12401 Bellingrath Gardens Road (251–973–2217; www.bellingrath.org), one of the finest private gardens in the country. Follow the signs to the gardens.

Magnificent in any season, the 900 acres on the Isle aux Oies River showcase a sixty-five-acre landscaped garden and a mansion filled with antique furniture and priceless objets d'art, including one of the world's largest collections of Boehm porcelains. It's hard to imagine that local Coca-Cola bottling pioneer Walter Bellingrath originally bought the property in 1918 for a fishing camp, later transforming it to its current old-world grandeur.

Focal points of the gardens include a Victorian conservatory, a large Oriental-American garden, bridal garden, a grotto with a spillway, and a bird sanctuary. Bellingrath Gardens is noted for cascading mums. In the fall, you'll see masses of them dripping from every wall, bridge, and balcony.

Retrace AL 59 and AL 193 to Dauphin Island and return to Fort Morgan and Gulf Shores by ferry. Be sure to be at the ferry landing and in line by 6:30 P.M., the last ferry of the day.

DINNER: Mango's on the Island, 27075 Marina Road, Orange Beach Marina (251–981–1416; www.calypsomango.com), has a mouthwatering menu that includes Caribbean and Creole selections featuring fresh seafood. Eat indoors or out overlooking more than a half million dollars in boats.

LODGING: The Beach House.

Day 3 / Morning

BREAKFAST: At the Beach House.

Spend the morning at the beach, then get ready for another outing.

Take AL 59 north to US 98 and go north to **Mobile.**

LUNCH: Rousso's Seafood Restaurant, 166 South Royal Street (251–443–3322), features gargantuan portions of fresh seafood in a nautical setting.

Afternoon

Mobile has flown several flags during its rich 300-year history. The site was inhabited by Native Americans when Pierre Le Moyne d'Iberville and his brother Jean Baptiste Le Moyne claimed it for France in 1702. Periods of English and Spanish rule followed, and Mobile became part of the United States in 1814. Mobile, as Alabama's only port, was the gateway to the world.

During the Civil War, Mobile was an important port for the Confederacy because it was through Mobile Bay that blockade runners were able to slip out to trade with the West Indies and Europe, which kept the Southern cause alive. The loss of Confederate battleships in Mobile Bay, followed by the fall of three nearby forts, resulted in the occupation of Mobile, one of the last ports to fall to Union forces, and eventually guaranteed victory for the Union in 1865. Economic recovery was slow in coming to Mobile after the war, but by the late 1800s shipbuilding had emerged as a major industry.

Mardi Gras Day is the opening of the **Azalea Trail Festival,** 35 miles of some of the largest and most flamboyant azaleas in America. Visitors look forward to seeing the Azalea Trail Maids decked out in pastel antebellum gowns cascading with ruffles and accessorized with picture hats and parasols.

Every tourist's first stop should be **Fort Conde Museum and Welcome Center,** 150 South Royal Street (251–208–7652), which also serves as Mobile's Welcome Center. Reconstructed to its 1735 appearance, the fort features furniture, costumes, artillery, and artifacts from that era. Guards in French costumes demonstrate flintlock rifles and relate Mobile's history daily. Closed Thanksgiving, Christmas, and Mardi Gras.

Called the Preservation City, Mobile has 4,000 buildings listed on the National Register of Historic Places. Seven historic boundary districts have been identified. If you are doing a walking or driving tour, architecturally or historically significant buildings are identified by colorful shields. Maps for the tours are available at Fort Conde.

The **Museum of the City of Mobile,** 111 South Royal Street

(251–208–7569); www.museumofmobile.com), having outgrown an 1872 townhouse, has moved into palatial new digs in the Southern Market/Old City Hall building. Documents; artifacts; antiques; early-twentieth-century costumes, including elaborate Mardi Gras costumes; and riverboat and Civil War memorabilia, as well as a collection of ornate horse-drawn carriages, depict the history of Mobile.

Retrace your route to Gulf Shores.

DINNER: For entrees with Southern flair, including jumbo seafood platters, pastas, and meals from the grill, visit **Jumbo's Grill and Sushi Bar,** 27267 Perdido Beach Boulevard (251–981–8889), on San Roc Cay. In addition to sushi bar favorites, there are sinful desserts—and they'll even cook your catch.

LODGING: The Beach House.

Day 4 / Morning

BREAKFAST: The Beach House.

Spend as much time as you can on the beach before heading back to Atlanta.

When the time comes to say a reluctant farewell to the romantic Gulf Coast, instead of retracing AL 59 to I–65, take a more leisurely route north on Scenic US 98, stopping along the way if you have time (see There's More). Return to Atlanta via I–65 and I–85.

There's More

Camping and outdoor activities. Adjacent to Fort Gaines is the 150-site Dauphin Island Campground (251–861–2742), which offers free boat launches, secluded beach, and walking trails that connect to the Audubon Bird Sanctuary.

Fishing. Dauphin Island is known for superb fishing. Excellent places to fish are the 850-foot-long Dauphin Island Fishing Pier, 1509 Bienville Boulevard (251–861–6972), and the East End Pier. Numerous charters take anglers out for deep-sea challenges. Dauphin Island is the site of nine annual fishing rodeos. A full-service marina offers amentities for those fishing or traveling by boat.

State park. Between Gulf Shores and Orange Beach is Gulf State Park Headquarters, 20115 East Beach Boulevard (251–948–7275), which offers 2.5 miles of beachfront, an eighteen-hole golf course, and lighted tennis courts as well as 6,000 acres of protected wilderness including nature trails and two freshwater lakes. There's also a resort hotel, restaurant, and pool.

Special Events

Alabama Gulf Coast

February or March. Mardi Gras festivities include parades in Foley (251–943–3291), Gulf Shores, and Orange Beach (251–968–6904).

Mobile

February or March. Mobile Mardi Gras. Parades occur daily (some during the day, some at night) through Fat Tuesday. (251) 432–3050.

Theodore

The following are among the most special events that occur at Bellingrath Gardens. For more information call (251) 973–2217.

January–February. Winter Wonderland features more than 50,000 blooming bulbs.

March–April. Spring Spectacular features more spring bulbs and azaleas.

November–December 26. Chrysanthemum Extravaganza features cascades of colorful mums.

Thanksgiving–New Year's Eve. Magic Christmas in Lights brings the magic of the season to life with more than two million lights, displays, nativity, music, and more.

Other Recommended Restaurants and Lodgings

Alabama Gulf Coast

The Original Romar House, 23500 Perdido Beach Boulevard (251–981–6156 or 800–48–ROMAR), a seaside bed-and-breakfast, is in a 1924 house.

Perdido Beach Resort, 27200 Perdido Beach Boulevard (251–981–9811 or 800–634–8001; www.perdidobeachresort.com), is a shell-pink Mediterranean-style palace with all the amenities of a large resort.

Locals recommend the following Gulf Shores restaurants and nightspots: the Pink Pony Pub, 137 East Gulf Place (251–948–6731), and Flora-Bama, 17401 Perdido Key Drive (251–492–0611), a joint that has to be seen to be believed.

Home port for Alabama's famous deep-sea fishing fleet, Orange Beach offers a wide variety of seafood restaurants: Tacky Jack's Tavern, Cotton Bayou Marina, 272006 Safe Harbor Drive (251–981–4144), for a hearty breakfast or dinner, and Voyagers at the Perdido Beach Resort, 27200 Perdido Beach Boulevard (251–981–9811, ext. 103), which serves Gulf Coast Creole cuisine.

Mobile

Malaga Inn, 359 Church Street (251–438–4701 or 800–235–1586; www.malagainn.com), housed in two 1862 Spanish-style town houses and an addition, has rooms furnished in antiques and reproductions. Pool, restaurant, and lounge.

Radisson Admiral Semmes Hotel, 251 Government Street (251–432–8000 or 800–333–3333), is a restored 1940s hotel that retains original architectural features and provides updated luxury accommodations as well as a restaurant, lounge, pool, and hot tub.

For More Information

Alabama Gulf Coast Chamber of Commerce/Convention and Visitors Bureau, AL 59 South, P.O. Drawer 457, Gulf Shores, AL 36547. (251) 968–7511 or (800) 745–SAND; www.gulfshores.com.

Mobile Convention and Visitors Corporation, 1 South Water Street, Mobile, AL 36602. (251) 208–2000 or (800) 5–MOBILE; www.mobile.org.

Orange Beach Chamber of Commerce, State 182, Orange Beach, AL 36561. (334) 974–1506.

Dauphin Island Chamber of Commerce, P.O. Box 610, Dauphin Island, AL 36528. (251) 861–5524.

INDEX